Also by Simon Spence

Still Breathing: The True Adventures of the Donnelly Brothers
(with Anthony and Christopher Donnelly)

The Stone Roses: War and Peace

Just Can't Get Enough: The Making of Depeche Mode

Immediate Records

Mr Big: Don Arden, The Godfather of Rock (Interviews and Research)

2Stoned: Andrew Loog Oldham (Interviews and Research)

Stoned: Andrew Loog Oldham (Interviews and Research)

Excess All Areas
A Biography

By Simon Spence

Aurum
Press

First published in Great Britain
2014 by Aurum Press Ltd
74—77 White Lion Street
Islington
London N1 9PF
www.aurumpress.co.uk

A catalogue record for this book is
available from the British Library.

ISBN 978 1 78131 264 3

1 3 5 7 9 10 8 6 4 2
2014 2016 2018 2017 2015

Printed and bound by CPI Group (UK) Ltd, Croydon, CR0 4YY

Dedicated to:
Anthony H. Wilson
Cultural Catalyst
1950 – 2007

Contents

'Only those who will risk going too far can possibly find out how far one can go.'

T.S. Eliot

'Show me a boy who never wanted to be a rock star and I'll show you a liar.'

Stardust

Prologue

It was June 1990 and Happy Mondays' third *NME* front cover in just under six months. The first, in December 1989, had trumpeted the arrival of 'Madchester' (replete with its own brightly coloured cartoon logo) following the Mondays' and The Stone Roses' joint and joyously counter-cultural appearance on *Top of the Pops* – during which a smirking Shaun Ryder, dressed all in black, had mimed smoking heroin. That moment had seen the two bands' 'hometown' of Manchester (though all six Happy Mondays had been raised in the neighbouring city of Salford) become the UK's 'music capital' and precipitated what the *NME* called a 'rock revolution'.

In fact it was bigger than that. Tony Wilson, the infamous boss of the Mondays' unruly record label, the celebrated Factory Records, said the band was spearheading a cultural revolution – and he was right. In March 1990, Shaun appeared on the cover of the *NME* for a second time, wrapped around a giant letter 'E', an unmissable reference to the dance drug Ecstasy. It was an image from a video shoot in Sitges, Spain, for the band's immeasurably catchy, supremely of the moment and, we know now, timeless single, 'Step On': the Mondays' first top five UK hit and the song that broke them worldwide.

'All movements in rock have been middle class until now,' Wilson said. 'This thing happening in Manchester is the only one created by the working class.' Alongside the city's musical contributions, hometown-boy-done-good Wilson was keenly aware and proud of Manchester's rich heritage of working-class, left-leaning political protest and the economic, scientific and cultural innovations that had impacted the world – from the industrial revolution to feminism, trade unionism to the invention of the computer and more. He saw Madchester and the Mondays as part of that grand tradition; an untutored, street-smart savvy and anti-establishment movement combined with a profound and inventive musical revolution.

There was no pretending, no posing, no marketing-driven, careerist showbiz fakery and false sentiment with the Mondays. Although Wilson idealised the band's humdrum roots in suburban Swinton, calling them 'scum', car thieves, robbers and drug dealers, the truth was enough: they were blue jeans and blue collar. They had something of the *Saturday Night Fever* vibe – it was innate and they were self-made and the scene was all about dancing, drugs and having a good time. Unlike the studied Stone Roses, everything to do with the Mondays seemed spontaneous and shot through with a genuine sense of enjoyment, to happen in the moment, the now – often it appeared by pure luck. Of course, this was not exactly true, because at the heart of the Mondays was a deep and dark artistic bent and a serious work ethic.

The Roses played their epochal Spike Island show in May 1990. Indie guitar bands that had copied the Mondays' rhythms such as The Charlatans, Jesus Jones, EMF, James, Primal Scream, The Farm, Inspiral Carpets and Flowered Up all flourished. None could hold a torch to the Mondays, who had already recorded two of the greatest British albums of the 1980s. The Madchester scene had formed around them but they wanted little to do with it and, like the Roses, shot the scene down in interviews. The Mondays were, above all, distinct, highly original, in the way of Roxy Music or The Velvet Underground, and there was a danger of that being forgotten.

Wilson enjoyed comparing them to the Sex Pistols and was seen as their Svengali, their Malcolm McLaren. He spoke expansively of Madchester as the world's leading youth culture and it threatened to drown out the deftness and many shades in the music of the Mondays. The term did adroitly sum up an atmosphere in a city where the smell of weed being smoked wafted around every corner and flares came dramatically back into fashion. But Wilson's 'movement' had essentially piggy-backed on, and packaged for guitar fans, the generational, cultural and musical revolution of Acid House, a burgeoning country-wide scene that combined illegal raves, the drug Ecstasy and stripped-back electronic beats originating from Detroit and Chicago. Acid was pure hedonism, but contemplated as part of a wider revolt against the ten years of Margaret Thatcher and Conservative rule that had climaxed with the recent Poll Tax riots in Trafalgar Square in London. The government had introduced draconian new laws to extinguish the liberated, lawless, all-night, outdoor Acid House parties that could attract upwards of 20,000 ravers and the police used undercover intelligence and brutal shows of strength to stamp them out.

Madchester was Acid House with guitars, bands not DJs, a distinct northern accent and a new wardrobe of T-shirts, flares, fringes and floppy hats. It was raving indoors at gigs – legally – or at The Hacienda, the ultimate Madchester club, co-owned by Factory Records and transformed by the Acid House scene. Happy Mondays had been regulars since it opened in 1982 and were at the very heart of the transformation, one that had now made it the most famous club in the world – the Madchester musical narrative was that by mixing Acid House music with guitar rock, the Mondays were creating a new dance/rock hybrid. 'The Berlin wall between dance and rock has come crashing down,' Wilson said. The real Berlin wall had fallen just months earlier and it was typical of the Cambridge-educated Wilson to try and frame historic world events or monumental works of art (Yeats, Shakespeare, Proust) in relation to the band he loved the most. Again, the truth was more complex. The Mondays had spent the past eight years immersed in the sounds of American dance music: electro, hip-hop, Motown, funk and disco.

The wilful, experimental, impulsive and Situationist-influenced Factory Records coursed through everything that was Madchester and Mondays. The label had dominated the Manchester music scene, operating a virtual monopoly, for the past ten years – defining the city's musical output. This was remarkable considering that two of the decade's most successful outfits, The Smiths and Simply Red, were from the city but not affiliated to Factory. Despite its often contrary nature, Factory was the UK's most successful independent record label of the 1980s, a decade during which 'independent' came to signify not just the means of production and distribution but an attitude and aesthetic and, to some extent, a distinctly left-field guitar sound.

Factory had risen to prominence in the late 1970s releasing the city's greatest ever band, Joy Division, who were firm favourites of the Mondays. After singer Ian Curtis committed suicide his band mates formed New Order and were among a new wave of mid-80s 'indie' bands, including Echo & The Bunnymen, The Smiths, The Cure and Depeche Mode, that enjoyed mainstream worldwide success. New Order had been instrumental in supporting the Mondays in their early years and they generated millions for Factory. Their recent Acid House-tinged *Technique* album had gone to number one in the UK and they were currently at the top of the singles chart with the official England football team World Cup song, 'World in Motion'. New Order also co-owned The Hacienda and they were considered Godfathers of the Madchester scene. But New Order were the rare example of an obdurate indie band infiltrating the popular culture of the 1980s, dominated as it was by glitzy heavy rock bands, pop acts and solo stars. Despite the odd blip of innovation such as The Jesus and Mary Chain, indie guitar rock had over the decade grown progressively predictable and straight, a hopeful strum at crossover success, or had ghettoised itself, exemplified by the underachieving, shambling, jangling C86 movement typically represented by The Pastels.

Madchester was a rebirth for indie; a musical movement Wilson hoped would have the impact of punk or challenge the prominence of American hip-hop as a cultural force. It was also a rebirth for the fortunes of the city. Manchester had been in a long decline following post-Second World War deindustrialisation and Madchester was reshaping the popular view (if not the landscape) of the city as a forever drizzling, depressing place full of abandoned warehouses, early death and unemployed people. Now it was being perceived as a vibrant place of opportunity, with a thriving music, club, fashion and social scene. The image of Factory Records too was altering — the standoffish, aloof attitude and minimalist aesthetic replaced by a colour-soaked and humour-splattered approach. The label, like the Mondays, stood at a crossroads. Both were leaving behind years of innovative, bewildering and colossal music and striding into the mainstream, the machine, the music biz, the establishment; the world of the Brits, the BPI, sales meetings, contracts, marketing campaigns and miming on TV shows.

It was going to be fun. Factory were renovating new million-pound offices and the Mondays had, in March 1990, headlined two consecutive and celebratory nights at Manchester's 10,000-capacity G-Mex venue, swiftly followed by a 12,500 sell-out date in London at Wembley Arena. 'The 90s belong to this band, nobody else can touch them,' wrote BBC 6 Music's Mary Anne Hobbs in the now defunct music weekly *Sounds*. Now the Mondays were due to head-line the Pyramid stage at Glastonbury on 24 June, the closing Sunday night of the three-day festival, and their third *NME* front cover celebrated the fact.

Before leaving for Glastonbury, they were photographed in Manchester's Heaton Park posing with a miniature Stonehenge, a reference to an infamous scene in the parody rock documen-tary *Spinal Tap* that had become something of a band obsession. Keyboardist Paul Davis wore a Greenpeace T-shirt. Bez, the band's totemic onstage dancer, typically, almost crashed his car arriving at the shoot, finishing a handbrake turn inches from drummer Gary Whelan's second-hand BMW as it pumped out Talking Heads on the stereo. Things were going so well that circumspect 28-year-old guitarist Mark Day had finally packed in his job as a postman. Head of A&R at Factory and the band's former manager, Phil Saxe, was predicting they would be as big as The Rolling Stones in five years. Like the Stones, they had taken on the mantle of the 'bad boys' of rock. Since the Pistols, British acts had kept a lid on their excesses, with drug taking only ever 'exposed' by the tabloids. The Mondays smoked spliff and drank in interviews and talked about dealing Ecstasy, taking heroin, speed, cocaine, crack, PCP and acid. The *NME* called them 'the nation's favourite outlaws'.

The band travelled to Glastonbury on Friday 22 June in a luxury double-decker coach full of girls, hangers-on, associates, minders and family. The air was thick with marijuana smoke, the band tripping on acid. The coach got lost and the driver reversed into a sign saying 'Glastonbury', smashing the back window. The band had requested 220 complimentary tickets for the festival but that was not enough for the band's extended entourage, who planned to tip up to Glastonbury for the ride. There would be a serious crew of over one thousand 'proper Mancunian lads' converging on the gentle, hippy festival. Manchester was said to be a ghost town that weekend. A yellow, laminated, 'backstage Happy Mondays' pass was copied in the thousands by, said Bez, 'entrepreneurs on the firm'. Many of the counterfeit passes were handed on to spivs outside the festival selling tickets. Close to £20,000 was reputedly made from the enterprise.

When the band finally arrived on the festival site, the coach immediately crashed into a tree and the front window of the upper deck was smashed. They passed the spivs selling tickets, many known to the band, who cheered and drew the band's attention to a naked couple having sex in a field. The fake passes allowed access to the backstage area and there were several clashes with security struggling to control the hundreds of Mancunians who evidently shouldn't have been there. A new security team had been employed that year at Glastonbury and they also clashed violently with the large contingent of travellers among the 72,000-strong crowd – the biggest ever at the time to have descended on the fields of Pilton. The festival spun out of control: on site there was profligate drug selling, men in balaclavas offering Ecstasy and crack, tent crime was rife and stallholders were reportedly 'taxed' by Mancunian gangsters.

On the Saturday afternoon Gary Whelan found a couple he didn't know having sex in the coach's luggage hold. Bez continued to swallow trips. Shaun went without sleep and spent Saturday night and most of Sunday in the hold smoking heroin. Rumours went round that he had pissed his pants, that Bez had finally lost it and that the Mondays were a mess and would be unable to perform. Shaun's younger brother, Paul Ryder, whose bass lines were central to the Mondays' songs and sound, lined up four pint glasses, half-filling each with vodka and topping them up with grapefruit juice. He'd been shovelling down the cocaine and drinking for two days solid and made himself vomit so he could drink his onstage quota of booze. He was feeling invincible.

The band were scattered around all parts of the massive site just minutes before they were due to bring that year's festival to a close and perform to 50,000 people, their biggest show to date. There was no half-hour alone backstage to prepare, no group hug, but that was never the Mondays' way. They were six young men — four of them former postmen — from the wrong side of town who should never have been in a band and even now, at the pinnacle of their success, they felt this deeply. Despite all the critical acclaim over the previous years, they were still insecure about their place in the rock 'n' roll firmament. They would always feel somehow dislocated. It was one of the reasons why they drank and took drugs — to cope with these insecurities.

Most other bands would have fallen apart before the set had even started, but the Mondays brought the backstage bacchanalia onstage, starting with 'Rave On' from the hit *Madchester* EP, which was received with an ear-splitting wall of noise from the crowd. 'Step On' followed, waves of energy hitting the band from the crowd, energy that never dulled during the Mondays' short, spirited 52-minute set. It was not polished but it was free from all rock cliché, and it throbbed — when it came to their sound system, the Mondays were known to be the most conscientious and free-spending band in the business. They were also one of the first rock bands to incorporate samplers and sequencers in their live show when the machinery was still in its infancy, delicate to use. There were no such glitches at Glastonbury, just drummer Whelan having fun triggering samples with his synth drums and keyboardist Davis trying to mess with Shaun's head pressing the handclaps button. The Mondays closed Glastonbury with their anthem for a generation, 'Wrote For Luck', as a bruised darkness fell on the summer evening. From the stage, on an incline a half-mile away, the band could see a merchandise van ablaze.

There were a record 235 arrests at the festival and £50,000 worth of damage was done that year. As a direct consequence the following year's Glastonbury was cancelled and when it was next staged, in 1992, a ten-foot fence had been erected around the site. The

Mondays were blamed for bringing much of the chaos; Michael Eavis, the festival organiser, said he never wanted them back.

A sublime Glastonbury headline set had been reduced to a story of gangsters, fights, drug dealing and mayhem over which the band had no control. Yet this was the paradox at the heart of the Mondays – a band whose lead singer had spent almost forty-eight hours doing heroin in a darkened coach's luggage hold before their biggest ever gig in the UK, whose bassist was coked out of his head and downing bottles of spirits, whose dancer was on another planet, who seemed to operate in a state of complete anarchy. How on earth could they achieve such potency on stage and in the studio? And not just once at Glastonbury or with 'Step On', but consistently for almost ten years.

It was difficult to fathom and the myth of the Mondays, which had already begun to loom large, would soon overshadow the complex realities – the practice and the dedication and the determination eclipsed by stories of chaos, stabbings, shootings, orgies, overdoses. The notion that came to define them – one they were not entirely innocent of advancing – was that they were the underclass, products of a prospectless council estate, who had no choice but to thieve, deal and rob, who were always 'out of it', who could not play their instruments properly and were simply on the make, in it for the money, chancers. But it could not have been further from the truth.

At Glastonbury the band had been brave enough to debut two brand new songs, 'God's Cop' and 'Kinky Afro'. Shaun made a mess of the latter, forgetting the words. He always had trouble remembering his lyrics, so his dad, Derek, who was instrumental in the start of the band and worked for them throughout their career, would write them all out for him and arrange them by his son's feet on the stage monitors. They were two of the Mondays' best ever songs. Unlike the Roses or New Order, the band's greatest work was still in front of them. After Glastonbury, the party rolled on to Ibiza, the Mondays becoming the first rock band to play the infamous KU club, and then America where they would blow the lid off New York's legendary Sound Factory and then record their third and best-selling album, *Pills 'n' Thrills and Bellyaches*, in Los Angeles.

Huge mainstream success lay ahead, more magazine covers (only Lady Diana featured on more British magazine covers than Shaun Ryder in 1990), bringing with it all manner of trials and tribulations for the band like no other. The craze for Madchester would wane and be replaced by another scene and a different hotspot; grunge rock and Seattle. But for a generation Madchester was punk rock and it was hip-hop, and it burst open the gates for a slew of guitar bands, including Oasis, Suede, Blur and Pulp, who would come to eventually overtake grunge and put 'indie' firmly and forever in the mainstream with Britpop. All these bands would tip their hats to the groundbreaking Mondays, a band who never have truly been given their due as one of the handful of great British rock 'n' roll innovators, a pure undiluted force the like of which we are unlikely ever to see again.

BOOK ONE

Pure Boys

1
Brothers

Contrary to the image of deprivation that Happy Mondays would come to sell themselves on, brothers Paul and Shaun Ryder lived in a decent-sized, privately owned semi-detached house with a garden and garage in a quiet cul-de-sac on a pleasant residential estate surrounded by fields and countryside. Kent Close was in Worsley, a well-to-do suburb of Salford, six miles north-west of Manchester city centre. It was not the sort of place where small children would spend their free time torturing animals, setting fire to schools, practising vandalism, petty theft and nicking cars, as Shaun would later claim he spent his childhood doing. Worsley had once been a historic cotton and coal-mining town but now looked more like a leafy village with a handful of restaurants and country-style pubs. Many of its mock Tudor buildings, including the grand Worsley Old Hall, were listed and part of a wider conservation area. Even in the mid-1970s when the Ryders first moved there, before the huge regeneration of Greater Manchester in the past twenty years, it was an attractive and desirable place to live, surrounded by countryside, including thirty hectares of woodland, and bisected by the Bridgewater canal.

At the end of the Second World War, when Salford pulled down its inner-city slums, five thousand new homes, split between four neighbourhoods, were built near Worsley in Little Hulton village and over 18,000 people were rehoused there. It was into this wave of modernist optimism, with a library, community centre, new shopping centre and school, that the Ryder brothers were born in the mid-1960s at their maternal grandparents' home. However, by the 1980s, Little Hulton had made the slow decline from working-class utopia to dystopia. As Thatcherism took hold in the rest of the country, certain council housing estates in Little Hulton became infamous 'no-go' areas, with high levels of economic and social deprivation and crime. This, alongside similar early warning signals on the larger overspill council estate in south Manchester, Wythenshawe, was both emblematic and symptomatic of decades of manufacturing decline in Manchester and Salford. The staunchly Labour-controlled Manchester Council meanwhile believed that the city's regeneration should be funded solely by public money, despite the government's insistence on only funding schemes with a significant element of private finance. The result was a chronic lack of investment.

Even as the band's status grew, it was easy to see how journalists were encouraged to paint a picture of a youth spent dealing drugs and burgling houses on a crime-ridden, drug-soaked sink estate. Poverty was rife, the city had been abandoned by Thatcher. Thanks to her flagship policy of selling off council homes, swathes of the population had been left behind in ghetto estates full of 'broken' families. Even local journalists were prone to stereotype the problems. As for those who came up from London to interview the Mondays as their reputation grew, Shaun Ryder never corrected their perception that the band's members had been lucky to get off the estate alive. Shaun would frequently state that they came from Little Hulton – even now they are commonly referred to as a Little Hulton band – where kids were called 'walking time bombs' and drugs and crime were simply 'a way of life' as there was nothing else to do. Later, when they made good, their fabled hard-bitten council estate background would see them viewed as a kind of Mancunian version of the Essex man, Thatcher's children: bought the council house, proletariat done good, in thrall to possessions and looking after number one. Neither perception was true.

'I was thinking about how many lies and exaggerations our kid has said over the years,' said Paul Ryder. 'Maybe it's something to do with being a lyricist and a character...or is he acting? This persona of being a hard man and getting into scrapes as a kid. What he describes is a completely different childhood to mine and from what I saw Shaun's was completely different from what he describes. He started saying things in the press, and it became, Wow, you must have been really troubled as a kid, but it wasn't like that.'

The truth was far more prosaic than the image of anarchy that Shaun liked to portray. Their father Derek had two jobs; he was a postman in the early mornings and part of a successful, semi-professional comedy duo at night with his friend Barry Seddon, playing clubs all around the UK, often in London. The pair also served up music, so the audience could have a dance, as a complement to their comedy routine: Derek on upright bass, Barry on guitar accompanied by a drum machine. Derek, who was raised in Farnworth, between Worsley and Bolton, had played in bands since he heard 'Rock Island Line' by Lonnie Donegan as a teenager and got hooked on the skiffle craze. To perform with Barry he'd retired a country band called Haphazard and an electric folk band called Cottonsong.

Many of the jokes Derek and Barry told in their act were left over from Derek's promising and lucrative television writing career, which had come to an abrupt end when his agent, Sonny Zahl, who also represented Ronnie Corbett, Dick Emery and Leslie Crowther, committed suicide. Derek wrote for *The Two Ronnies* among other shows, earning £100 to £150 per script. He felt an affinity with Corbett over their similar stature: 'I thought I knew the problems of being small and exaggerated them for comedy effect,' he said. Derek had a good few years with the script writing, resisting Zahl's demands to move his family to London; he wore flash handmade suits and coats and took his wife and two young sons to Bournemouth for holidays in four-star hotels. 'Lots of money,' said Derek. 'We were living the high life.'

Derek married Shaun and Paul's mum, Linda, when he was nineteen and became the first person in his family to own his own home on the back of a 100 per cent mortgage offered by the council. He made a profit selling the house after a few years and moved up the housing ladder. The family moved around a few times, and each time Derek made money, bought a better house and a better car. In many ways the family was the image of comfortable middle-class respectability. A strict Roman Catholic, Linda had been a primary school teacher before becoming a school nurse at the local Catholic primary school, St Mark's, which her sons both attended. She also played piano. 'She had this little electric organ that my dad bought for her,' said Paul. 'But he used it more than she did. He would play Beatles tunes on this organ. Because Mum's a teacher with little kids, she just ended up doing nursery rhymes [on the organ] and she did them very well.'

Derek had enjoyed piano and saxophone lessons as a child, and was self-taught on guitar, bass, banjo, piano accordion and mandolin. 'I'm a great believer in self-tutoring,' he said. 'I lived in the library. Anything I wanted to know or do I got a book out.' Derek's father had been an engineer and his mother a cotton mill worker, and he had trained as an engineer himself. He was obsessed with music, musical instruments and equipment: as a kid, he'd been a hit doing Everly Brothers numbers at the local cinemas between films with a pal of his, chiefly because he had discovered how to wire two extra microphones up to the standard one. 'We had three mics, so we were the kings,' he said. 'Everybody else sounded like shit.' Before getting married he'd made a small fortune running local discos, putting together his own sound system. He understood the importance of having the correct sound.

Paul and Shaun would often see and hear Derek and Barry rehearsing cover versions for their set in the front room at Kent Close. 'I thought they weren't taking any notice,' said Derek. But it was in this vibrant musical atmosphere that the brothers started to draw their first inspirations. Among their parents' record collection, Shaun and Paul found 1950s rock 'n' roll – The Everly Brothers, Chuck Berry, Little Richard, Jerry Lee Lewis and Fats Domino, plus country & western, Irish folk music and 1960s hits by artists such as Tom Jones. Linda and Derek shared the same taste in music. 'We were both Stones people,' said Derek. 'Shaun and Paul flogged their albums to death, and The Beatles'.'

'The first records I ever heard were my mum's records,' said Paul. 'A Buddy Holly album, Elvis, The Beatles and Stones – they were four albums that stuck out to me when I was seven or eight.'

Their home was musical; records and live music in the house and *Top of the Pops* as well, religiously. 'My dad put that on so we always watched it.' Both Paul and Shaun recall being struck by David Bowie performing 'Starman' on the show in 1972. 'That turned me on to something different,' said Paul. 'I just stood there staring at the telly, thinking wow, where's he come from? My prize possession became this Bowie T-shirt and I wouldn't take it off.'

The brothers were close but different, and in those formative years can be seen the seeds of what they would become as musicians. At Christmas or birthdays, Paul would ask for a cassette deck or new speakers, things that were practical and permanent. Shaun, meanwhile, would want clothes and shoes, stuff that came and went, his primary concern being how he looked when he walked out of the house. 'When I opened mine, it looked big, shiny and expensive,' said Paul. 'And he didn't think what he'd got was as much but he always looked smart.'

Music was an ever-present part of the brothers' upbringing. If they were not listening to their parents' records, being taught on the piano by their mum, or listening to their dad and Barry play, they were being played new sounds by members of their extended family. Their nana Annie, Linda's mum, had two sisters who lived nearby, Winnie and Mary, and their children came to play a significant role in Shaun and Paul's lives. When on babysitting duty, Winnie's daughters would fill the brothers' house with Motown. 'They'd bring a little record box full of Motown seven-inches to play,' said Paul. 'They'd play Motown all night and that really rubbed off on me, all those great bass lines. Then they got into reggae and that's the next thing they'd bring round – all these reggae albums, I-Roy and U-Roy.'

Shaun and Paul were closest to Mary's two youngest kids, Matt and Pat Carroll. They had a huge record collection at their house thanks to their seven elder siblings. 'There were a couple of thousand albums in the living room,' said Paul. The four boys worked their way through a musical treasure trove: Roxy Music, Sly & The Family Stone, Commander Cody, The Byrds, Flying Burrito Brothers, Link Wray, The Tams, Gram Parsons, Elton John, Townes van Zandt, Otis Redding, Bunny Wailer, Gregory Isaacs and more.

The exposure to all these great, diverse music styles at an early age was a bedrock and a lasting influence for all four boys. Later, when the Mondays were just beginning, Shaun would say it was a love for all different hues of music that led to him bonding with Bez. 'We were both unafraid to say I like The Specials but I dig Tom Jones and Showaddywaddy and Buddy Holly, to say what we really liked.'

As with most lower middle-class Irish Roman Catholics, church was a central tenet in forming the Ryder family's values, and something that Linda held very close to her. But it was here that the brothers displayed their first signs of rebellion. As soon as Paul was old enough to attend by himself, he'd pop his head in to see what colour the priest was wearing and get off: 'I could say, "Yeah, I've been to church, he was wearing green".' He preferred exploring the slag heaps, fields, woods and streams around Kent Close, acquiring an air pistol to shoot rats at the local sewage works. Shaun recalled making 'a few bob' collecting and bagging up horse manure and selling it door to door 'round all the houses on the estate' as plant fertiliser.

Shaun and Paul went to a Roman Catholic high school, St Ambrose Barlow in neighbouring Swinton, a former district of Worsley that had developed into a substantial mill town and coal-mining hub but was now parochial, old-fashioned and in decline. Shaun flunked his first-year tests and was placed in the bottom class. 'I always got words mixed up,' he said, explaining how he had to read the same line three times before he understood what he meant. In fact he was dyslexic. The school brought in a specialist to observe him and to decide whether he was left-handed or right-handed. The decision was made on the seemingly random basis of which hand Shaun used more frequently to pick up objects. 'When he wrote he would write one line normally with his left hand and then switch the pen to his right hand and write the next line in reverse, right to left, then switch the pen back to his left hand for the next line so his writing snaked down a page. It was weird,' said Derek. Shaun wrote poetry that showed exceptional talent, imagination and originality. 'He was accused of plagiarism,' said Derek. 'The teachers wouldn't believe he had written these wonderful poems. So Shaun stopped writing them.'

'I was branded a thickie,' Shaun said, and took on the role of class joker. He was disruptive in class and canings, he said, were commonplace. He grew increasingly frustrated in the bottom sets. In the third year he clearly recalled thinking, 'I haven't learned a fucking thing since I've been here.' He started to skip school, spending time at the cinema, impressed by films like *Enter the Dragon*, *Dirty Harry*, *The Exorcist*, and particularly the David Essex films *That'll Be the Day* and *Stardust*. The latter, released in 1974, saw Essex's character embark on a successful rock career, before alienating his band mates, becoming a drug addict and finally dying dramatically of a heroin overdose.

'Shaun wasn't interested in school because he was original and they weren't used to original at schools,' said Derek. 'They couldn't deal with him.' But Derek believed his son's lack of formal education and writing the way he did was to his advantage when it came to being in a band. Shaun often wrote phonetically, and his incorrect spellings, allied to his ambidextrousness, enabled him to make unique and fast-flowing leaps of imagination; words, sounds, themes and concepts that on the surface appeared unrelated were imbued with meaning when put together in a song lyric. 'It fascinated me,' said Derek. 'He couldn't remember his lyrics and every song from day one, I wrote the lyrics out for him. One day I wrote them all out properly, proper spelling and everything and he said, What the fucking hell's this? He spelled words a different way and when I spelled them the correct way he didn't know what they were. Words that began with a C he would begin with an S. I had to write them out exactly how he'd written them and spelled them. When we were doing the big gigs, people who worked for the venue, stage staff, would see the lyrics and laugh.'

Paul joined St Ambrose Barlow in 1975 when his brother was in the third year and he got to know many of Shaun's friends, mixing with this older crowd of 'funny characters'. He was a talented rugby player, playing the coveted scrum-half position for the school team. 'I was delighted about that,' he said. 'It got you out of all kinds of subjects.' Another fringe benefit was free tickets to go watch the local Swinton rugby league team play. A broken nose would turn him off playing but Paul went to watch Swinton every Sunday for years.

Like his brother, Paul was not academic. 'Paul was quite clever but lazy at school,' said Derek. 'Like Shaun, he couldn't be arsed either.' He formed his own circle of pals at school and started getting drawn into petty theft, the most notorious examples of which involved robbing parked Carlsberg beer trucks. 'The trucks had a canvas side,' said Paul. 'So you'd cut it just enough to get your hands in and then pinch crates and crates and crates of Special Brew which we then sold.' The crime made the local paper, the *Swinton Journal*, and brought extended bragging rights: 'We were in the playground going, Yes, we made it in the paper!' Among Paul and Shaun's school pals, shoplifting was another sweet thrill, just for the hell of it, getting something for nothing. And, at the time, it was seen as an easy touch. You just needed the balls. The brothers, particularly Paul, became adept shoplifters, and neither thought to stop: it seems as though, whether it was stealing clothes or records, they were rarely, if ever, caught.

Neither Paul nor Shaun had a need to steal as they were well provided for. Derek recalled buying Shaun a drum kit he wanted and setting it up for him in his bedroom, cutting shapes from carpets to deaden the sound so as not to disturb the neighbours. Of course, Shaun removed them as soon as Derek and Linda left the house. He recalled Derek being a strict dad who kept him in line via beatings: 'I was scared of him until I was fifteen.'

In late 1976 punk swept through St Ambrose like a rampaging fire. With Paul in his third year and Shaun in his last, the sight of the Sex Pistols on TV, in their infamous December 1976 interview with Bill Grundy on the live, tea-time *Today* show, left an impression that would still be referenced years later. 'Punk had massive impact,' said Paul. 'I saw the Sex Pistols on TV and it was like, Wow, never seen that before. I really liked the punk ethic of you can do anything you want, you can even do this if you want, be in a band like us. That stuck with me for years. It changed my life.' Paul, who had shown little interest in his brother's fashion habits, immediately went out and bought some drainpipe cords and suede boots.

Over the next couple of years the Manchester music scene started to develop an impressive reputation against a backdrop of social and economic hardship. The punk gigs made going into the city centre a slightly safer proposition. It had a reputation as a fearful place, to be avoided like the plague, dirty and horrible, full of piss-stinking dark alleys and regular kickings, with what club nightlife there was dominated by beery blokes and women dancing around handbags. Unemployment, strikes, high inflation, the lack of public spending, immigration, also saw a rise in the popularity of the British Movement and National Front among alienated working-class youth in Manchester and Salford. Anti-fascist groups sought them out, often leading to ferocious street battles. The empty, crumbling buildings and, yes, the rain only added to the sense of depression and violence.

In 1977 the brothers attended their first punk gig — Buzzcocks, Manchester's pre-eminent punk band, from whom Paul had copied his cords and suede boots look, at the Elizabethan Ballroom in Belle Vue. They saw local Granada news anchor Tony Wilson at the gig. At the time the future Factory Records founder was presenting a music show on Granada called *So It Goes* that featured live performances from the best punk bands of the era, including the Sex Pistols' first such appearance. Later that year Paul and Shaun saw American punk pioneers The Ramones play with fellow Americans Talking Heads at a new Manchester punk venue, the Electric Circus. 'We saw Joey Ramone outside the venue and were buzzing,' said Paul. 'We watched Talking Heads for half an hour, and I said, that's not punk, that's something else, that's really, really good.' They saw The Ramones again the following year, in 1978, at the Free Trade Hall and there was teenage talk of forming a band — cousin Matt had a beaten-up guitar — but it was an unlikely pipedream and talk was all it remained. There were no bands from Shaun and Paul's part of Salford. The trendier parts of south Manchester, such as Didsbury — dubbed the Chelsea of Manchester, and thanks to its bohemian reputation more intimidating to the brothers than even the city centre — seemed to be the city's musical breeding ground.

Shaun was glad to leave school at sixteen in 1978, and in what would become typically misleading fashion, designed to shock and amuse himself, he told his career advisor he wanted to star in pornographic films. Instead, his dad got him a job in the Post Office as a messenger boy delivering telegrams.

Based in the centre of Manchester, it was here that Shaun bonded with the teenage 'Perry Boys' from the tough inner-city areas of Salford and Manchester. Perry Boy was an emerging, fashion-obsessed youth cult often linked to the football terraces. It was not long before Shaun was wearing his hair in a side parting or 'flick', shopping for rare Adidas trainers, Pod shoes, Lois jeans, Peter Werth jumpers and Fred Perry polo shirts. This was an expensive and uniquely working-class look confined to Manchester, Salford and Liverpool, where it was dubbed 'Scally', and not one that he could sustain on his Post Office wages alone. Shaun thought of himself, in a Levi suede jacket and beige Farah slacks, as 'fashion brave'. This was also when he started smoking marijuana. Shaun called it a 'brilliant time'; the Post Office uniform made him look older and he enjoyed afternoons in city centre pubs, smoky places full of shady underworld characters and strippers. He confessed to stealing credit cards from the post and buying new clothes with them. Many of the early Perry Boys were still into punk, but Bowie and Roxy Music, chiefly for the haircuts, were also key influences.

The Perry Boys quickly grew to be feared in Manchester, roaming gangs turning the city centre into a treacherous place at night. They were often violent and frequently criminal – many travelled to various European cities on robbing sprees, often timed to coincide with a Manchester United match. Paul, who followed his brother and became a Perry Boy, went regularly to Old Trafford, largely to watch the sharply turned out, well-organised hooligan firm fighting their rivals – sometimes on the terraces or the pitch. Liverpool FC were United's chief rivals on and off the pitch as scalpels replaced fists and boots. 'It was all about who was dressed the best, who their top lad was, who was our top lad,' said Paul. 'A lot of people were getting cut up. The atmosphere before a big fight was fearful. Piccadilly bus station at night was like that too.'

Pips nightclub in the city centre, where various musical genres clashed in a strange world of passageways and caverns set around an open courtyard, was one of several popular hangouts. 'The disco room at Pips was mega,' said Paul. 'The soul room was fantastic. The Bowie room had been just freaks dressed up in white make-up and flamboyant gowns, with a Ziggy haircut, and that crowd dropped away as we filled it up with the Perry Boys, lads from Middleton, Blackley or Ancoats – a good little crew.'

Credit for introducing the two brothers to what Shaun would say was one of the key cultural touchstones of his teens, belongs to Shaun's then girlfriend Denise Lomax, who also worked at the Post Office. Joy Division's debut album *Unknown Pleasures* (released in June 1979) became a major obsession. Shaun liked the way they dressed – 'They had a slight Perry Boy thing going on,' he said – and their darkly poetic, intense songs, bleak and brutal, seemed to have swallowed the horrors of Manchester whole and spat them back out. Crucially to Shaun and Paul, this critically acclaimed and increasingly popular band were local, from Salford. Their records were released by the new Factory Records, also local, having been formed by 'that bloke off telly' they'd seen at the Buzzcocks, another local band. It was this triumvirate that made their pipedream of forming a band seem a 'more realistic prospect'. 'I knew I wanted to be in a band and it didn't seem such a ridiculous proposition any more,' said Shaun. Denise also tuned them in to John Peel's Radio 1 'alternative' music evening show, where Paul discovered Thin Lizzy.

Derek and Linda Ryder had surrounded their children with music without ever forcing it upon them, but by the time Paul was sixteen, Derek realised that their own musical interest was starting to rub off. In 1980 he bought Paul his first bass guitar: 'I was playing upright bass and then Paul came and said he wanted to play the bass. I didn't want to teach him but I knew somebody who gave lessons. He came down and Paul had his first lesson. Afterwards Paul said to me, I don't want any more lessons. I said why? He said it's all scales...it's not interesting enough. He wanted to play something.' Derek asked his son what he wanted to play. 'He said "Transmission" by Joy Division' – a Factory single released in October 1979. 'We got in his bedroom, listened to it and I worked it out and showed him. He mastered that and then sent off for some self-instruction tapes and he was away. He could play. He didn't know what he was playing but he could play.'

'I can't remember thinking, I want a bass,' Paul said. 'Somehow I ended up with one.' He thought it would be easier to learn than the guitar as it only had four strings. 'It was just me and a little amp. I sent off for two cassette tapes from an advert in the back of *Melody Maker* or *NME* — "Teach yourself bass with my cassettes". My dad taught me a few bits — he was a jack of all trades on musical instruments — and I listened to these cassettes.' At one Thin Lizzy concert at the Manchester Apollo Paul recalled being at the front of the stage when guitarist Scott Gorham 'flicked out his guitar pick and my mate caught it. Then he flicked another out and my mate caught it again and gave it me. So I learned to play bass with Scott Gorham's guitar plectrum.'

Over the years since leaving school in 1978, Shaun and cousin Matt had frequently talked of forming a band. In 1980, Matt, with his second-hand acoustic guitar and with Shaun providing the vocals (his drum kit long since sold), made their first fumbling attempts at a musical career. They used Derek's Korg Mini Pops drum machine and were encouraged by Derek and Barry. 'We couldn't play but Barry showed us two chords to play over and over,' said Matt. 'We tried to cover a Joy Division song. We never had a name for the band. If we did it might have been No Exit, but that was just a name I had made up at school for a punk band that never existed.'

Matt and Shaun's 'band' was largely a pose, an excuse for childish high-jinks, often with Paul and cousin Pat tagging along. 'There was this pub in Walkden they used to go to,' said Derek. Another run-down suburb of Salford, Walkden was a former coal and cotton town like neighbouring Swinton, but smaller and even less attractive. 'They only went there because he served them underage. They said to the landlord if he got a jukebox they'd get all their mates to come down. So the guy got a jukebox in and a few months later me and Linda went down for a night out and that jukebox had every song that we both loved. It was fantastic. Then three weeks later I found out it was so fantastic because it was my fucking records that they'd taken down to put on the jukebox. I paid to listen to my own records and I never got them back.'

In 1980, Paul finished at school, and joined his brother at the Post Office as a messenger boy. While Shaun had been promoted to become a postman with his own round, he and Paul, with his dyed-red flick haircut and more reserved than his brash brother, stayed close. 'There was lots of spare time,' said Paul. 'One day Shaun and our mate from school, Andrew Jackson, who was in Shaun's year and also worked in that office, put rat poison on their sandwiches and gave them to pigeons and the next day there were reports of pigeons dropping out of the sky.' The incident, Paul said, has been exaggerated in all further retellings.

Together Paul and Shaun continued to go and see groups play live in Manchester, and they were among the twenty or thirty who saw a very early Depeche Mode play Fagins club. They also went with their cousins Matt and Pat to gigs including Teardrop Explodes, Human League and Adam and the Ants at the Apollo, a traditional venue for bands who had started to become popular. Matt had become friendly with a bouncer at the venue who'd let them in after the show started for a reduced rate of £1. The four read the music press and were keenly aware of how such bands were being critically received or where they were in the charts. They formed their own opinions, thinking they could do better than the trendy Adam and the Ants and loving the arch pop of increasingly unfashionable Depeche Mode. Obsessing over music and fashion, they were unusual among their work colleagues and local pals, many of whom were already contemplating settling down.

Bands such as Orange Juice, a recent discovery of Paul's, and Echo & The Bunnymen were now among the favourites at Kent Close. 'We got brought up on the same albums,' said Paul. But Shaun was slightly ahead of him on the indie scene. 'He'd bring records home that I hadn't heard of and then three or four months later everyone would have heard of the band. He did have some really bad choices as well; had a kind of prog rock thing going on there for a while.' Shaun had the nascent indie scene sussed, picking up fast on any original guitar band that emerged, but his tastes ran to more adult-orientated rock too and, despite his dyslexia, he enjoyed reading books on icons such as the Stones, Hendrix or The Doors. It all seemed a long way from sitting in his front room in Worsley with Matt and Paul, repeating the few notes they knew and trying to come up with one-liners that made them all laugh. Perhaps it was time to grow up.

Life, on the whole, was fairly settled for both brothers, as both were living at home and working locally. The Post Office wage was good and would pay for clothes, records, cigarettes and nights out in Swinton – a pub crawl along 'the top road' and then on to the local club, the Wishing Well, where you could drink until two in the morning. 'Same thing every Friday and Saturday night,' said Paul. They were over the thrill of teenage petty crime but, unusually for the period and place, pursued their love of marijuana.

Despite their music, fashion – and narcotic – interests, there was part of both Shaun and Paul that was deeply conventional. Shaun was on his way to marrying Denise. Paul had a steady girlfriend. They both could have settled down to work at the Post Office for the rest of their lives, gone down that traditional route like most of their friends – job, wife, mortgage and kids. But they were also their father's sons. And while Derek was unashamedly conservative, his evenings performing on stage with his friend Barry, as they toured up and down the country, sometimes not getting back until long after midnight and needing to work the following day, were something that he would continue long after the brothers had left home. As the pair grew out of their teens and their sense of imminent freedom from the family home became a growing reality, it was this side of home life that would burst most violently into flames.

2
Guitar

Mark Day first encountered The Beatles as a five-year-old on a black and white TV in his mother's corner shop when they played on *Top of the Pops* in 1966. But it was not until 1981 that he met the Ryders and abandoned his dream of becoming a footballer for good.

'Daysy', as he came to be known, had struggled through his secondary education, like Shaun, with undiagnosed dyslexia. At sixteen, he left Wardley High School in Swinton with only a C grade O-level in Technical Drawing. He got a job as a labourer at Pilkington Tiles in Swinton and worked there for a year before his dad, a Post Office inspector, got him a job at the Post Office as a messenger.

He lived with his parents in a two-up, two-down terrace in Swinton, the former industrial town gone to seed since L.S. Lowry had lived there, obsessively painting its giant redbrick mills and cobbled backstreets. It was more urban, much rougher, than Worsley, with a large, modern town hall, a small claustrophobic shopping precinct and some large and notorious council estates. Day's home was not particularly musical but his mother had aspirations in that direction. She had installed a grand piano in their tiny living room. 'A fucking massive grand piano,' said Day. 'She never used to play it but she was insistent on having it. It was shoved in the corner, made the room look really small and just got in the way.'

Day's own musical tastes were, unlike those of the Ryder family, at odds with his parents'. Once he had discovered the Beatles and the Stones, he quickly progressed through Deep Purple, the Michael Schenker Group, UFO and Pink Floyd to Genesis and Emerson, Lake and Palmer. Much to his mother's horror he managed to see Queen play live three times at the Apollo.

While the piano in the living room stood unused, his mother would constantly moan that no one in the house was musical. Day, aged seventeen, took this as a challenge. 'I'll fucking show her,' he said. 'So I went out and bought a £5 guitar, a little shitty one, and went from there.'

He sent off mail order to an address in the *NME* for a guitar teaching tape by Jack Wilcock. 'I couldn't read music but this Jack Wilcock tape was totally different – it was the first format of tabs or music by numbers.' The guitarists he was influenced by were wide-ranging: Schenker, Brian May, Dave Gilmour, Hendrix, Jimmy Page, Randy Rhoads and even American virtuoso jazz guitarist Joe Pass. After years of struggling to pay attention at school, he had found something that allowed him to focus for more than fifteen minutes: 'Most of my time was spent listening to records on my record player – lifting the arm up and putting it down again over and over on a certain part of a song. I used to slow the record down so I could hear if the sound was a slide, a pull-off or a stretch.' This dissection of the songs led to a deep interest in their sonic structure and every weekend he would tape the Top 40 and try and work out how all the songs were put together. 'I was always fascinated by why this song was so good, why did it get into the top ten.'

At eighteen, around the time that Shaun got his first post round and Paul became a messenger, Day was promoted from being a Post Office messenger boy to having a proper delivery round. He was transferred to a sub-office in Farnworth, Bolton, and would get up at 4.30 a.m., finishing work at one in the afternoon. He was on £30 a week, gave his mum £5 for food and board, and apart from playing guitar there was little else to distract him. He had yet to form any clear ideas as to what he was going to do with his life.

It was while working at Farnworth that he met Derek Ryder and his perennial sidekick Barry, who were both based at the Post

Office there. 'They'd come in and still have make-up around their faces from doing their act the night before,' said Mark. 'They were always messing about because they hadn't had much sleep and sometimes they'd still be pissed.' One break-time, Barry saw Mark reading the *NME*. 'We started talking about music. He said I want you to meet Derek, he's got two sons who are in a band.' The two got talking and Derek invited Mark to his mother-in-law's bungalow in Swinton for an audition.

At the time that Mark Day was introduced to them, Shaun, Paul, and cousin Matt Carroll were not much of a band. By now Paul – who usually went by his nickname, Horse, as in Horse Ryder/ Rider – could play rudimentary bass, and had an ear for approximating bass lines from records; Motown bassist James Jameson was a big influence. Of the three he was the most gifted musically, but that wasn't saying much. 'I could hear a record and copy it but I could never quite get what I was trying to copy – not being able to copy fully the bass lines off Motown records or Thin Lizzy records.' Shaun and Matt's roles were less clearly defined and neither seemed to take the 'audition' entirely seriously, with Shaun just a few months away from marrying Denise and looking at buying a house. Typically his flippant attitude masked a growing desire to make the band work. He hoped it would be 'a way out' of the drudgery of his job. 'I didn't want to be a postman,' he said. 'It was great being a messenger boy but being a postman was six days a week, getting up early for fifty-odd pound a week. Once you became a postman, then that was it – the fun ended in that game.'

'I turned up in a Queen T-shirt, with a proper guitar case with a brand new Aria Pro II guitar in it,' said Mark. 'And Matt turned up with his guitar in a plastic carrier bag. I thought I'm in here.' Derek set up a little PA system for the vocals and the drum machine, and the first song they ever did was Joy Division's 'Transmission'. 'I'd never heard it before. But I thought, Oh this is interesting – two chords, "radio, live transmission". That was the audition and they said, Right, you're in, but change your T-shirt.'

After Christmas, in January 1982, Day offered the attic at his parents' home in Swinton as a place to rehearse. He and Shaun were almost twenty and Paul and Matt eighteen. 'You couldn't stand up in the attic,' Day said. 'You had to go up some ladders. It was a converted loft that wasn't converted properly if you know what I mean. My mum and dad would be downstairs, they could hear everything we were doing, the neighbours could hear. The first name for the band we had, which was my idea, was Something in the Attic.'

The rehearsals would take place once a week, midweek, and were painfully slow going. 'I had to be the singer because Shaun was too shy to do it,' said Day. 'He'd just sit around listening. He couldn't play anything. I started writing my own lyrics and songs. They'd take the piss.' After a few rehearsals the band's name changed to Avant-Garde – a suggestion of Matt's, who left after a few more rehearsals. 'Matt used to come along every week and play the same thing over and over again,' said Paul. 'Then he went off on his own journey and left us the name.'

'It was a relief he'd gone to be honest,' said Day, who was by far the most advanced musician among the group. 'It felt I was trying to teach Matt to play guitar when I wanted to focus on Paul and Shaun. I was a bit bossy, trying to get them to gel as a group and play together. It quickly got to the point where Shaun had had enough of me singing and he said, Right, I'll fucking do it. Then we started doing cover versions, because at least the template was laid down.'

Day was methodical, dedicated and patient with the less talented members of the band, and they attempted several cover versions including a joyously camp Depeche Mode song, 'What's Your Name?', from the band's 1981 debut album *Speak & Spell*. 'A really good pop song,' said Paul. They also had a go at two Joy Division songs, 'Shadowplay' and 'New Dawn Fades' (both from *Unknown Pleasures*), and 'I Fought the Law' – The Clash's version. 'They'd suggest a song and I'd have to go away and research it,' said Day. He would work out his part and then show Paul where he should be on the fretboard. 'We were learning as we went along. I never thought we'd get anywhere. For me, it was more about having friends. I didn't have any real friends so it was quite nice to have people come round and for us to play music together and for them to introduce me to different bands.' After playing for a while, they would go to the Morning Star in Swinton for a pint, while Day was also introduced to marijuana. It 'changed my way of thinking about things', he said. 'But we didn't socialise at weekends; we weren't like best mates.'

'Mark listened to a different kind of music to me and Shaun, he dressed differently, but he could drink – that was a plus,' said Paul. 'I really liked what he played. I couldn't describe it but I knew it was different. I thought, this is great; who cares if he doesn't come from the Perry Boy side of town – and after hanging about with us for a while his dress sense changed.'

It was clear even in these early, scratch sessions that the Ryder brothers were gradually forming an idea of the kind of music that they wanted to play. By the time Day joined they had moved away from trying to simply copy Joy Division to building new songs around the records they liked, and as the relationship with Day developed they started to feed him the kind of music that they wanted to create. They gave him a stack of records to listen to, including the first Orange Juice album, *You Can't Hide Your Love Forever*, released in May 1982. 'They don't sound like anyone else on that album,' explained Paul. 'You can see their influences but they don't sound like them which was always my ethic.'

'They'd say listen to this, listen to this,' said Day. 'It was all jingle-jangly, very chorusy and phasey. I changed my style to more of an indie style. They were trying to educate me to the indie side of it. I just went with it really – working out how the guitarists got that sound.' In the attic Shaun messed around with his microphone – a present from his father – and Matt's wooden guitar amp to create an impenetrable reverb and echo effect on his vocals, or just feedback noises, as Paul and Day tried to come up with original music. 'We'd go on for hours with this little square drum machine going,' said Day. 'We would just jam. Horse would keep repeating a bass line he made up and I'd get ideas. I'd tape what we did and in my spare time I'd listen back to it and try and improve my guitar part or come up with new parts – we didn't have names for these songs we made up, so we called it whatever was the common denominator that we could remember it by – like "Phase Song".'

Shaun wasn't convinced. He couldn't take the weekly attic sessions seriously. With his wedding looming, he simply enjoyed the excuse to smoke a few spliffs, mess about with silly noises and have a few pints afterwards. Shaun said his fiancée Denise thought he should 'grow up' and that the band was 'childish and wank'. Part of him thought the same. Meanwhile Derek continued to encourage them, suggesting they cover 'Feelin' Blue' by Creedence Clearwater Revival. 'It was dead simple, three chords, but it really worked,' he said. 'It sounded impressive with somebody who couldn't really play and Shaun's vocals were really good, really going for it.' But when Paul looked up from his bass, flushed from the progress they were making, and praised what they had done, the contrary Shaun would dismiss it as 'shit' and roll another joint. They regularly clashed.

'Paul was driven and serious,' said Day. 'Shaun was an animal on whatever substance he could get. They were always fighting. There'd be a disagreement and something personal was said, so they'd go outside, into my back yard, take off their best tops and have a fight. I'd have to go out and referee. Then they'd come back and continue rehearsing but it wouldn't go so well after that. They were opposites. I could easily have walked away.' After three months of this there was little to suggest that the band would have any staying power, but the sound they were producing was becoming more refined and ambitious. Against all the odds, particularly the ability of the brothers to break out fighting at the first opportunity, as Shaun's wedding approached the three members of Avant-Garde were spending sufficient time rehearsing to realise that they had to make a decision about their collective future. And what they decided was that they needed to dump the Korg Mini Pops and get a real drummer.

3
Drums

Gary 'Gaz' Whelan was brought up on a diet of Little Richard, Elvis, rock 'n' roll, gospel and soul music, but his real passion was football and he had shown prodigious promise as a youngster. A bad accident, in the local park, when he was eleven briefly halted his progress and would have a severe effect on his childhood. 'I put my left arm behind my back and it snapped at the elbow,' he said. 'My bone came through and my bicep muscle came out. I went into shock.' The nerves in his arm were badly damaged and Whelan wouldn't recover feeling in his two middle fingers until he was sixteen. The accident put a stop to classical guitar lessons and left him deeply traumatised. 'I saw my first child psychiatrist when I was eleven,' he said. 'And after weeks of treatment they said, We know what it is you're suffering from but there's nothing we can do.' The paperwork said 'Phobia of thoughts', and Whelan was diagnosed with obsessive-compulsive disorder (OCD). 'Everybody has these intrusive thoughts but they go; mine don't,' he said.

As a result of the accident, in 1977 Whelan started at Wardley High a few months after everyone else. Once there, he quickly befriended fellow Manchester United and punk fan Paul Davis. 'He was absolutely hilarious, on a completely other planet,' said Whelan. 'He was an amazing artist too.'

Like many teenagers of his generation, and not just in Salford or Manchester, the first record Whelan bought was punk masterpiece 'Ever Fallen in Love' by the local band who'd impressed Shaun and

Paul, Buzzcocks. The single mixed dirty subversion with classic pop hooks. In his third year at Wardley he switched from punk to Mod – during the brief Mod revival sparked by the release of the *Quadrophenia* film in 1979 and the Two Tone ska/punk explosion – and went to his first gig, The Specials at the Apollo in Manchester. 'There was only one other person at school who became a Mod and that was this older kid called Bez,' said Whelan. 'This goggle-eyed skinny kid who used to march about the school, a complete lunatic – we all used to keep out of his way. Some of his friends were absolute nutters.' Bez was two years above Whelan at Wardley High, two below Mark Day. 'It was Bez's year that had ruined the reputation of the school and then my year were also pretty bad.'

After six months of being a Mod, Whelan became a Perry Boy as the craze spread from rough inner-city areas to the suburbs. He was back playing football, playing for England Schoolboys, and he followed Manchester United fanatically. In their final year at school, late 1981, he and Davis – later to become known familiarly as PD – formed a band. 'PD wanted to be Sid Vicious,' said Whelan. 'He was obsessed with Sid, so he wanted to play bass. I wanted to play guitar but I couldn't because I hadn't got the feeling fully back in my fingers, so I had to pick drums up. My nana bought me a drum kit and I set them up in my bedroom. I was obsessed with The Beatles and Ringo Starr was my first influence – I tried to copy him but I couldn't because I was right-handed.' (Starr was left-handed although he set up his kit right-handed.) The band didn't do much, but word of Whelan's drum kit reached Shaun, via Denise Lomax's sister Bev who was in the same year at Wardley as Whelan and Davis.

'Bev would say, Oh, our Denise's fella Shaun has got a band and they want you to join because I've told them you've got a drum kit,' said Whelan. 'I'd seen Shaun about in Swinton. He was four years older than me so there was a big difference. He had dyed blond hair and I'd see him wearing a suit; to me he seemed a bit Bowie-ish.'

At the same time another pupil in Whelan's year, Nigel Day, also passed on a similar message; his brother had a band just starting out and wanted Whelan to come and play with them. 'I'd gone to primary school with Nigel and when we joined Wardley High, his older brother Mark had been a prefect and a heavy rocker,' said

Whelan. 'Me and Nigel used to take the piss out of him. He was just one of those straight guys – he was like forty years of age when he was fifteen. It didn't seem plausible to me that it could be the same band Bev was talking about. I just didn't see how Mark and Shaun could be in the same band. I sort of dismissed the whole thing. I was just about to turn sixteen and was discovering girls and drinking – so I wasn't really bothered.' When Mark Day came knocking on the door of his Wardley home, he hid. 'I was saying, Don't answer it – I don't want to be in a heavy rock band.'

Both Crystal Palace and Everton were interested in signing Whelan, but he had no interest in moving south. 'Everton wanted me back for a last trial. I had to be in Liverpool Saturday morning for 8.30 a.m. On the Friday before the trial my dad said, If you go out to the pub tonight, I won't take you. Football had been an obsession for me and my dad, for so many years. I went to the pub and he didn't take me – then he didn't speak to me for three or four years after that.' As it happened, both clubs had warned Whelan not to play football in the street with his friends. A twisted knee doing just that put an end to Whelan's hopes of being a professional footballer. 'I wasn't dedicated enough,' he admitted.

With a career in football increasingly unlikely, music was Whelan's only other hope of escaping the life mapped out for him. His hair cut in a short back and sides, left longer on top and flicked into a fringe, wearing Farah slacks and a Lyle and Scott jumper, he picked up his snare drum and walked the short distance to Mark Day's. 'Paul and Shaun were there,' he said. 'Mark didn't say much. Paul was very quiet, insular, very moody. I could see straight away Paul and Shaun were different. Shaun was the loud one, the mouthy one. He had this echo on the microphone and I couldn't understand a thing he was saying.' Shaun said he had seen Whelan about because he lived near his nana's in Swinton but had not spoken to him due to the four-year age gap. He knew Whelan was 'good at football' and he 'seemed all right'. What swung it for Shaun was that the schoolboy not only had a drum kit but a side parting, a nice jumper and a smart pair of trousers. 'He'll do,' Shaun said.

After a bash about in the attic, Shaun invited Whelan to his nana's bungalow, close to Whelan's house, and toasted him joining the band with whisky. 'Shaun and Paul were even more obsessed than me with haircuts and clothes,' said Whelan. 'They were Perry Boys like me but Shaun and Paul had put a twist on the look. They didn't wear trainers, they wore "Festivals" – blue beach shoes from Marks & Spencer – without socks. They wore big Sabre cardigans and chunky knit Sabre jumpers. They looked different to every other Perry Boy I'd seen and I liked that.'

While the new band, still called Avant-Garde, were celebrating their status as a fully formed ensemble, Mark Day's mother was not impressed with Whelan's snare drum adding to the noise in the attic. 'She was worried her ceiling would collapse,' Day said. As it turned out, their next-door neighbour was the caretaker of All Saints primary school, just around the corner. An arrangement was quickly brokered whereby the band could rehearse there every Thursday evening in exchange for £5. 'In the very same room I learned to read and write in when I was five,' said Whelan. 'Shaun had given me a cassette of songs to learn. My mum, who was an ordained white witch and often had clairvoyants at home, let me have time off school to learn them. She was happy for me to be channelling my energy into something. She had hopes I was going to do something with the football and with that going by the wayside, she saw something in the music.

'The first song we ever played together as a foursome was a song by Depeche Mode. It was the first one I'd learned off the tape, dead easy. I took another couple of weeks off school to learn "Shadowplay" and "New Dawn Fades". Then I took another couple of weeks off school and in the end I just ended up leaving.'

As soon as he turned sixteen, in February 1982, Whelan signed on the dole – part of a generation of school leavers facing unemployment on a mass scale. In 1979 Margaret Thatcher had run for government on the slogan 'Labour Isn't Working'; but in 1982, after three years of Conservative rule, with the country in recession, the number of unemployed had doubled – to over three million for the first time since the 1930s – and manufacturing was down thirty per cent. The Labour stronghold of Manchester was hit hard.

Of all the members of the band, Whelan was the one who conformed most closely to the image of being from the badlands that the press would return to repeatedly through the Happy Mondays years. After leaving school, he hung out in the pubs in Swinton with a tough gang of lads, some of whom had terrorised Shaun and Paul amongst many others. 'I was actually trying to skip rehearsals because I wasn't that interested,' Whelan said. 'Every Friday I'd go to the Bull's Head and next door to the Wishing Well where there were loads of local girls.' Drinking, he found, temporarily lifted the symptoms of his OCD. One night Whelan came out of the Wishing Well and got into a stolen car driven by a friend of his. 'I didn't realise he'd stolen it until I got in,' he said. They were both arrested and charged. 'Another night this gang were all going to my friend's house to try heroin for the first time – injecting it. Heroin had just made a big sweep around Manchester and Liverpool – certain areas were hit hard and Swinton was one of them. I wasn't planning on trying it but after a few drinks and with peer pressure, you never know. On the way there, Paul pulled up in his car and took me to rehearsals.'

In May 1982, all the band – although they weren't advertising themselves as such – attended Shaun and Denise's wedding. 'I'd had three or four rehearsals with them by then,' Whelan said. The newly married couple moved around five miles from Kent Close into a house on a new estate in a village called Astley on the outskirts of Leigh, in the commuter belt between Manchester and Wigan. Between Shaun's job, his wife and the mortgage – the pillars of middle-class respectability – the weekly rehearsals in All Saints primary spluttered sporadically on, with no great sense of purpose, and little awareness of where they were aiming musically. It didn't help that Shaun couldn't drive and relied on lifts from Denise, Day or Paul, and when Whelan was given his first taste of marijuana, and then LSD, it looked like the band would peter out as quickly as it had formed.

Of all the band members it was Paul who Whelan grew particularly close to, spending time clothes shopping in Liverpool, or seeing local post-punk band The Chameleons at the Manchester punk venue Band on the Wall and Orange Juice at the newly opened Hacienda, the UK's first ever superclub. Financed by Factory Records and the label's flagship band New Order and based on New York club Danceteria, it was a highly stylised, futuristic and spacious two-storey venue with multiple bars and alcoves, chiefly filled by live bands with the odd funk or electro club night or weird fashion party. It had a reputation for poor attendance, bad sound and pretentiousness. Nonetheless, booker Mike Pickering had great taste and consistently booked cutting-edge New York electro or hip-hop artists, as well as the best in upcoming British music, alongside Factory's own acts. Paul felt at home here and was a regular from the moment it opened. There was no entrance fee from Monday to Thursday and the bar charged pub prices. Newly married Shaun stayed home and Whelan noted how his musical tastes were 'darker' than Paul's more pop tastes. 'Shaun listened to Bowie, Joy Division, Sex Pistols and The Doors and Stones,' said Whelan. 'Paul was more into Echo & The Bunnymen, Stax, Motown and Northern Soul and he always loved pop music.' Whelan fell somewhere in the middle and grooved on the Bunnymen, Talking Heads and A Certain Ratio (ACR). And it was now, in hindsight, that the voice of the band was beginning to emerge. Not in the sporadic rehearsals, but on shopping trips, listening to records, at gigs and on the floors of the nightclubs as the modern Manchester music scene started to take shape.

Meanwhile, with overtime, Shaun was working harder than he had ever done before, from five in the morning until six at night. 'He came into rehearsal once and he had this big sling, it looked like, round his bollocks because he'd got a hernia through carrying heavy sacks,' said Whelan. 'He was a proper hard worker, Shaun – he cracked on he wasn't, but he was.' Denise still thought the band was 'a load of shite', said Shaun. The idea of settling down and growing up made him uncomfortable and he said he was 'smoking a hell of a lot of weed' – something his new wife did not approve of. 'I was getting more into the band,' he said.

Talking about the band's formative years, Whelan's lasting impression was that 'I felt I was meeting two people who were like me. I'd always been in gangs at school and fitted in but always felt alone – felt weird. These two kids were exactly the same, outsiders, but very good at fitting in, chameleon-like. I got a lot of reassurance because at the time I was thinking, Oh, maybe I am weird. English literature had been my favourite subject at school but I pretended I didn't like it to fit in. I exaggerated my accent to fit in. When I met Shaun and Paul I didn't feel the need to do that. The only thing we didn't have in common was those two weren't into football and I was obsessively into Man United, going to away games and home games. I was never a hooligan, a fighter at football, the group I went with were more thieves – the grafters.'

One thing Whelan found impossible to share with Paul or Shaun – or anybody else at the time – was the extent to which he suffered from OCD. 'You had to hide it,' he said. 'It was the kind of situation where you can't show your weaknesses and if you do you're finished. It was probably at its worst between the ages of seventeen and nineteen. I'd have about fifty pairs of boxer shorts because if my toes touched any part of the boxer shorts when I put them on they'd have to go in the washing pile. It could be an hour before I got out of the house; it was ridiculous.' He had a problem with touch: 'If I touched something with my right hand I had to touch it with my left hand. So playing drums could be a problem. I constantly smelled of TCP. I couldn't have physical contact with anyone. I had a real fear of germs. Listening to music I'd do things like press play on a song and I'd have to have a pure thought for that and I'd go back and press play again and again until I got the pure thought so no one would get harmed. It's frustrating because you know it's ridiculous, completely irrational, but you just can't stop yourself.'

All four members of Avant-Garde were enthusiastic but none seemed especially talented. Even their most gifted and diligent member, Mark Day, the eldest at twenty-one, would fog up in befuddlement after a few tokes on his hash pipe (he didn't smoke cigarettes). Paul, now eighteen, had a determined attitude but remained lethargic, twenty-year-old Shaun wrestled with married life and at sixteen, Whelan was virtually a novice with raging hormones and OCD. Their repertoire of cover versions sounded, frankly, awful. Key then to their ongoing development, indeed continuation full stop, was Derek, who every week at rehearsal in the school hall would set up his and Barry's powerful PA amplification system and loan them other equipment so that Shaun could hear himself sing above the band's cheap bass and guitar amps and the sound of drums. It gave their badly played and limited repertoire a power they frankly could not have mustered any other way. 'I gave them a bit of what the audience would be hearing and feeling,' Derek said. 'If they'd have just gone in that room without the stuff I had, if Shaun had been there without the mic and PA, it would have just fizzled out – it wouldn't have happened. I had standards and I wanted them to have that standard musically. I wanted them to know how important it was to have a great sound, it makes a big difference.'

Derek already thought the whole thing was a little strange, as Paul and Shaun had never played anything before, but he went along with it. And he had to laugh, in late 1982, when, as he set up the PA system and other equipment in readiness for his sons' band to rehearse for the umpteenth time, they told him they weren't going to do 'Feelin' Blue' that week. 'They said we've written our own stuff,' he smiled. 'I said, what, in a week? They said, yeah. So I said all right, play us something. They started and I was gob-smacked. It wasn't perfect but the feel of it was out of this world and it was completely original. I said, All right, just get on with it then. We used to use the drum machine for Gary, to keep him in time. I'd put handclaps on or a bit of percussion.' Paul would be trying to play a bass line, probably from a Motown record, but could only get so far because he had no musical training; when it came to a bit he couldn't work out, he came up with something else that made it original. It was the same with Day, said Derek: 'can't quite do it, comes up with something else. And Shaun . . . well, he was always a bit special, a one-off.'

4
Happy Mondays

There was only one rule that the band applied to writing music, and that was that the moment it started to sound like someone else they would scrap it. It had to sound different, and that rule applied to the lyrics too. Shaun had started to write, and one of his very first efforts, 'Saigon', was about the Vietnam War – a subject they were obsessed with, constantly watching films like *Apocalypse Now* and *The Deer Hunter*. 'We thought "Saigon" was a great song,' said Whelan. 'But Shaun hated it, he'd cringe at his lyrics – "From the size of the needle locked in your arm to the Russian roulette and the funny farm in the back streets of old Saigon."' Another of the early songs, called 'Red', was 'a Bo Diddley kind of thing'.

As for what they meant – the quality that would come to define the lyrics, which at times seemed both over-burdened with meaning and impenetrable – they were deeply personal to Shaun. 'I knew exactly what he was talking about but they were all cryptic,' said Paul, and the band quickly learned not to ask too many questions. Shaun's response was always to deny the words meant anything, or to challenge the others to write them. In time, he would become so skilled in obfuscating their meaning that they would touch something different in every listener – a wonderful asset. For now, a laddish one-liner would deflect the band from probing his deeper feelings.

'My job was to keep lifting the song up, keep propping it up, the scaffolding, before it collapsed,' said Day. It was his role on guitar to give the songs melody. 'It was all a learning curve – I started to understand about rhythm and lead and tried to incorporate the two by doing different tunings. I was experimenting, trying to work out how to do stuff that's not been done before. I'd jam at home, spend hours trying to make it different and interesting. I never got into Shaun's lyrics early on because I was more focused on getting the music. Some of it could be very personal. I didn't like to challenge him – sometimes we did. I'd say, that's a great line that, what does it mean? And he'd say it and we'd all have a laugh.'

Just as Paul was Horse, Day was now routinely referred to as Moose: 'It's when they started taking drugs. My eyelashes were long. I'd burnt them when I was doing a bong or hot knives and they grew back dead long. I didn't mind nicknames.'

'We thought that's what makes a band – being a unit,' said Whelan. 'The three of us were tight. Mark did his own thing. We would just jam tunes, Paul would play the same bass line over and over, I'd try and get a groove and Moose would be trying out guitar parts and Shaun would be on the floor scribbling lyrics. Sometimes he'd just sing a load of nonsense, made-up stuff. It had me in stitches sometimes what he was saying.'

It was a sign that the band were moving into a more solid form that the rehearsals were becoming more regular and had started to follow a pattern. Derek would set up the equipment, Shaun would wish he'd then leave them to it – though he often didn't – Paul would be the one to proactively start new songs, trying new bass lines he'd made up at home, and Day would continue to try and improve the guitar parts on the songs they'd already written. 'They wrote everything together,' said Derek. 'Nobody came into rehearsals and said, Here's a song. They didn't write like that, everything came from a jam. Shaun would say, You know, on such-and-such record, you know when the guitar goes, play something like that. It was all organic. Shaun used to sing absolute gibberish to whatever was played, anything to start off with, but there would be certain words or sentences that made sense or were right, so he would take them, put it there and build the rest round it…but not sitting down and writing it, it was through making things up, saying anything, shouting something.'

Lyrics and melody aside, at the post-rehearsal sessions in Swinton's Morning Star pub, just over the road from the primary school where they rehearsed, the name of the band was often a topic for discussion.

Having called themselves Avant-Garde for most of 1982, they changed for a couple of weeks to Penguin Dice. Then, in January 1983, Paul saw Echo & The Bunnymen perform 'The Cutter' on *Top of the Pops* – the band's first top ten hit. 'I thought it was amazing,' he said. 'The Bunnymen were really cool and some of my bass lines were very influenced by Bunnymen bass lines. There was a line in "The Cutter" that I thought said "the happy laws".' (The line was actually 'Am I the happy loss'.) 'We were in the Star talking about the name and I thought that would be a good name.' For a few weeks after that they called themselves The Happy Laws until finally, after a beer and a smoke, they settled on Happy Mondays – the Mondays part of the name often thought to be a loose homage to New Order's 'Blue Monday' single, the biggest selling twelve-inch of all time. It wasn't. In fact, Paul, who came up with the new name, said the band were close to changing the freshly minted moniker in the wake of the phenomenal success of 'Blue Monday' in the spring of 1983.

Also under discussion at the Star was Paul Davis, who Whelan hadn't seen since leaving school almost a year previously. Shaun recalled Davis, who lived near Kent Close in Worsley with his parents – his father was a high-ranking police officer – approaching him in the street, calling Whelan 'a dick' and proposing the band would be vastly improved if Whelan was booted out and he joined. 'When Shaun found out we'd been best friends at school he found it really funny,' said Whelan. 'PD wanted to be the bass player. I hooked up with him again and said, Look, I'll try and get you in this band but bass player's taken, maybe keyboards – we haven't got a keyboard player. We didn't really want one, but maybe. He started to come to rehearsals just to hang out.'

'He was a very clever lad but completely hatstand,' said Derek. 'He marched to his own drum more than anybody else [in the band]. He used to hang about when they were rehearsing and one day he said, I want to be in the band. At school Gary used to look

after him because he used to get picked on because he was different, not like anybody else. One day in the room he said, I want to
be in the band and I said, Well, what do you want to play? The bass.
Well, we've already got a bass player, Paul. Well, I'll be the drummer
then. You can't, Gary's your mate, he's the drummer. Oh well, I'll
be the keyboards then, so he bought a little keyboard.'

'PD used to spend a lot of time observing,' said Mark Day. 'He'd
just come down to rehearsals and watch. He'd get on with us and
get into the music. I said, Look, instead of just sitting around do
something, play keyboards. We just let him run riot on the keyboard. He never played the same thing twice. He was funny and
he helped the spirit of the band, because if things got serious or
argumentative a one-liner from him would cut it all to pieces and
we'd end up laughing. He also had a melodic touch, would float in
at the right moments. He came up with great riffs but the problem
was he'd do it once and then he couldn't get it exactly right again or
he'd come in with it at the wrong place, he'd forget. But we were all
guilty of that. He was a wild card within the music and it worked.
He'd do stuff that worked even though he's not playing it in time
or anything, it actually flirts with the song – bits of brilliance he'd
come up with.'

'He'd say something and we'd go four down, two across…
cryptic,' said Whelan. 'He was the least musician-like of us all but
PD's contribution to the band was a lot more than he's been given
credit for.' The addition of Davis on keyboards had an extraordinary
impact on the newly minted Happy Mondays. He had no musical
training but a canny ear for simple catchy melodies, and his surreal
way of looking at the world extended to his approach to music:
with him in the band, Happy Mondays would never fall into a
predictable routine. In the beginning Derek would help him with
keyboard lines, writing the notes on the keyboard and putting
stickers on it to help Davis out. Then he would improvise and
develop the melodies. To see him play with his right hand and then
use a finger on his left hand to play in between the notes his right
hand was playing was an eye-opener and sounded like somebody
doing live overdubs. 'It gave our music something else,' said Paul.
'PD was just starting out and he'd play something that was not

obvious at all, it was like he was in his own world just listening to the drum and putting his own thing down. It was really good, took the music somewhere else completely.'

'He was a character,' said Whelan. 'It was that funny side of him that clicked with everyone.' It was over drugs that Davis and Shaun really bonded, however, as PD always had a joint on him and was more of an experimenter than any of the other band members. They became best friends, but only for a short honeymoon before their relationship came to an abrupt end, to be replaced by a simmering and mutual distrust and dislike. None of the other band members could ever get to the bottom of what had gone on. 'Shaun always used to say, He's the craziest kid I've ever met in my life and I've met some nutters,' said Whelan. 'PD would just turn up out of the blue at his house, at crazy hours. I don't think Shaun was particularly bothered but his wife wasn't happy. He was spending more time with PD than his wife.' Shaun would later tell the *NME* that, during this period, Davis had overdosed on heroin at his house and Shaun feared that he was dead.

As part of his integration into the band, Davis became an enthusiastic Perry Boy convert. 'He used to draw pictures of himself in a Post Office uniform,' said Whelan. 'Because a lot of Perry Boys worked at the Post Office he made that connection and wanted to be a postman. He ended up working at the Post Office in Manchester. The four of us would drive round in Paul's car – a bright yellow Escort we called the Egg. We'd give Paul a pound for petrol money, go to Moss Side to the [Big] Western [pub] and get pound wraps of weed and smoke that. Then we'd go down to Shaun's house and spend time there or go to the pub, just the four of us. We spent a lot of time together, talking about music and clothes and listening to music.'

It was around this time that Shaun discovered Funkadelic, which had a lasting impact on the direction of the fledgling band. The pioneering American funk outfit had recently split after thirteen jaw-droppingly out-there albums. Even their most commercial album, 1978's *One Nation Under a Groove*, had track titles such as 'Promentalshitbackwashpsychosis Enema Squad (The Doo Doo Chasers)'. Shaun enjoyed the playful, bizarre lyrics that were the band's trademark, often featuring made-up words or plays on exist-ing words, abnormal song structures and the always ferociously rhythmic grooves, regularly extended way beyond traditional lengths. 'Shaun was always playing us Funkadelic,' said Whelan. 'Shaun was the leader just by dint of the fact he was the eldest.'

By the late summer of 1983, the band realised that if they were ever going to launch themselves properly then they would have to break out of the safety of their rehearsals and play to a live audi-ence. It was Derek who pushed them to do it; he was put in charge of arranging the logistics, and in September 1983, they played their first ever gig at the Wardley Community Centre in Swinton. Derek also set up the equipment, including his PA, tuned their instru-ments, and soundchecked them, since none of the band members had the faintest idea of how to deal with the technical side of putting on a live set. There was no stage and Happy Mondays played for twenty minutes in front of the same number of people. Paul claims he needed three pints and two joints to get through it past his nerves. For Day, 'it was the most nervous gig I'd ever done; you had all your mates stood around the outside. I was shaking in my boots.'

The reaction was mixed. Derek thought they sounded 'fan-tastic', but some of their pals struggled to get their heads around the mix of badly played funk and scratchy guitar rock, or Shaun's cryptic words and discordant delivery. It was not an easy listen as there were no singalong choruses or any real tune to whistle. The problem, Whelan surmised, was Shaun's voice, a nervous gruff bark which put people off, to which the band's advice was 'listen to Bob Dylan and John Lydon'. The word seemed to be either that he couldn't sing, or that the music was appalling. Or both. But it was a sign of the self-belief that was starting to form amongst them that they wouldn't be deterred.

Derek next recorded the band 'as a booster'. He hired an expensive four-track reel-to-reel recorder for the day and set it up in Shaun and Paul's nana's bungalow in Swinton. This recording, known as 'the Bungalow tape', was only ever intended to be heard by the band and their pals. 'I had Gary in the bedroom, microphone on the top of the wardrobe on a stand hanging over his entire kit,' said

Derek. 'Paul was in the hall with his bass. Moose was in the kitchen. All the doors were open so they could see one another. Shaun was in the living room with PD.' Six tracks were recorded: 'Delightful', 'The Egg' (named after Paul's car), 'Hold Back the Night', 'The Happy Side of You', 'New Day' and 'These Words of Mine'. The bass dominated, Shaun demanded heavy echo and reverb on his voice, and Day indulged himself in long guitar solos but, with the first two tracks particularly, there was something unmistakably original and deeply promising about this earliest recording. 'I think Gaz was in the toilet with his drum kit,' said Paul. 'We were all in different rooms of this bungalow but we managed to pull it off.'

As the year moved on, Derek started to take an increasingly active role in the band's arrangements. Having gone from supplying the equipment to recording their first demo tape, he now took it upon himself to arrange Happy Mondays' second gig, much to the band's evident pleasure since it meant one less thing for them to think about, and more time to be spent in the pub, smoking and imagining instant stardom. He'd entered them in a Battle of the Bands competition he'd seen advertised in the industry *Stage & Television* newspaper and on 24 October 1983 packed up the band's equipment in a hire van and drove them to the Blackpool General Post Office club to compete against Dance Vision, Mindsoared and Sensible Shoes & the High Heels. Mindsoared, a heavy rock band, owned the 'fantastic sounding' – according to Derek – PA that all the bands would use. 'Their keyboard player had a bank of keyboards like Rick Wakeman,' he said. 'The guy was telling PD about the keyboards, saying he could use them and PD said no, it's OK, I've got my own, and he got out this little Yamaha thing, only about a foot long, and opened the lid up.'

'We played three songs,' said Paul. 'Mindsoared owned the lighting rig and PA so it was obvious they'd come first – which they did. And we came last.' But, at the end of the night, on one side of the room were the winners and their pals, with the judges, and on the other side of the room was the entire audience, sat around the Mondays. 'They loved it,' said Derek. 'They were right on it.'

'There weren't many people there and we tried to bribe the judges,' said Day. 'It was just gaining experience, getting used to playing in front of an audience; what it's like and how it works – call it the apprenticeship stage.'

Encouraged, in early 1984, Derek booked time for the band in a studio in Wigan. 'It was a place called LE Agency,' said Paul. 'They were an agency for cabaret bands on the northern club scene; they represented my dad and Barry.' The fourteen-track studio in an old beer cellar underneath the agency's offices (which were in an old pub) came with an engineer and cost the band a reduced rate of £30 for a full day. Derek set them up in the live room and 'they just went for it. It was just like the Stones did in their early days, record live, we captured that.' The band re-recorded 'Delightful' and 'The Egg', plus a new song called 'The Weekend Starts Here'. The results, if still thinly recorded, eclipsed the Bungalow tape and sounded musically and lyrically singular, full of intrigue and promise. The six-minute version of 'The Egg', on which Shaun's vocals were recorded with echo and reverb through cousin Matt's old amp, and Mark Day showed off his fancy fretwork, set a template for what was to come: a hypnotic, repetitive, relentless strutting rhythm with the bass dominating, light keyboard flashes, smart guitar arpeggios and Shaun's James Joyce-like, stream-of-consciousness, non-linear narrative that followed no normal song pattern. This demo tape was the one the band and Derek would use to try and get more gigs and to potentially attract record company interest.

Derek sent the demo to *One Two Testing* magazine, which alongside pop star interviews and reviews of guitar and recording equipment had a page devoted to reviewing demo tapes. To everyone's surprise the demo was given a write-up: 'Our first ever review,' said Paul. In it, the band's name was called 'excruciatingly twee', but 'the emphasis on bassier tones', it was said, gave the demo 'an odd individuality and quirky charm'. 'Delightful' was picked out as 'the most attractive track' with a 'tight rhythmic groove'. Shaun's singing style was compared to 'a melodic David Byrne' and the band 'evocative of Talking Heads'. The review concluded: 'Happy Mondays have the songs, the ability and the distinction to make more of a noise than they already have. Can't wait to hear more.'

Of the band, it was Paul who took the initiative when it came to hustling the new demo tape, getting it to local DJ Tony Michaelides, a local John Peel figure who played 'The Weekend Starts Here' on his Sunday night Piccadilly Radio show. 'My next mission was to get us on at The Gallery,' said Paul, 'and to get the band's name in the *Manchester Evening News* in the gigs list.' The *Manchester Evening News* was the biggest-selling local daily newspaper, while Paul and Shaun were regulars at the Saturday funk, soul and rare groove night at hip club The Gallery. 'Me, our kid and Paul Davis were the only white faces in there apart from a few white girls. We sat in the corner just smoking weed.' Paul knew that there was a space upstairs at The Gallery where various hopeful local bands, and occasionally visiting acts, played. On 29 February 1984 he and Whelan had been to see Liverpool band The Farm play there. 'They were the first Perry Boy band,' said Paul. He owned a copy of their twelve-inch single, 'Hearts and Minds', which had a photograph on the sleeve of the band in Perry Boy gear: 'I was gutted because they beat us to it.'

'There were no bands dressed like us before that,' said Whelan. 'But we were listening to electro and hip-hop' – artists like Afrika Bambaataa and Man Parrish, and the *Street Sounds Electro 1* album – 'and bands from the south Bronx were wearing Adidas trainers and jumpers and tracksuits. We said, Fucking hell, they dress like us.' Paul took a demo tape to the booker at The Gallery and secured the Mondays a support slot with Lloyd Cole and the Commotions on Thursday 15 March. It was the Mondays' first central Manchester gig. Cousins Matt and Pat, who had enrolled on a graphic design course at Salford Technical College, designed a black and white poster for the gig, while Paul Davis designed a colour poster featuring his own caricatures of the band. 'He went around Manchester putting them up with decorator's paste,' said Paul. 'One of them he stuck on a road sign and it was still there two years later.'

The gig was listed in the *Manchester Evening News*, the band's name visible for all their pals, girlfriends and family to see (unlike the specialist *One Two Testing* magazine), much to Paul's satisfaction. But before they had a chance to celebrate their triumphant arrival on the Manchester scene, Lloyd Cole and the Commotions pulled out of the gig when their debut single, 'Perfect Skin', began picking up radio play, destined for the Top 40. In the end only about twenty people turned up. 'Someone gave me speed, first and last time I ever tried speed,' said Whelan. 'I finished the set and they were only on the second song. Shaun and Paul were looking at me like, fucking hell, what's going on? After the gig, we all went downstairs to the reggae night.'

While Shaun called the gig 'crap' and 'felt a bit embarrassed' by the poor attendance, it was the first time that they had performed on a proper stage with proper equipment. For the first time they sounded like a real band. What they needed now was better songs.

Paul was now on deliveries out in Walkden and life at the Post Office was infinitely duller and harder work than when he'd been a messenger. He'd optimistically sent off the demo tape to a long list of record labels but had only rejection letters in return. 'Paul would send stuff out willy-nilly,' said Derek who, via a contact, targeted Steve Edney, the director of A&R at London Records, owned by the Polygram conglomerate, and home to best-selling new wave synthpop chart stars Bronski Beat, Blancmange and Bananarama. The label had a reputation for taking risks and Edney was often seen in Manchester checking out local bands. 'I sent him a tape and he loved it,' said Derek. 'He came up to Manchester to see them rehearse in Swinton.' It was an old Victorian school hall the band rehearsed in and the gable end window was huge, thirty feet high. 'I introduced him to the band,' continued Derek. 'He stood there as they started playing and half a brick came through the window. He said, Does this happen all the time? I said, No, they must be getting better, it's usually a full brick.' Edney exclaimed, 'Oh shit, my car,' and went running outside, but the vehicle was intact.

Edney told Derek he liked the music but not the image. Derek was disappointed: 'They had their best gear on. Nobody went on stage in coats like Shaun or Paul did. People didn't understand that. They went on stage in what they wore all the time, none of this dressing-up stuff…' The way they dressed was eventually to become an image in its own right.

A few days later London Records sent the band a polite letter declining to sign them – in it Edney advised the band to work on their 'image', or rather to get one. 'When they came up, they'd asked, What's this look?' said Whelan. 'What do you go on stage with? We were saying, This is the look. They wouldn't have it.' The best-selling British acts of 1984 were Frankie Goes to Hollywood, Culture Club, Duran Duran and Wham! Even the leading 'indie' bands, New Order, The Smiths, Orange Juice and Echo & The Bunnymen, had an attractive, slightly alien sheen to them. The Mondays would not, could not, change. They felt they were at the very cutting edge of street fashion and it was the mainstream that was out of kilter.

They were not pliable, and it was not what a major record label was looking for: they weren't even dressed in the classic Perry Boy style any more, a cultish look that was beginning to take off, under a new moniker, 'casuals', in the London suburbs in a highly stylised blaze of flick haircuts and heavily logo'd and pastel-shaded sportswear. In Manchester, the look had moved on and grown a lot scruffier. Now it was almost a smackhead or slacker look. Paul wore tracksuit bottoms and the band all had a blue snorkel coat with fur around the hood, which was worn off the shoulder with just the bottom button fastened. Paul Davis took it one step further and put a psychedelic twist on the look that he could have easily lifted from The Mamas & the Papas – a goatee beard and a paisley shirt. His risqué taste would rub off on the other band members, who would adopt goatee beards and similar shirts (in tune with the then current wave of new 'Paisley Underground' bands from America – a kind of indie scene made up of bands such as Dream Syndicate, Green On Red, Rain Parade and The Three O'Clock, whose music the Mondays listened to). Still, it was not exactly the New Romantics. 'It was the Duran Duran era but there were no New Romantics where we lived,' laughed Whelan.

'I always thought I had a good dress sense and so did our kid and Gaz,' said Paul. 'In those days, which were the Boy George days, we used to get A&R men coming down and they'd see us in our trainers, trackies, Adidas gear and side partings. They'd say to us, You've got no image, and we'd go, This is our image, but these guys didn't see that. They wanted Duran Duran-type things.' Although the band was desperate to sign to a record label, their take-us-as-we-are attitude remained off-putting. The one label they felt – or hoped – might be alive to their look and sound was Factory

Records, the local label behind Joy Division, New Order and The Hacienda, but, frustratingly, they did not know how to get a foothold in this fashionable scene. Life went on: the day jobs at the Post Office, the girlfriends – in Shaun's case a wife and mortgage – and the dreaming.

On Saturdays they would head for the city centre to shop for clothes and breathe in the scene. At the very epicentre of the new Perry Boy look was a stall called Gangway, located on the upper level of the municipal market in the Arndale Centre. The Arndale, a giant shopping mall with a two-storey market hall, had recently been completed to replace a maze of old Victorian buildings but its bile-yellow façade and sheer size were widely disliked; *The Economist* called it the 'ugliest shopping mall in Europe'. Gangway was run by Phil Saxe and his brother Leonard. It sat in the market alongside stalls selling clothes, haberdashery, confectionery, videos and more. Although the market was brightly lit, clean and well managed, it was, like the rest of the Arndale, plagued by gangs of marauding young men, often football hooligans. Saxe kept 'a big iron bar' behind his stall and was not afraid to use it.

Saxe was thirty-three and had grown up in inner-city Stretford, the eldest son of one of the few Jewish families in a district famed for being the home of Manchester United. His father owned a tailor's and outfitter's and sent the young Saxe to study Hebrew and the Torah at South Manchester Synagogue. 'I didn't see the point of any of it,' he said. By the time he was fourteen he was dressing Mod – short hair, mohair suit, brogues – and was a fanatic for soul music and rhythm and blues, Atlantic and Stax – Otis Redding, Wilson Pickett, Eddie Floyd, Booker T and Solomon Burke.

On Saturday afternoons he would travel to the centre of Manchester, to the Mogambo coffee bar. 'It was where all the black guys, usually half-caste, the Scottish guys [from Salford] and the cooler Jewish kids would go,' he said. 'People would carry album covers as a sort of badge of who you were. We'd be carrying Freddie Scott's *Hey Girl* album or a Bobby Bland album and we'd look down on people carrying The Temptations and The Four Tops.' At night he headed for Manchester's hottest clubs – the Jungfrau, Oasis and the infamous Twisted Wheel. 'From the age of sixteen to nineteen,

I did lots of amphetamines. Every Saturday night, more and more amphetamines.'

The Saturday all-nighter at The Twisted Wheel had been a Mod Mecca but by the time Saxe started going there, in 1968, most of the original Mods had drifted away to a new club, The Magic Village, which championed the psychedelic scene. The Wheel now attracted kids like Saxe, working class and drug-fixated, specifically amphetamine – purple hearts, blueys and yellow dexamphetamine. 'It was a distinct little subculture,' said Saxe. 'If a girl went there she must be a slag, if a bloke went there he must be taking drugs.'

In 1969 Saxe started DJing at the Wheel's Saturday all-nighter, playing records imported from America, 'faster and rarer stuff' than anywhere else in the city or indeed the country. 'It was faster because of the drugs,' he said. This was the birth of the Northern Soul music and dance movement. Called Discotheque at the time, it was based on records not bands, a uniquely northern sub-genre that would become celebrated for the athleticism of the all-night dancing (spins, backdrops, flips and karate kicks), style of dress (huge high-waisted baggy trousers), drugs (speed) and the unearthing of obscure black American soul music (the rarer the better) with a heavy beat and fast tempo. 'People were leaping about on the dance floor,' said Saxe of his original night at The Twisted Wheel. 'I was wearing brogues or pumps, parallels – basically what became semi-flares twelve years later – and Brutus short-sleeved, checked, button-down shirts. We all used Brut, stolen from chemists alongside the amphetamines, to cover up the smell of sweat from dancing.'

The Wheel closed in 1971. 'The music kept getting faster and faster and in some ways it was getting awful,' said Saxe. 'We'd play Irish dance bands as long as it was fast.' But he'd started something and the scene spread to new venues, famously the Blackpool Mecca and Wigan Casino, and its popularity peaked in the mid to late 1970s when Wigan Casino was voted by *Billboard* magazine the number one discotheque in the world, ahead of New York's celebrated Studio 54. It was not difficult to see echoes of the scene at The Hacienda during the Madchester era.

After The Twisted Wheel closed, Saxe sold his records, bought a flat, got married and landed a good job at the Co-op as product and brand manager. His musical tastes radically changed, although they remained deeply specialist as he mined a particularly influential strain of American underground rock: The Velvet Underground, Iggy Pop, The Modern Lovers. He also fell under the spell of early David Bowie and flounced about the suburbs and the city centre with his best friend, eighteen-year-old Mike Pickering, a fellow Bowie devotee who had grown up next door to his wife, Jean. In the late 1970s, Saxe left Manchester for a job in Hull, as marketing manager for Humbrol, the manufacturer of model kits and paints, and while there he studied part time at Hull University for a business degree. He returned to Manchester in 1983, and he and Jean and their two young children lived in a nice house in Bramhall, an affluent suburb of Stockport. Saxe began teaching part time at Salford University, and then came the market stall, which was part of his father's clothing business. Gangway, he said, was popular with teenagers from a demographic he described as the 'scally sort of element...I called them The Boys: tough lads, unemployed, into a bit of blagging [shoplifting/robbery]. They'd come out of Strangeways prison and straight down here.'

In early 1984, three savvy, tearaway teenage girls from inner-city Salford came to Gangway and started a new era in Manchester cultural history. They were from poor families and could not afford the then popular stretch jeans or very tight ice-blue jeans that fashion-conscious girls in the North-west, particularly Liverpool, wore. Without money, these streetwise Salford girls drew on their resourcefulness and attitude to mark themselves out, awesome in their self-contained, self-assured disregard for what anyone else might think (there should really be a statue to them). 'They were aged about fourteen or fifteen,' said Saxe. 'They had what we called palm tree haircuts, hair scraped back and bunched up and tied on top of their heads.' The girls asked Saxe, Did he ever get any flares in? Saxe was taken aback: flared trousers had been poleaxed by punk and nobody wore them any more. The girls were insistent: they wanted some cheap flares.

Saxe got a lot of his stock from a firm called 'the Iranians' who bought huge packages from companies like Levi's, £100,000 worth at a time, sight unseen. Market traders like Saxe would go into their warehouse and sort out what they wanted. 'So I went in and found some flares – paid sod all for them. The girls came in the next day, tried them on and all bought a pair each. Then, over the next week, people started coming to the stall, a couple more girls, the odd boy, all asking, have you got any more flares?'

Ultimately, although there would be peaks and troughs and lean periods when the style was kept alive by a handful of lads, this was the genesis of the look that would come to characterise Madchester five years down the line and from there sweep the nation. 'After the girls, Happy Mondays were the first group of boys to come in looking for flares, that's how I met them,' said Saxe. 'I didn't know they were in a band but they looked a little different to the other lads that would come to the stall. They had paisley shirts on, flowery shirts, and little beards. It was Shaun and Paul, Gaz and PD and a few of their mates. They looked a bit like beatniks, like Shaggy from *Scooby-Doo* with these little goatees, baggy jumpers and now the flares.'

Soon Gangway was making serious money, upwards of £1000 on Saturdays. Jeans with twenty- and twenty-five-inch bottoms started flying out. They were quickly superseded by semi-flares; eighteen-inch cord Wranglers, parallels like Saxe had worn at The Twisted Wheel and that became the width of choice, again led by the Mondays. 'We were the only people serving this group,' said Saxe. 'You're probably talking about four or five hundred people.'

'Phil was like the Andy Warhol of the Perry Boys,' said Whelan. 'He had a very Jewish sense of humour, and he was a United fan, so I got on with Phil straight away.' Saxe enjoyed talking to all his customers, and he and the Happy Mondays found they shared common music tastes in The Velvet Underground and Talking Heads. The band was also impressed with Saxe's love of the record label Stax and his keen appreciation of Otis Redding, a favourite of Shaun's. When they discovered he was the original Northern Soul DJ, they were even more impressed. But still hurting from their rejection by London Records and the poor showing at The Gallery, the Mondays did not tell Saxe they had their own band. They feared he would take the piss, something Mancunians seemed born to excel at. Saxe did not mind the band ribbing him over his slight lisp and the psoriasis on his hands: Davis's nickname for Saxe was 'the blistered rabbi'. He gave it them back. When Davis turned up at Gangway having gone for the whole George Harrison cord look – cord shoes, cord trousers, cord jacket, cord cap – Saxe responded with, 'Fucking hell, you look like John Inman.' 'But he looked great,' said Saxe. 'He was really stylish, spent ages getting a pair of jeans, used to walk past the mirror again and again to see how they fell on his shoes, really concerned about it.'

Paul Ryder was equally at home in the Arndale market. While at school he'd held down part-time jobs in three different trendy clothes stores in the shopping mall. 'Phil had different clothes to what any high street chains were selling,' he said. 'His stall was a meeting place. He had a kind of community of people around the stall from all different parts of Manchester. We ended up getting lots of friends from places like Hulme and Blackley. We became friends with a couple of lads from Moss Side who'd chased us round the Arndale.'

Saxe's culturally alert brain, led by his marketing man's nose, began to wonder what he could do with the emerging scene that was forming around his stall. 'No one else in the country looked like The Boys,' he said. 'It was a really distinctive look, really underground, a real subculture, and it had blossomed really quickly.' What he started to think was that these kids should have their own bands, make their own music. It would be a similar thing to The Who, who had come out of and represented the nascent Mod culture in the early 1960s. Saxe felt a band made up from members of 'The Boys' would also be a suitable riposte to what he saw as the 'awful, pretentious, art music' that everyone was into in Manchester at the time.

This was 'typified by Factory Records who dominated everything', he said, thinking of bands such as Joy Division, New Order, A Certain Ratio and The Durutti Column – bands, ironically, that the Mondays liked and to a certain extent hoped to emulate.

Saxe was on the lookout for something different and thought he might have found it when he discovered a lad working on a stall in the Arndale market who had a band of his own. He went to watch them play at a regular night at The Hacienda promoted by his old best friend Mike Pickering. It was called the Hometown Gig, and would feature four local unsigned bands each week. Saxe saw The Hacienda as an extension of its benefactors at Factory Records, 'an awful place…a middle-class arty scene. It was full of people wearing suit jackets with shorts and long socks and shiny shoes or wearing big fur coats.'

Saxe was equally unimpressed by the band he had come to see. As he turned to leave he bumped into Shaun and Paul, and had an epiphany. 'To see these working-class lads from Salford in The Hacienda was really odd,' he said. 'They stood out. I said, You're customers of mine, what the hell are you doing here?' They sheepishly admitted they had a band and were thinking of trying to get a gig at one of these unsigned band nights. 'I was amazed to find out that they had a band,' Saxe said. He explained to them how Mike Pickering was his best pal and could get them on. Shaun and Paul were not the kind of men to look a gift horse in the mouth. 'They said, Can we give you a demo? I said, Yeah, drop it in at the stall.'

Wow, thought Saxe, driving in his van over to the Iranians' warehouse with the Mondays demo on the stereo. 'I loved the stuff,' he said. 'I was listening to "The Egg" and thinking, this is unbelievable and different. I was really convinced this tape was something astounding; I don't mean commercial, money-wise, I just mean artistically. I loved the fact they had a working-class background coming from Salford. I thought that was really great.'

After the disappointment of missing out on a deal with London Records, and struggling to land any more gigs, this was just the break that the band needed. Saxe asked Mike Pickering to listen to the tape with a view to the band playing at the Hometown Gig night, which would take the band into the relative big time. Playing at The Hacienda was fast becoming the hottest ticket for emerging bands, a rite of passage in the city for any local band hoping to make it, most notably the now huge Smiths. Such a gig would bring them not just under the spotlight of Factory Records' tastemakers but a host of music business movers and shakers looking for the next big thing. Shaun, since his teenage infatuation with Joy Division and latterly his admiration for New Order, had always wanted to be on the same label as those bands. The Mondays were keenly aware that, as well as booking bands for The Hacienda, the now 26-year-old

Pickering was head of A&R at Factory and an influential figure in Manchester. He had his own hip electro band, Quando Quango (on Factory, naturally), and DJed on Friday nights at The Hacienda's electro/hip-hop and funk club night. The Mondays were regulars at this sparsely attended but musically cutting-edge night.

'Mike said, I don't need to have a listen to it, if you like it, I'll put them on,' said Saxe. 'I went back to the Mondays and said, I've got you a gig at The Hacienda. They were dead chuffed.' In the space of just over two years they had gone from being musically illiterate, playing in Mark Day's mum and dad's attic, to steadying themselves to play the most important stage that Manchester had to offer. They knew how big a deal it was and they knew that they couldn't make a mess of it.

On the night they played alongside a poet dressed as Paddington Bear and a band playing Eastern European folk music, not what they had expected. They steeled themselves, for they had rehearsed hard for this moment and played without drugs and booze in their system despite a ferocious attack of nerves. They had never delivered their short twenty-minute set with more clarity. The fifty or so people milling about the cavernous space of The Hacienda offered them a smattering of applause. The world did not stop.

'So they did the Hometown Gig night at The Hacienda and no one paid any notice,' said Saxe. 'When I went down to the changing room afterwards, Mike said, I know why you wanted me to put these on, you want to manage them. It never occurred to me. I then thought, Yeah why not? I went to them and said, Can I be your manager? They had Derek and he thought he was the manager. But when I asked they all said, Yeah, dead keen. The only qualification I had as far as they were concerned was I had a business, so I must know more than they knew.'

5
Factory

Saxe started driving out to Swinton to watch the band in rehearsal. Derek, who had been helping them out in a quasi-managerial role, accepted his presence with good grace. Derek had never wanted to be in control; everything he'd done for the band so far, from driving them around, setting up their equipment and trying to get gigs, to sending out demos to record companies, was done 'because somebody had to do it'. 'And then along came Phil,' he said. 'He knew they were different and they thought he could sort something out with Factory.' With Phil as manager, Derek simply continued to do what he was doing for the band, handling their equipment and sound.

In this early period, hanging out with the band, Saxe found them to be 'lovely lads', advising, 'Take all those stories about the band, or what they were up to, in those days with a pinch of salt.' He said their criminality went as far as 'a bit of shoplifting' and he was 'not bothered in the slightest' about them 'smoking draw' (marijuana), which they nicknamed Denis, after footballer Denis Law, or dropping the odd tab of acid. 'I'd join in,' he said. As he got to know the band individually, he noted how guitarist Mark Day was unlike the others, 'not one of them', 'a little bit of an oddity'.

Saxe was the first person who brought a clear vision to Happy Mondays, who only knew that whatever they did they didn't want to be postmen. What he saw in them was the potential to be completely distinct from anyone else, and he told them in no uncertain terms that to succeed they couldn't be a 'me-too' band. They had to have their own piece of the market. While Saxe is keen to stress that his role in the Mondays' progress wasn't life-changing, it's clear that without him they would have scratched around for far longer before breaking out.

His first move as manager was to feed them Northern Soul cassettes and tell them to make their music more danceable. The music on the cassettes was familiar to Paul and Shaun from their youth but Paul, in particular, now began to appreciate it more. 'I started copying the bass lines off Northern Soul records and not quite getting it right and turning it into my style of playing,' he said. 'I never thought that Phil was trying to create this scene around us but looking at it from the outside, it was like that.'

'When Phil first saw us he said we reminded him of The Velvet Underground straight away,' said Whelan. 'Not so much musically, we just did. That was by default, we didn't consciously try and be like them; we weren't that smart or bothered, it was just how it happened. We never took it seriously. We were flippant about it.' But if there was one band they wanted to be like – though they never uttered the name – it was The Velvet Underground. They were 'just the coolest band, the way they looked, the image and everything'. Of course, many on the indie scene at the time dressed in black boots and black jeans in imitation of The Velvet Underground – the Mondays didn't want to look like them, 'but we loved the music'.

Unlike London Records, Saxe saw the Mondays' image as a definite bonus. He knew that if they could attract an audience from the hundreds of similarly dressed Boys who swarmed around his shop then a live performance by the band would be more than just a gig, it would be a happening. He thought they could spearhead this movement. Manchester's Perry Boy movement had been highly visible, their violence terrifying many, including Morrissey, while the look had inspired his foil in The Smiths, Johnny Marr. This new development of the look, with a band to front it, had the potential to make a significant impact on the city's music scene, and perhaps more widely. Don't change was Saxe's message, don't become like other bands.

'We were having our own scene amongst ourselves,' said Paul. 'Mike Pickering got it bang, straight off. We did that one Hometown gig at The Hacienda and he put us through to the next round of the competition in December 1984, advertised as "The Year's Best of The Hometown Gig (In our opinion)". But the day we were supposed to play, Mark got a nosebleed and we couldn't do it – he had to go to hospital, we were gutted. He always suffered from really bad nosebleeds.' Day blamed it on nerves, and it was not unusual to see him playing with tissue stuffed up his nose. In any case Pickering suggested to Saxe that Happy Mondays record a single with Factory. Saxe called it no big deal, since 'anyone could record a single with Factory in those days', but it suddenly put Happy Mondays, long-time admirers of Factory acts, on the same page – if not the same headline – as homegrown legends Joy Division, New Order and A Certain Ratio, plus the upcoming James, who Pickering had recently brought to the label and who the Mondays also admired.

The immediate benefit was free entry to The Hacienda. 'They were fixtures and fittings from that time,' said Pickering. 'Phil said to me, I'm going to start a movement with these lads. Phil pulled the Mondays together. I thought they were raw and very good. Shaun had a great voice that reminded me of Feargal Sharkey.' Shaun was still working on his vocal styling; each recording, each gig he learned new tricks and techniques. For now, he admitted, he was 'still trying to impersonate Ian Curtis a bit'.

Pickering may have been head of A&R at Factory but the title was grander than the job. He'd been brought into the Factory set-up by his best mate, and fellow Manchester City fan, Rob Gretton, the infamously tenacious manager of Joy Division and New Order. Gretton grew up on the vast Wythenshawe council estate and was fiercely opposed to London major music business schmaltz. He was one of three forceful personalities who dominated Factory Records. The label, despite its outward success, was based in a one-bedroom first-floor flat in Palatine Road, Didsbury and had a staff of two. Gretton, who enjoyed the same modern American black dance sound as Pickering and was the driving force behind The Hacienda, was in many ways the nemesis of Factory's co-founder

Tony Wilson. Certainly they argued a lot. The flamboyant TV presenter Wilson saw Factory as 'an experiment in popular art' (the
label was known for conceptual pranks such as giving catalogue
numbers not only to records but to events, posters, Christmas gifts,
even a cat) and loved to pursue avant-garde projects. Gretton was
more solid, preferring real bands with conventional songs.

Wilson, however, had the backing of the deep-thinking, conceptual genius behind Factory, Alan Erasmus, a black actor who had
co-founded the label with Wilson. Erasmus, whose flat in Didsbury
the label ran from, described the politics of Factory as the 'politics of
the absurd'. He could be relied on to trump any Wilson whim with
an even more fantastical vision for the label. He was also pragmatic,
sorting through the hundreds of tapes Factory would receive every
month from aspirant bands. He would say if it didn't grab him in
the first few seconds, forget it. Pickering had to answer to these
three men – all heavy marijuana smokers – when it came to his
request to record the Mondays. 'I said to Tony, I've got this band.
Tony said, Darling, you want to sign them then you sign them. Rob
said, I want to see them.'

Gretton was a busy man, and under incredible pressure. He
was ploughing New Order's cash into The Hacienda, which was
losing money hand over fist. New Order were said to be already
owed £200,000. The worldwide success of 'Blue Monday', and the
band's album *Power, Corruption and Lies*, had recently been followed
by a second top ten album, *Low-Life*. The fastidious Gretton worked
relentlessly on the detail of this success, which included touring the
world in support of the new album. He was also about to become
a father for the first time. He arranged for the Mondays to piggy-
back on a New Order UK date at the end of January 1985 at the
1000-capacity Tiffany's venue in Leeds.

Over Christmas 1984 and through the first few weeks of the
new year, Saxe paid for the band's first professional rehearsals to
get them in shape for the New Order support, where the Factory
cognoscenti were expected to give their verdict on the band. The
rehearsals took place at Spirit near Manchester's Piccadilly Station,
a basement set-up that also housed a basic eight-track studio. The
recently formed and still unknown Stone Roses, then an aggressive,

punky psych-rock five-piece with a chip on their shoulders over Factory's dominance of their home city (they even had a song about the label and Wilson), also rehearsed at Spirit. The Mondays were serious about this opportunity. Paul had got a new Peavey bass amp for his twenty-first birthday and Mark Day also bought himself a new amp. 'It just became a bit easier to work things out,' said Paul. 'You could hear things better.'

'We were living our dream,' said Shaun at the prospect of supporting New Order. All the band were determined to do their best, and inevitably they argued over what songs they would play. Shaun wanted to include a Beatles song, 'If I Needed Someone' from the *Rubber Soul* album, but Mark Day couldn't get it right. 'They wanted to do it, I didn't because I wasn't sure about it,' he said. 'I used to get in rehearsals, have a joint and I got into a dream.'

The excitement and pressure caused tension, particularly among the Ryders. Derek was often at rehearsals, taking care of the equipment and sound, and Shaun was already fed up with his presence: 'You don't want your dad around when it's your little gang trying to make music, do you?' He and Derek exchanged words, and the disagreement escalated into a scuffle during which Shaun stabbed his dad with a pen before storming out. The band went to the chippy, and when Shaun returned he and Paul argued. Another scuffle ensued, Shaun ending up with chips and gravy on his head. Scuffles between the brothers were commonplace and always ended the same way, with Paul coming out the better. The root cause, however, always seemed to be Shaun. If he was not fighting with Paul or Derek it would be someone else in or around the band. 'There's a saying that goes, if you come across three wankers a day, then it might be something to do with you,' said Paul. 'Shaun always found five wankers a day and never got the hint.' These skirmishes between the band members, sometimes developing into full-blown fights, would occur frequently and 'usually over nothing', said Derek. 'It was nothing serious, always daft things. So it was forgotten and finished with. Not going on for weeks or flaring up over the same thing.'

At the end of January 1985, two years after the band had become Happy Mondays, they played only their fifth gig, in front of 1000

New Order fans packed tight into the sweaty Tiffany's club. New Order's star was still on the rise and they would soon be playing much larger venues, but already their fan base was fervent and devoted. As if to emphasise the speed of the Mondays' ascent, Day's most memorable recollection from the evening was watching New Order play. But for Paul it was a life-changing experience. The Mondays were playing through a huge PA with proper foldback, and it was the first time that he had heard monitors the way he wanted them on stage. Now he knew what the band could actually sound like.

After the gig – at which Rob Gretton concurred with Pickering that the Mondays were worth recording – the band sat down in The Cat pub in Swinton for an interview with the *Swinton Journal*. 'Shaun was taking the piss out of me,' said Mark Day. 'I was the main target if he couldn't think of anything or was trying to be witty in front of his mates. He used to say all sorts of shit that wasn't true. My mum read something about me being a heroin addict and got very upset about it. That caused a rift.' Day stormed out of the interview. For Shaun, however, creating the right image was as important as the music. 'I understood that from the start,' he said. 'If it was just about the music, we would never have made it.'

Day was a down-to-earth and likeable character, but at six months older than Shaun, aged twenty-three, he was not as easily influenced as the other, younger members of the band. Shaun found him 'a bit dull' and 'too square'. While Shaun dreamed of imitating the bad boys of rock, such as the Stones or The Doors, and saw rock 'n' roll as an escape from the mundane, Day was level-headed and discussed pensions and forming a mail order company should the band not provide a decent income. It was obvious whose vision appealed more to Paul, Whelan and PD. Those four also shared a passion for clothing, indie guitar bands, and funk, disco and soul music. It was Shaun's gang but he could never get Day to dance to his tune. It was annoying, a thorn in Shaun's side, but Day was, the singer admitted, 'a very good guitarist'.

This was evident on new demos the band recorded between 17 and 24 March 1985, in the ramshackle Spirit studio. The studio was often used by students, overseen by in-house engineer Tim Oliver, to learn the rudiments of recording. If a band agreed to be recorded by students they would get a free demo. The Mondays did just that, with Derek keeping a keen ear on proceedings to make sure Paul's bass – already a signature motif – was loud enough. The band recorded seven tracks: 'Comfort & Joy', 'The Weekend Starts Here', 'Oasis', 'You and I Differ', 'This Feeling', 'Anyone With a Battle' and 'Delightful'. The band was especially pleased with 'Oasis', a new song that had come from a jam in Whelan's bedroom. It was named after the popular underground city centre market where Whelan's eighteen-year-old pal, Si Davis, worked in a sports shop selling rare trainers. 'Oasis was the name of the café at the back but if you said Oasis everybody just went into the marketplace,' said Paul. More than five years later, fellow Mancunian and huge Happy Mondays fan, Noel Gallagher, would go further and name his band after the same underground market.

The band and Mike Pickering used the demo to whittle down the tracks they would choose to record for their debut release. Pickering booked time in the new state-of-the-art Square One studio in Bury and asked Spirit engineer Tim Oliver to assist him with production. Derek came along to set up the band's equipment and help Paul Davis with his keyboard parts. Manager Saxe was also present. 'It was a low-key thing as far as Factory were concerned,' said Saxe. 'Tony [Wilson] probably didn't even realise we were doing it.' But this was what the band had been waiting for. They cut band favourite 'Delightful', 'This Feeling' – a track Pickering liked – and the new song, 'Oasis'.

It was a safe selection, but this would be the band's worst ever recording. Everyone present, including Pickering who had never produced a band before, seemed excessively keen to appeal to the Factory bosses, on 'Delightful' ripping off New Order's drum sound and combining it with the scratchy indie guitar work of James. They were trying too hard to fit in with prevailing trends, and the straight indie guitar pop of 'This Feeling' was indistinguishable from any number of instantly forgettable bands starting out and trying to sound like Orange Juice. 'We didn't like "This Feeling",' said Whelan. 'It was a bit twee. We were forced to put that on there. Factory even wanted "This Feeling" as an A-side. We hated it because it was too nice, just a set filler.' Only 'Oasis' hinted at what the Mondays, as a whole, were truly capable of as the members locked into a heavy circular rolling groove and they all came alive. As a package the three songs were not exactly earth-shattering, but the odd flash of delicate guitar work from Day and Shaun's decidedly odd lyrics would be sufficient to intrigue Wilson, Erasmus and Gretton.

Working with Pickering was the first time that anyone had been able to disentangle the Mondays' music and they could hear each part with absolute clarity. It made them nervous and they played the songs at a speed they had never done before, too fast. The flash studio environment was intimidating and their bravado dropped away. They felt exposed as the novices they were and looked to Pickering for guidance, offering little creative input of their own. But Pickering too was unsure of himself and apart from the 'electro' sound he got on Whelan's drums, he did little to enhance the band's sound. The music on the tracks was recorded first, leaving time for Shaun's nerves at recording his vocal for the first time ever to grow. He was already disappointed with the band's sound; not only was it too fast, but he wanted it to be 'spacier and a bit dancier'. When it came time to record his vocals he prevaricated, protesting he didn't want to be in the studio. 'I can be quite difficult in a situation like that,' he said.

'We were all insecure,' said Whelan. 'That attitude of not wanting to be there, it's a nice security net, a get-out clause. If you fuck up, or don't come through, well we didn't give a fuck anyway, whereas we really did.' Shaun, when he did, sang winningly, putting in the most distinctive performance of all the band. He was already using repetition and playing with the sounds, and hence the meanings, of words. Hearing his voice, strong, rhythmic and out front, was the real revelation of this recording session. On 'Oasis' he ad-libbed, throwing in some bastardised Tom Jones, singing, 'It's not unusual to be loved by anyone. It's not unusual to be fucked by everybody.' It gave the track a life it might not otherwise have had.

'From day one, I knew Shaun was special,' said Paul. 'Shaun doesn't sound or write like anyone else. I didn't want the band to sound like anyone else and when he came along and did vocals and lyrics, I thought this is great because he doesn't sound like any other singer.' From ad-libbing in the rehearsal room, Shaun would take a spark and set a fire, but he said his words would never be 'about one person or situation' but 'snippets of stories'; about his own experiences or stories he'd heard, which he would then string together to make a song. This was less in evidence on these early tracks: 'Delightful', for instance, can be read as a comment on his disintegrating relationship with wife Denise. He had also taken on board advice from Saxe, who had drummed into him his theory of the importance of counting on Northern Soul tracks. 'People like to understand what's coming next,' Saxe said. 'If someone goes one, two, three, four you know it's five next.' On 'Delightful' Shaun had counted from one to six, followed by the surprising line, 'I can count your teeth'. Saxe also impressed on him the need to use information people could relate to in his lyrics – reference points such as the names of towns – but Shaun took no heed of that advice.

After the recording, the band were invited to play two further shows with New Order, at Salford University and in Macclesfield. Despite their reservations about the tracks Pickering had produced, Shaun and Paul hoped they would soon be able to pack in their jobs at the Post Office for life in a rock 'n' roll band. Day had no such illusions: the Mondays had no recording contract with Factory, who were offering the Mondays no money, and there was no guarantee of recording again for the label. Whelan and PD were just happy to go along with it all and see what happened.

Shaun's home life was now a constant frustration. His wife did not like him taking drugs, either alone or with band members and assorted pals who came round to drink beer and listen to music. 'She would go mental,' he said. He started calling her Bull and she began to realise she had made a mistake marrying him; he was not the 'growing up and settling down' type. It was not an easy time for Shaun and he could be moody and unpredictable. The band would meet at Whelan's house before gigs. He was on the phone one day when Shaun came in. 'We'd been arguing about something and he attacked me while I was on the phone,' said Whelan. 'So we ended up fighting and my mum had to split us up. We did the gig and he was on the microphone holding his hand up saying, Look what I've done on his head. His thumb or finger was knocked out. We nearly started fighting again.'

'Supporting New Order was huge for us,' said Paul. 'One of New Order's sound guys, Eddie [Hallam], did the sound for us and a little further down the line he ended up being our sound guy. They were great shows and afterwards I couldn't believe people liked us. I was surprised. I thought we were too left-field for people to like.'

The Mondays played to capacity crowds of just over one thousand each night, although not everyone was entirely happy with their performance. 'We tried to do the Beatles one live at the gig,' said Day. 'I knew it was shit and I couldn't remember it properly so I didn't want to do it. There was an argument on stage. It was rubbish. I knew it would be but they wanted me to do it anyway and afterwards it was my fault for not learning it.'

'It was mad, a total mess, but brilliant,' said Bernard Sumner, New Order's guitarist and singer. 'The Mondays didn't look or sound like anyone else I had ever seen on stage. Ever since Joy Division went with Factory, we had been mixing with a lot of middle-class people like Tony, Mike Pickering, Vini Reilly, of the band Durutti Column, and virtually all the other acts on the label. Suddenly this band appeared who were on the same wavelength as us. We were both from poor backgrounds and lower working-class families in Salford. We had the same attitude. A lot of Manchester bands at the time were very po-faced and pretentious.'

The first time that Tony Wilson saw Happy Mondays he described them as a 'shambling bunch of scallies', which neatly summed up the band that New Order could most closely associate with. Despite his love of the high arts — he had a degree in English from Jesus College, Cambridge — and passion for politics, Wilson had been invigorated by punk, and ascribed much worth to working-class authenticity in music. His roots, he liked to think, were in working-class Salford, despite having been raised in comfortable middle-class Marple near Stockport. He was unfazed by the Mondays' rough edges, their laddishness. He took perverse pride in affording opportunities to bands no other record labels would touch and saw the Mondays less as a band than a concept. They were similar, he felt, to a project Factory had long persevered with, although little success had been evident: The Stockholm Monsters, who Wilson described as 'working-class bastards from the north of Manchester who had a bit of funk and a bit of spunk about them'. In fact, Wilson had just been punched in the face by a member of The Stockholm Monsters during an argument. So, while he was not at all taken with the Pickering-produced Mondays tracks, describing them as sounding too 'indie', he felt the hooligan-tinged image of the band had appeal.

Wilson's involvement, however, with the Mondays was minimal at this stage. He had a whole host of other concerns. In April 1985, his second wife, Hilary, with whom he'd recently had a son, had been hospitalised following an attack with a carpet knife by a woman who was said to be an obsessive stalker of Wilson's. He juggled running Factory and managing the label's acts, The Durutti Column and A Certain Ratio, with a high-profile TV career as one of the main anchors on *Granada Reports*, the regional evening news programme, and was also hosting a new late-night Channel 4 panel discussion show, *After Dark*.

There were many misconceptions about the man dubbed 'Mr Manchester' and Wilson seemed to actively thrive on them. The 35-year-old had started his TV career fronting a regular, short, light-hearted segment of *Granada Reports* where he would be tasked with undertaking stunts such as feeding alligators and leaping out of helicopters in the sea. He became known as 'The Kamikaze Kid' and an unlikely sex symbol. He yearned to be taken seriously but spoiled his chance to work on Granada's high-profile current affairs programme, *World in Action*, due to a reputed drug incident. Instead he became known as the face and attitude of Granada music show *So It Goes*, which gave live debuts to a host of punk and post-punk bands including Joy Division. He was Granada's golden boy, six foot, with long hair, charm and an egocentric image, often seen at the city's gigs smoking dope.

He'd started Factory in 1978, in partnership with Alan Erasmus, after the pair had initiated a post-punk club night of the same name. Working closely with three other partners, Joy Division manager Gretton, graphic designer Peter Saville and record producer Martin Hannett. Wilson put up the money to make Joy Division's first album and they were the label's great success until Ian Curtis committed suicide. Since Curtis's death, New Order had become the label's biggest-selling act and their success funded all manner of less successful bands and art projects, including The Hacienda. The label was widely admired for its stark graphic style and uncompromising musical output. Behind the scenes it was ramshackle. Saville had relocated to London, Hannett was suing the label, Gretton had his hands full with New Order, Erasmus travelled to Russia, hoping to hook up with classical musicians in pursuit of his own personal project, to be called Factory Classical, and Wilson juggled regional fame, his traumatised wife and a busy TV career with management of the label.

'It was Mike Pickering who we dealt with,' said Paul. 'Tony kept his distance for a while – he didn't come down to rehearsals, he didn't phone anyone up out of the band.' The band were allowed complete control over the sleeve for their debut single on Factory and it was designed by Central Station Design – Shaun and Paul's cousins Matt and Pat Carroll and Pat's girlfriend Karen Jackson. They came up with a graphic of a green hill and blue sky – in line with Factory's practice of rarely, if ever, including a photo of the band on their own record sleeves. In small print, on top of the hill, were the words 'Happy Mondays Fac 129 Forty Five', and the twelve-inch only release, featuring 'Delightful', 'This Feeling' and 'Oasis', thus became known as *Forty Five* (the speed at which it was to be played on a record deck, as opposed to 33 rpm).

With their debut on Factory imminent, Paul left his job and signed on the dole. 'I said to my dad, I'm quitting the Post Office to be in the band. He just said, Alright then. Anyone else it would have been, you've got a job for life son, you get a pension after fifty years. My dad was like, OK, cool.' Paul celebrated his freedom with a two-week acid binge that sent him into such a haze that eventually he didn't know where the trip ended and the world began. It was the last time he did it, saying later that it left him seriously damaged, with his head 'never the same' again.

Shaun too was now on the dole. The Post Office had suspected him of pulling scams, including dumping a load of Yellow Pages instead of delivering them, and put him under investigation. He'd played cat and mouse with the Investigations Branch for a few months at the start of 1985 but his errant behaviour and attitude to the job had incensed many older postmen. They were waiting for him to slip up so they could report him. Not that it seemed to bother him as he took to dropping acid before doing his round in Walkden. Though impossible to substantiate, he claimed to have been hauled before a disciplinary hearing after – in an inversion of the usual dog/postman routine – he picked up a small, yapping dog while tripping and bit it. It seems more likely that he got into trouble simply for taking drugs on the job. But whatever the reason, he was suspended and then sacked. Although this was the final nail in the coffin of his marriage, with Denise again raging at him, he was unfazed. He had savings, Denise still worked to cover the mortgage and it left him more time to spend on the band, smoking marijuana, drinking and listening to music.

Free from work, and with his marriage in tatters, Shaun became friendly with a young and lively local character dubbed Little Mini, whose activities included small-time drug dealing. It was Mini who supplied the black microdots that had sent Paul funny in the head. The pair even took a coach trip to Amsterdam together but while Mini arrived home safely, Shaun was busted at customs trying to bring back some hash and porn magazines, which resulted in a court appearance in Reading two weeks later. Paul drove him down, and Shaun escaped with a conditional discharge which would be wiped from his police record if he didn't reoffend in the next year.

Little Mini was part of a slowly growing entourage that the band were starting to gather around them, many of whom they'd met at manager Saxe's Arndale market stall. He danced on stage with the band at their next gig at the International club in Manchester supporting Flag of Convenience, who were essentially Buzzcocks minus singer Pete Shelley. But the performance did not gain the kind of attention that they had hoped for, local writer Mick Middles giving the set the thumbs down in his review for national music weekly *Sounds*: 'Happy Mondays spent twenty minutes supplying us with positive proof that Factory's roster is little more than a den full of hippies these days. If their maudlin strumming didn't confirm this, then the band did as they searched the crowd for "draw" after the set.' Middles was the pop columnist for the *Manchester Evening News* and he was not alone in feeling that Factory had become a self-congratulatory clique riding on the back of New Order. He saw the Mondays as the latest in a long line of self-indulgences on the label's part.

The Mondays' debut Factory release, *Forty Five*, slipped out in September 1985 with little fanfare. Factory did not believe in traditional record industry promotion such as press or TV adverts, nor did they employ a specialist press officer or radio and TV record plugger – preferring to let the music and Saville's graphics speak for themselves. It was an anarchic gesture, political grandstanding that was a form of inverted promotion in itself. Mike Pickering was one of many pushing for better, more traditional marketing at Factory. The *NME* reviewed the release alongside two other Factory singles, by Section 25 and The Stockholm Monsters, and called lead track 'Delightful' 'an okay piece of rocky pop'.

To give the single some promotion, Saxe arranged for the Mondays to be interviewed by two local magazines, *Muze* and *City Life*. Although both articles praised the band's intriguing lyrics, Shaun was not present for either interview – he 'didn't do' interviews. He was, the band said, 'too volatile'. In the *City Life* interview Whelan was quoted as saying: 'We're not anti-social but we don't know any other groups because they're all shite.' Paul said: 'Nobody knows how to take us.'

The single sold poorly, in the hundreds not thousands, chiefly to hardcore fans of New Order or Factory, but the lead track was played on the John Peel show on Radio 1, an important and exciting step for the band. On air Peel called the band 'unusual' and said he 'liked' the song. Factory was on good terms with Peel and began arranging for the Mondays to perform a live session on the show, one of his regular and popular features. Despite the poor sales, *Forty Five* even charted, reaching number seventeen in an indie chart compiled by Jumbo Records in Leeds and published by the *NME*. The band was overjoyed. They had a record on what they considered to be the coolest label in England, and that to them was making it. And they finally met Tony Wilson. 'He was like God in my world,' said Day. 'He was absolutely brilliant,' said Whelan. 'He said, You're the way forward, you're the new thing, your image is you have no image. He was lovely, but we were saying, Well we have got an image. When we'd go to The Hacienda people would look at us when we danced. We stood out.'

Wilson extended his charm but little else. And not everyone in the Factory family shared his generosity of spirit. Many were looking at the Mondays in the wrong way. Some of the lesser-known acts on Factory's extended roster, who shared Wilson's pretentiousness but lacked his sophisticated self-awareness, and were experimenting with arty guitars and electronic beats (and all of whom seemed to wear dowdy, Joy Division-inspired long over-coats), simply viewed the band as thugs. There was also a growing snobbery among many Factory musicians who increasingly valued 'musicianship' and were experimenting with 'sophisticated' jazz. To them the Mondays were déclassé. Gretton and Erasmus were busy and there was a growing sense of insecurity at the label. Bands now storming the indie charts, such as Jesus and Mary Chain, The Smiths, Cocteau Twins and The Cult, were on other hip indie labels (Creation, Rough Trade, 4AD and Beggars Banquet respectively). It was seen as a slight against Factory that they had failed to pick up The Smiths, who were from Manchester and had become the UK's biggest guitar band. The Mondays were simply seen as another mistake made by a label who were losing their sense of direction and identity. 'For the most part we were viewed with huge sus-picion,' said Whelan. 'We were not the usual Factory types.' They were lucky then that, alongside Pickering, they had the firm and unstinting support of one other member of the Factory staff.

Tracey Donnelly was in her early twenties, an attractive and eager new member of the Factory team. She had previously worked in Swing, the hip hairdressers in the Hacienda basement, and at the club itself, behind the bar, helping with ticket sales and organising the club's first merchandising. She now worked full time at the Factory office in Erasmus's flat, replacing Rob Gretton's wife, Leslie, who was pregnant. Donnelly had noticed the Mondays starting to gather a crowd around them at The Hacienda, but did not share the trepidation of many towards the band who looked more like a gang than a group of musicians. This was in part because Tracey was the sister of the notorious Donnelly brothers, young tearaways Anthony and Christopher. Said to be affiliated with the city's much-mythologised crime firm, the Quality Street Gang, the pair travelled Europe on the blag, bootlegging merchandise at concerts by the likes of U2 and Michael Jackson: they were 'proper boys'. Tracey hooked them up with the band, and they became part of the Mondays' still small but impressive Manchester audience of 'Pure Boys'.

Tracey became a leading champion of the band within Factory, also spreading the word amongst the Manchester club scene, and the band spent increasing amounts of time in her office where she kept the Factory vinyl and tapes. That is until she realised everything she was giving them, including sought-after enamel badges bearing the Factory Records logo, were being sold off at Record Peddler in exchange for albums. It did nothing to dim the fondness she felt for the band, Saxe and Derek. The financial situation at Factory was eternally precarious, a result of the decision to have no contracts with its bands, while owning a superclub with no punters and operating with a cash flow that made the label an accountant's nightmare. By 1985 New Order were still the only band making money for the label and The Hacienda. Factory's primary concern – and Tracey's – was therefore taking care of New Order, as well as finding 'the next New Order', who would fill the growing financial hole. Tracey was the only person at the label who saw the Mondays as having the potential to occupy that role.

At the end of September 1985, the band found themselves bottom of the bill at a six-band Factory-dominated line-up for a Saturday night gig, in the Cumberland Suite of the inner-city Belle Vue greyhound stadium. In an event advertised as the 'Manpower Music Festival', A Certain Ratio headlined above Inca Babies, Kalima, Jazz Defektors and My American Wife. 'I think we ended up going on second,' said Paul. 'Our kid came on stage and he said, Welcome to the fucking Gong Show.' The comment left both audience and band in hysterics. But once they had pulled themselves together they played one of their best sets to date, reinforcing the belief amongst a small but growing number that they could deliver on their potential. For the band, the more they saw of the inner workings of the Manchester scene, the more their confidence grew.

In October, Saxe, who was running the band's growing day-to-day interests, organised a statement gig late on a Sunday night in Corbieres, a tiny city centre venue the band knew well. He coupled the Mondays with a hip new band called The Weeds. 'Fifty pence in,' Saxe said. 'Corbieres could only hold about seventy people but those seventy people who came to the gig were the coolest people in Manchester.' Singer with The Weeds was Andrew Berry, Hacienda DJ and the hippest hairdresser in town. He ran Swing in The Hacienda's basement, cutting the hair of, among others, New Order and The Smiths, and DJed with Mike Pickering on Friday's Nude night. It was Berry who gave Whelan the 'Brian Jones' haircut that he would later nurture in public.

'It was heaving that night at Corbieres,' said Paul. 'There was no stage, we just set up on the floor. There was no microphones on the instruments or anything.' The air was thick with cannabis smoke, the atmosphere electric. Word went round that Andrew Berry's best pal, The Smiths' guitarist Johnny Marr, was amongst the crowd. The Mondays had a tight circle of twenty lads all dancing frenetically in front of them. Bob Dickinson, an influential Manchester journalist who'd already interviewed the band for *City Life*, reviewed the Corbieres gig for the *NME* in glorious terms: 'with perspiring, resounding frustration they thunder the sound of northern council estates . . . theirs is a mixture that threatens not to gel – genteel guitar, thwacking bass, twiddly organ and mule-kick drumming – with under-mixed vocals.' He singled out 'Oasis' and 'Delightful' as key tracks, ending the review with: 'The Mondays find their feet with furious happiness.'

'It wasn't their technical ability,' said Berry. 'It was their focus and their determination to find the centre of the music by creating an atmosphere and a vibe. Mike Pickering described them to me as "pure", meaning without any previous influences as though they had been locked in a time capsule and not been tainted by anything that was around in the media or current popular culture. When you think about it, no one looked or sounded like the Mondays when they first came out.'

It had taken the direction of Saxe to put Happy Mondays on the right track, and Pickering to bring them into the Factory fold, but on stage they were left to their own devices. It was pure Mondays, and it was pure Shaun who, in the process of learning the art of holding a stage, had dropped all pretence of the shyness that had punctured the band's early rehearsals. They had found their voice, and there was nothing quite like them, not in Manchester, Liverpool or London, where a new wave of melodic 'jingle jangle' indie guitar bands such as The Weather Prophets were starting to tour the circuit and were seen as the next big thing. The question was, did the Mondays have what it took to get to the next level? The answer came in the form of one man, who was to define the Mondays for years to come but who had the most indefinable role in the history of the band – in the history of *any* band: Bez.

6
Bez

Before Bez walked into the life of Happy Mondays he was plain Mark Berry, with a reputation as a shoplifter, fighter and joy-rider, a boy who had behaved so badly at school that he repeatedly reduced teachers to tears. Bez's father John — a detective inspector in the Criminal Investigations Department (CID) who worked as head of security at Manchester Airport — and mother were both from Liverpool and lived in Walkden, while he had one sister, a university graduate training to be a lawyer.

Bez had left school at sixteen in 1980 and got a job as a labourer in a warehouse, and by seventeen he was unemployed and living locally in a shed in a friend's garden. He then committed an audacious robbery at Worsley golf club, coming away with a few thousand pounds in cash and a huge stash of Slazenger golf jumpers, highly coveted by Perry Boys—which he foolishly attempted to flog around his home patch in Walkden. It wasn't long before he was arrested, charged and bailed to a probation hostel in nearby Eccles. Before his case came to court he did a runner, ending up living locally in a tent, but was soon re-arrested and sent to a young offenders' institute in Stoke for six months. He found the regime unbearably harsh, leading to what he called 'a mental breakdown'.

Towards the end of his sentence he returned to Manchester, living in a halfway house under the supervision of a probation officer. He started taking speed and smoking weed heavily, robbed the house and again did a runner.

Bez next hooked up with a friend who was planning a wages van robbery. After this was aborted, plan B involved a house rumoured to hold a large wad of cash. The burglary was botched, the police were alerted and Bez was arrested again, this time to be remanded in Strangeways – a prison renowned for its barbaric conditions. After two months he was shipped out to a closed borstal in Wigan where he mixed with some of Britain's most vicious and unpleasant young men. In total, since being arrested for robbing the golf club, he'd spent eighteen months either locked up or on the run – a nihilistic episode he hoped was at an end.

In 1984 Bez found himself back in Walkden where he developed a fixation with needles – 'injecting anything', he said. Heroin had flooded the area and pals were developing bad habits. He took off on the Magic Bus for Greece and spent the next few months travelling through Europe. He lived on his wits and made friends easily. Finally he ended up in Morocco, staying with a local family in Tetouan. He smoked the strongest dope he'd ever come across, experienced a spiritual awakening, and visited the mountains where the weed was grown and smuggled out. After a month his grandparents sent him enough money to pay for a return home. Unfortunately the cash went missing in transit and Bez ended up living in a cave with a psychiatrist who Bez said had 'lost the plot'. Bez spent time in the cave, 'deep in the cover of the mountain', nursing a fever before returning home to his nana's in Wigan.

He was soon back living in Walkden and in trouble again. While the Mondays were recording their debut single for Factory, he found his flatmate using an angle grinder to open a stolen safe. Bez hinted at a desperate robbery, the proceeds of which were intended to pay off a large drug debt as he was now dealing drugs to friends. Bez was making casual money, collecting and selling abandoned pallets with another friend who had a van, when he met Happy Mondays. 'He was,' said Saxe, 'the luckiest man in the world.'

'Me and Shaun were getting weed off Little Mini and for months he was saying you've got to meet my mate Bez,' said Paul. 'He kept going on about me and Shaun meeting Bez. At the time Bez was still living in this cave. After a few months, Mini said right, Bez is home, and we just clicked within ten minutes of meeting one another.

Mini said, I knew you three would get on. It was his attitude. I liked his free spirit. I wasn't tied down to any nine to five – I suppose that was me being a free spirit.'

Since Shaun had lost his Post Office job in the summer, he and Denise had both recognised their differences were irreconcilable. They had decided to split up and had recently sold the house they had bought together, described by Shaun as 'a Lego-land, semi-detached Barratt home', and with his share of the money Shaun was living in a rented flat in Boothstown, another residential suburb of Salford near Worsley. Having found out about his stretch in Strangeways, he was reputedly cautious at having Bez visit him at first – and Bez was as good as his reputation. He always seemed to be around petty crime – gold chains snatched from a girl's neck or small-time weed busts. Nonetheless, Bez was handsome and charming and fell easily into the Mondays' extended circle. 'Bez had travelled round the world and lived in a cave, original hippy,' said Whelan. 'He was the genuine article.'

Bez had attended the Mondays' Corbieres gig, bringing with him an ample supply of hashish, cannabis and cocaine. The band that night, he noted, were 'funky as fuck, chaotic but together…a lads' band for the lads'. He was still with them the next day when they'd been listening to the tape of the show at Shaun's new flat, where Paul was now virtually living too. The tape was played back endlessly over spliffs and drinks, and each song carefully evaluated. 'We were serious,' said Whelan. 'But we wouldn't admit it, not even to each other. We'd go, Yeah, don't give a fuck what it sounds like. Bez changed a lot of that. Bez would come in and listen to stuff and say I love that or I like that. Bez was the one who would be allowed to tell everyone, us and other people, that it was good.' Shaun, two years his senior, became firm friends with 21-year-old Bez. Shaun called him a 'maniac', a 'force of nature' who created chaos wherever he went. 'But there's a very likeable side to him,' he added, 'and he's great company, especially if you're getting wasted.' Bez started spending more and more time at Shaun's flat; Shaun was later to claim that they would support themselves by robbing handbags in local pubs. Bez's enthusiasm for music – of all stripes – and the Mondays was infectious. His happiness, as he tagged along with the band on visits to The Hacienda, to Saxe's stall or his new shop in the Arndale market called Somewear in Manchester, or to Andrew Berry's hairdressers, was almost combustible.

For Bez, the Mondays' next gig, on 3 December 1985, support-ing New Order at The Hacienda, could not come fast enough. New Order were playing two sets at the venue that night, and the first, in the early evening, was filmed and shown live on the BBC2 televi-sion show, *The Old Grey Whistle Test*. The Mondays were the support act for the band's second show, due to start at midnight. Early in the evening Bez and Shaun took acid and, according to Bez, Shaun 'got the horrors', insisting he would only go on stage if Bez joined him. 'Shaun said, Can I have my mate Bez dance on stage with us?' said Phil Saxe. 'I said, Oh don't be fucking stupid, that'd be daft, he'll look like a go-go dancer. Then the first time they did it at The Hacienda, instead of people walking out and going to the bar, which they normally did, people stopped and laughed. So I thought, maybe that will be alright and we should have Bez. You'd added something comic to it. It was just that Shaun was shy and he wanted someone up onstage to help him be the front person.'

'Bez had been buzzing about Shaun,' said Derek, 'and Shaun felt it'd be good to get him up on stage and it worked. Shaun just wanted to stand there and sing, he didn't want to do anything else.' He had handed Bez maracas to shake, a sound that he himself nor-mally added to the band's percussive sound. But he wasn't the only one who benefited from Bez's stage presence; Paul, who suffered from stage fright, also admitted that Bez helped to take the focus off him since everyone would be staring at Bez, hunched over, doing the boxer-type shuffle that was the signature dance of many of 'The Boys' in Manchester. And while most of the band thought that Bez would hang around and dance for a few songs and then disappear as quickly as he had emerged, they slowly came to realise that he was the missing link.

In fact there was far more to the story that it was Shaun's bad acid trip and onstage shyness that had led to him pushing Bez up on stage. It may have suited Shaun's growing image as a wayward, drug- and drink-fuelled, Bukowski-esque character to believe that, but in reality it was a far more predetermined and calculating move on his part. The band, he felt, were sounding good, the songs were getting better, but something was missing, and Shaun – determined to push the Mondays forward – knew what he wanted. Bez looked good and was a standout character. The comment from London Records that the band had no image had stuck with Shaun, and Bez would 'add to the image' and 'help us get recognised', he said. 'I brought him on stage at The Hacienda to lift things up, because no other bands had anybody dancing with them. It was something different.'

It was certainly different to the current indie guitar scene, even if, as Whelan noted, Shaun's favourites Funkadelic 'did the same thing'. Bez 'was really important', said Paul, and Shaun's cunning and sense of purpose, although often errant, underpinned the development of the Mondays. But it was the hard-working, unsung band members who would be key to their future.

7
Boardwalk

Sunday 6 January 1986. 'The first band practice of the new year,' noted Mark Day in his diary. 'Singer is too good to practise. Paul D, awkward bastard, refused to change voicing on keyboard. Horse lost his temper – another punch up. I had to intervene. Gary said he wanted nothing to do with it. I will have to go into extra training as it's going to be a rough year for Happy Mondays.'

The rehearsal was at The Boardwalk, a new location found, and paid for monthly, by Saxe. It was not far from The Hacienda and the band's 'office', the antiquated Peveril of the Peak pub, and coupled a small live venue with rehearsal rooms in the basement. Other acts who rehearsed there included fellow Factory bands James, Jazz Defektors and A Certain Ratio. The Mondays took the smallest room, recently vacated by Simply Red, who had just signed a big-money deal with Elektra Records, so they didn't have to share with anyone else – meaning they could leave their equipment set up.

'We'd turn the light off so it was pitch black and try and play,' said Paul. 'It didn't really go beyond two minutes because nobody knew where their fingers were supposed to go. We were getting in there at midday and not leaving until nine at night and all we did was jam. No song would ever get started until there was a bass line there. I'd get the bass line together in my bedroom, take it to the rehearsal room, plug it in, make it loud and fine tune it and then everything else came on top of it. We'd always record our sessions straight onto cassette to listen back to the guitar, so we could pick the mega bits Mark Day had just done. He'd always say, Oh that bit, that's really easy – well it's fucking genius, dude, just keep playing that bit there and get into a groove on it. We could play before but once we'd been in The Boardwalk, hours and hours and hours, we got really tight.' They rehearsed six days a week, every day apart from Saturdays. The Boardwalk became their place to meet up and hang out. But they knew they had to play – play and get better.

The Mondays worked together as a team and there was a vibrant, positive atmosphere in The Boardwalk. The band would sometimes take inspiration from what they heard coming through the walls from the other bands rehearsing. They grew prolific, writing so much stuff 'it was unbelievable', said Derek. Shaun and Paul's dad would still help Davis out with keyboard parts, help operate the new Roland CR800 drum machine that kept Whelan in time and was used for extra percussion, and record every rehearsal to listen to before transferring parts he felt were good onto another tape to hand back to the band for them to develop. Davis gave up his job at the Post Office, leaving Mark Day as the only band member with a full-time job, though his work as a postman did not inter-fere with rehearsals. The guitarist began to grow as a creative force. He'd spent a week's wages (£30) on a wah-wah pedal to enhance his and the band's sound. 'I got [the idea] from Jimi Hendrix,' he said. 'It gave the music that funky sound, American soul, disco feel.' Day admitted he wasn't 'technical' and 'didn't know what I was doing half the time', but he knew what he wanted and 'knew what sounded good'.

Now that Whelan – who was benefiting from the tutelage of A Certain Ratio's noted funky drummer, Donald Johnson – and Paul were locking into a distinct bass-heavy sound and rolling drum groove patterns, Day was allowed to experiment with melody. 'Mark's a genius as far as I'm concerned,' said Derek. 'He is one of the most underrated guitarists. You try and work out what he's playing on those tracks. He had a book with thousands of guitar chords in it and he knew every one of them and he invented some more himself. He really worked at it, sat there cross-legged on the floor working out parts, overdubs, everything.' Day said he strove to find something different to enhance each song and would flick through the book, dropping in a chord at random to try it out. That's how he came up with the guitar melody for a new song that Paul and Whelan were working into a Funkadelic-style workout, 'Freaky Dancin'', a song that would become a band favourite. 'An inversion of a major seventh, slide into a major ninth trying to get it funky,' Day said.

The band were yet to make any money from their music, living hand to mouth on the dole, and were still having to juggle the complications of their private lives. Shaun was making attempts to patch up his relationship with Denise and was frequently irascible or argumentative, and the band had to learn to deal with his mood swings if they were going to have any chance of getting his lyrics recorded. This was easier said than done since the fights that had plagued early rehearsals became increasingly vicious, with no one left untouched (both Paul and Whelan claimed Shaun had bitten them during scraps). Meanwhile, Paul's girlfriend was pregnant, which brought with it the additional financial stress of trying to make ends meet from a band whose singer more often than not refused to sing at rehearsals. This added extra spice to live performances, as it was left to the rest of the band to work around Shaun – a skill that they honed on the road until it became a sixth sense.

Although it was Paul who made sure rehearsals continued on a daily basis, it was clear Shaun was the leader of the gang, devilishly handsome and always in the best street-smart clobber, the frontman with an increasingly stylised way with words who was growing more confident and original in his lyrics. On new song 'Kuff Dam', he sang 'You see that Jesus is a cunt, never helped you with a thing you do or you've done'. Although he would have suggestions for the music, referencing tunes he liked, he never got involved in the hard slog of putting the songs together. 'We always wrote the music the same way,' said Whelan. 'Me and Paul would jam for a while, get a groove going, get a song going, Mark would put some guitar on top, and then Shaun would sit down and write lyrics to it.' Shaun never got involved in the music and the band never got involved in his lyrics; this was the way it worked. 'All Shaun ever said about the music was, Make it dirtier, or Speed it up,' said Whelan.

As the Mondays' music came close to how they wanted to sound, like nothing that had come before but echoing the intensity and darkness of Joy Division combined with the elongated grooves of black dance music, Shaun took it a stage further with distinctly unique lyrics and strange vocal melodies that seemed familiar but were somehow twisted out of shape. This was a band already far away from following the traditional verse/chorus song structure. Alongside 'Freaky Dancin'' and 'Kuff Dam' came new songs such as 'Olive Oil', its title inspired by a girl the band knew 'with big eyes and big feet', also known as 'peepers and creepers', and 'Cob 20', named after a school friend of Paul and Shaun's who rode his sister's Raleigh Twenty. Shaun usually titled the songs and, like the aforementioned examples, the titles frequently had no relevance to what the songs were about, a deliberate ruse to further obfuscate direct interpretation. Sometimes he simply stole and bastardised snippets from lyrics of other bands he liked or took them as his own. 'Freaky Dancin'' for instance was the title of a 1981 song by Cameo, an American funk band the Mondays listened to. The band had by now discarded many of their early primitive efforts but kept returning to 'The Egg', with Day now using a blue bottle slide on the song, growing convinced it would be their next single.

This was partly as a result of the encouragement of Bez, who now often sat in on rehearsals. The band drew inspiration and confidence from their new friend, who would groove along and nod his head in time to songs he enjoyed. 'He didn't actually speak,' said Paul. 'If his head was nodding, that was it, it's cool.' Bez was slowly making his presence felt. 'The taste master was Bez, believe it or not,' said Whelan. 'He had a good musical knowledge and was into all sorts of music. He'd travelled round the world, he was into all sorts of folk music.'

But Mark Day still couldn't work out what Bez actually did, or why he was coming to rehearsals. Musically he didn't contribute to anything, he just sat around, stoned, nodding to the music and pointing out the bits that he liked. At least, thought Day, you could guarantee he always had a joint on him to share around. But he was the kind of person who seemed to perennially attract problems. Things came to a head in late January 1986 when he was seen shoplifting food and then getting into Paul's car. They both had to report to the police.

For the members who were responsible for holding the band together in practical matters, the inclusion of Bez also meant one extra person to taxi about in Day's Vauxhall Chevette. A typical day spent trying to rehearse would start with them picking up Shaun in Boothstown, then Bez, who took an eternity to get out of his new flat in Little Hulton, and then waiting for the pair to score enough drugs to see them through the day. When the rehearsal was over it would be exactly the same routine in reverse. Of those days Mark Day's memories are of complete exhaustion and of people endlessly knocking on the door of his parents' house – where he still lived – wanting to be driven down to Little Hulton to score smack. While Bez clearly brought an ingredient that the band knew they were missing, he also brought additional chaos which, between Shaun's increasingly shambolic behaviour and the fights, the band didn't need if they were going to make good on their promise as the next New Order.

Over the weekend of 15–16 February 1986 Happy Mondays recorded their second Factory release at Strawberry Studios in Stockport. New Order's singer and guitarist Bernard Sumner, to whom Saxe had recently grown close, was producing the session. On the Saturday the band laid down guitar, drums and bass for two songs, 'The Egg' and 'Freaky Dancin'', with Whelan finally getting the drums right at 5 a.m. Originally 'Freaky Dancin'' was supposed to be built on a steady and slow tempo, but after hours of trying to get it to work, Sumner had to concede that a stoned groove of varying tempo was the best they could capture. Sumner was helping to develop New Order's increasingly polished and precise electronic sound, and played the Mondays the band's upcoming single 'Shellshock', which displayed these qualities to impressive effect and would be an eighth Top 40 single for the band. Although Sumner was in effect a 'pop star' and the band had good reason to be in awe of him – being long-time admirers of both New Order and Joy Division – they were at ease in his down-to-earth and humorous company.

The Mondays took their work seriously, having been left

disappointed by the sound on their previous Factory single, and abstained from drugs and booze during the recording. 'Not even pot,' remarked Sumner, who said he was in the studio producing the band 'as a favour to Phil'. Tony Wilson had called him 'one of the finest producers to ever come out of Manchester' and he had produced or remixed, often uncredited, several Factory acts. The Mondays particularly liked his recent production of Marcel King's 'Reach For Love', a smooth electro soul song he'd made with ACR's drummer Donald Johnson. Shaun had seen Johnson, who Sumner often worked with, creating expansive musical worlds via computer-triggered samplers in ACR's Boardwalk rehearsal room. Shaun was fascinated, and a seed was planted that would later germinate with the Mondays' use of samplers and sequencers. But for now they didn't have the wherewithal to incorporate such elements into their sound and Sumner resisted the temptation to overload the recording with electronics – although 'The Egg' would feature keyboards that could have come from a New Order track. He said his intention was to try and capture the Mondays' 'rawness'.

On Sunday, Tony Wilson popped into the studio. It was his first real contact with the band. He was beginning to formulate how he could sell them beyond their 'scally' image. Although their Factory debut had been largely run-of-the-mill indie guitar rock, when Sumner played him back what the band had recorded so far – with both tracks over five minutes long – he heard 'black stuff, dance stuff'. 'I know they're a group, a rock group, but they're something else,' he said. Wilson dubbed them a 'white soul act'. It was a description he would quickly drop when it provoked only laughter, but he wouldn't be the last to try and fail to name the 'something else' in the Mondays' music.

Mark Day added further overdubs to both tracks using Sumner's own guitar and Shaun put down his vocals. He was already all over the tape, shouting abuse at the other band members and responding to their angry replies with further wisecracks. 'One of the funniest things I've ever heard,' said Sumner, who rued the fact that this 'banter' was deleted and not kept for posterity. One snippet that featured Shaun shouting 'Shut up Gaz, we're starting', and then a more exasperated 'Ronnie!' – his nickname for Whelan, after Liverpool footballer Ronnie Whelan – made it through to feature at the start of 'Freaky Dancin''. The song's lyrics concerned a topic Shaun would return to again and again – heroin, a drug he'd dabbled with and had a real taste for. 'Freaky Dancin'' is often thought to be a song about Bez, but in fact it is about the drug and its effects on his relationship with Denise. It was a scruffy song, but it had a groove, however shambolic, and a neat vocal melody. However, it was 'The Egg' that the band were really into – its slow, laidback feel, its surreal storyboard of words, silky bass line, strong drumming and melodic twists.

The session went on through the night and would finish at ten the next morning. When they were not recording the band would watch porn – *Animal Farm* was the latest sex video nasty doing the rounds. It was not this though that would be remembered as the Mondays' depravity started to take on mythical status. Wilson, who saw himself as 'executive producer' on the session, went out to the nearby McDonald's to pick up food for the band. Sumner had a Chinese takeaway delivered but only took a couple of mouthfuls before declaring it vile and throwing it in the bin. The band dived in after it, hungrily stuffing it in their mouths. Unlike many stories about the Mondays, this one was true. 'We were all starving,' said Paul. 'We had no dole money left. Bernard had four mouthfuls of his orange chicken whatever and threw it in the bin...it was whoaaa, straight in.'

Following the recording, Saxe had organised for the Mondays to play support to The Colourfield, a band formed by former Specials and Fun Boy Three frontman Terry Hall, based in Manchester and best known for their hit 'Thinking of You', on four UK dates – the Mondays' first 'tour'. Shaun insisted Bez come with them, which continued to cause friction amongst the other band members; they felt he was just a madman, even though he did bring a passion to the stage that was otherwise missing.

In preparation for the tour Derek Ryder, who was still working closely with the band, made a flight case for their equipment out of plywood and 'shopping trolley wheels'. He also hired the Transit van and, while still getting up at 4 a.m. for his job as a postman, he drove the band everywhere. At the gigs he set up their equipment, tuned the guitars and then ran to the mixing desk to do the sound. Then he would pack all the gear away at the end of the night and ferry the band around before going back home and straight out to work again. Meanwhile Shaun and Paul's mum Linda, who chose not to attend these early concerts, was always on hand with mountains of sandwiches. Happy Mondays may have been about to do their first tour, but they were still on the dole. Mark Day even hid secret supplies of food in his guitar case – until the rest of the band found out.

The first gig was at Hull University. The band's rider was a paltry one can of beer each, and the crowd didn't warm to them. It didn't help that Mark Day was stoned and had a fit of giggles on stage, while Bez danced sporadically and looked so out of it he frightened the audience. After the next gig in Reading they all slept in the van at a service station. 'We had this great big brown sofa top from Gaz's house in the back, some sponge and we all had a sleeping bag – real rock 'n' roll,' said Paul. It was a bitterly cold February and they woke up to find ice on the inside of the van windows.

By the time the tour reached Leicester, the Mondays were stoned and tripping and tired. They got into the venue early and lay on the floor in the bar to sleep, and they were still there when the door opened and the audience poured in. The band finished the set in chaos. Later that night Saxe threw a can of beer at Shaun as the tensions that had been rising throughout the previous three days on the road came to their natural, violent conclusion. At some point Shaun threatened to sack PD, but it was, apparently, just banter. The only person who managed to stay out of it was Bez, who was off his head half the time and according to Saxe probably didn't know where he was in any case.

The trouble was that when they did the gigs they never wanted to be there. They knew when they got it right live, got into their groove, they were at their best, but they still lacked the confidence to feel that they could pull off a proper set. Even though they'd been together over three years, they had only done fifteen gigs and there was still a huge amount for Shaun to learn about interacting with an audience.

On the last night of the tour in Newcastle, Shaun didn't bother to soundcheck – 'as usual' said Day – and the crowd response was poor. The tour ended on a downbeat note when The Colourfield threw a party back at a hotel and the Mondays were initially turned away. They left to head back to Manchester in the early hours. Matt Carroll, who'd tagged along for the gig, was sick coming back in the van, which pretty much summed up how they felt the four dates had gone.

Back in Manchester, Bez joined Paul and moved into Shaun's Boothstown flat. Politely described as bohemian, it was a one-bedroom flat that none of them cleaned. It was, according to Paul, 'awful' – they were eating baked beans cold out of the tin, with no one bothering to impose any order on the place. A real problem over the coming months as the band started to do more and more badly paid gigs further afield, was that one of them was always away the day he had to sign on, which meant no money. In the end they got one of their mates to do it for them in return for a fiver. Life remained unremittingly grim, but there was always something on the horizon to look forward to, to keep them going.

On 1 April 1986, months after he'd played 'Delightful', the band finally travelled to London for the first time, to record a live session for John Peel's Radio 1 show. Peel's backing was crucial for any indie band in an era when there were few national outlets for the music. Shaun and Paul had grown up listening to the show and hoped to make a good impression. Unfortunately Day had dislocated his arm playing football. While he managed to get through a support slot with New Order in Brighton, he turned up with the band at the BBC studios in Maida Vale with his arm in a sling.

The session would be recorded live and broadcast later. Derek set the equipment up in the studio and was furious when BBC engineer Dale Griffin, former Mott the Hoople drummer, who was in charge of recording the session, grabbed hold of Whelan's drum kit and dragged it across the room. Derek kicked off. 'If something broke we were fucked,' said Derek. 'We had no spares. I had to look after stuff.' Next, Griffin started bossing the band around. 'The guy there was very BBC, we're doing it our way,' said Whelan. 'So we had a bit of a fall-out.' The Mondays downed tools. 'Fuck it, they weren't doing it,' said Derek.

It was a disaster. A call was made to Saxe back in Manchester and John Peel was informed of the situation. The telephone in the studio rang and Griffin was summoned to it. Peel, on the other end, made it clear he expected the Mondays to be recorded. Griffin was forced to apologise and then didn't speak another word, recording the band in silence.

It was a measure of the Mondays' fortitude that they were prepared to forfeit the chance of their most significant national exposure to date rather than tug their forelock to a puffed-up BBC gatekeeper. It said even more about them that they fed off this drama to record easily their greatest moment to date, delivering an astonishingly assured seventeen-minute performance, playing 'Kuff Dam', which seemed now to be another song about heroin, 'Olive Oil', 'Cob 20' and 'Freaky Dancin''. The sound was epic, percussive, and the pace of the songs supremely measured.

The session was broadcast on 9 April. The band knew they were going to be on and were crammed into Day's car, parked outside the Big Western pub in Moss Side, where they had just scored a bag of weed. They knew that the show was influential within the music industry, had been responsible for helping launch innumerable bands, including The Smiths, and it would not be just the Factory cognoscenti listening in to judge them but 200,000 listeners. It was a big moment, though they pretended to one another that it wasn't. They hushed one another as Peel introduced 'Kuff Dam'. The band fell silent. 'We were all quietly stoned,' said Whelan. The song finished, they looked at one another. 'We were quite surprised. We said, Fucking hell, why can't our recordings sound that good.' The spliffs started to taste sweeter after each of the four songs they'd recorded were played by Peel over the next two hours. They were walking on air. But what seemed such a big moment for them went largely unnoticed, did little for their popularity. Even though they were on the fabled Factory Records roster, it would take much more to make them stand out from the hundreds of indie band wannabes.

8
Out

Out Promotions had recently been appointed to handle Factory's press, radio and TV promotions – an event of sufficient importance at the label to warrant a catalogue number: FAC161. Dave Harper ran the press side and American-born Nicki Kefalas the radio and TV side. Harper had worked at Rough Trade Records and Kefalas for Scott Piering, when he was manager of The Smiths, and as a receptionist at Rough Trade. 'I had to go on a night out drinking with various directors of Factory to clinch the deal,' said Kefalas. 'We went to the Russell Club and I met Hurricane Higgins; it was an all-night session.' She had little experience in radio and TV plugging, 'but they were quite forward thinking in those days and they just wanted someone who got the music'.

Kefalas and Harper's company would grow quickly to handle the cream of British independent record labels, representing, alongside Factory, 4AD, Creation and Mute. Harper recalled meeting the Mondays for the first time in London, hoping to glean enough information to write a press biography. 'Phil Saxe did all the talking,' he said. 'They just sat there looking suspicious.' It was clear that the band would never have got anywhere without Saxe, who was at the time not being paid for his work. Harper was accused by Paul Davis of being the devil and by the rest of the band of talking shit, at which point Saxe suggested just turning the tape recorder on and letting them give their own account of themselves. The result, when transcribed, was a mash of funny stories that was then sent out to the music press. According to Harper, 'It went down really well, best press release ever.'

'Freaky Dancin''/'The Egg' was released on 7 June 1986. Central Station Design again handled the cover, sticking with strong block colours and shapes, this time overlaid with a freakish, screaming cartoon figure in solid black. Locally, 'The Egg' was creating a minor buzz. The *Manchester Evening News* called the song a 'compelling piece of music which rolls along at a rare pace. The singer's sardonic delivery flowing from beneath a massively dominant bass...they will step to the forefront of the Manchester music scene during the course of this year.' John McCready in the *NME* dismissed the single: 'It sounds like something A Certain Ratio might have made before Donald Johnson was drafted in to stamp on their toes and make them dance,' he wrote.

The single performed poorly, not much better than their first effort, selling 'bugger all' in Saxe's words. He remained fervent in his belief that the Mondays were a completely original band that could affect a cultural shift, a Velvet Underground for the 1980s. But he felt this needed communicating more widely, with more urgency, so that their audience could be given an opportunity to grow. 'I thought, this is music that no one has ever heard before,' he said. 'But people would look down on us. We were scallies and they were all serious musicians. It was all very negative in Manchester to the Mondays.' Brimming with frustration at what he saw as the lack of local support, Saxe crossed swords with local DJ Tony Michaelides. 'I nearly attacked him,' he said. 'I said, You fucking bastard, why aren't you playing "Freaky Dancin'"? I couldn't believe someone who's meant to champion new music wasn't playing it. He said, Well, it's not a very good record. I said, It's different, it's vibrant, it's the best thing that's ever happened to Manchester. I was evangelical about it all.'

A Factory-organised art and music festival called The Festival of the Tenth Summer took place in Manchester in July. It was intended to celebrate the city's culture with specific reference to the Sex Pistols' first performance there in 1976, an event Wilson maintained had changed the course of Manchester music history. The Festival of the Tenth Summer was typically Factory and consisted of ten 'events' incorporating art, fashion, music, merchandise and film, spread across several venues, with a climactic show at the 10,000-capacity G-Mex Centre featuring A Certain Ratio, OMD, The Smiths and New Order. The Mondays played a night titled 'Back in the Cellar' at the small Rafters club and the gig was reviewed positively in both *Melody Maker* and *NME*. In *Melody Maker* Paul Mathur, a pal of Factory's new PR Dave Harper, wrote: 'The current Freaky Dancin' gobstopper and its father Delightful crackled and ripped in the heart of a set which made electric guitars and voices and mad, mad eyes great again.' Stan Barton, in the *NME*, noted the band's 'fruitcake of a maracas player' and wrote of an 'instantly appealing set, delivered with an arch deadpan humour' and 'a quirky charm'.

While in Manchester, Paul Mathur interviewed the Mondays for a full-page feature in *Melody Maker* – the band's first major piece of press. It was notable for the band's refusal to speak at all during the interview. Mathur wrote that the Mondays were so reticent about doing interviews they'd failed to show for one the previous week. He also called 'Freaky Dancin'' 'the best single of the year'. Saxe – 'described by some as the Malcolm McLaren of the Perry Boys', wrote Mathur – did all the talking. 'They didn't like doing interviews,' said Saxe. 'They wanted me to do the interviews. I loved what they were about. I was sort of like a preacher. They wouldn't talk and they needed someone to champion them.'

Saxe did what he could for the band but he was a novice too, and the gigs he booked for the band around the country, in an attempt to win a crowd outside Manchester, were ad hoc. They travelled to London on 23 July for a first gig in the capital with, if not high expectations, the hope that they might have generated some sort of a buzz. It was a miserable, unseasonably cold day, and raining, and the pub venue Saxe had booked them into, The Cricketers in Kennington Oval, had not even bothered to advertise the gig. The band the Mondays were due to support had cancelled at short notice and the venue's owner told Saxe there seemed little point in his band playing. They were ready to head back to Manchester but Derek, who had driven the hire van to London, had other ideas. In return for food and drink, instead of a fee – which was only £50 – the band would play. Derek set up the equipment, the band did a soundcheck and then started on the beer. A few hours later, with the crowd still not in double figures, the drunken band had to be shoehorned on the stage. 'We thought fuck it, go on then,' said Whelan. 'We jammed the gig, played one song for seven or eight minutes because we were all off our nuts.' One of few people there to see the Mondays that night, unbeknownst to the band, was Sorrel Downer, a female journalist from *Melody Maker*. Over the course of the gig she became a convert to their cause, as fervent about the Mondays as Saxe. The Mondays' luck was turning.

In her review of the gig, Downer called the band 'manic pied pipers, whipping the sane and blasé into grinning gibbering, jerky party-lifers'. She mentioned the band's flares, their 'anoraks' and nonchalant indifference on stage, picking out Bez as a 'true star'. She next made 'Freaky Dancin'' single of the week in *Melody Maker*, calling it 'irreverent, exciting and sort of accidental'. London was proving a happy hunting ground for the Mondays. Three days after playing The Cricketers, they returned for a gig at the Clarendon Hotel Ballroom in Hammersmith supporting hot indie rock band The Weather Prophets, whose recent single 'Almost Prayed' had been an indie number one hit. The Mondays were reviewed again, this time in *Sounds* by Jonh Wilde – a journalist Factory PR Dave Harper had corralled to the gig. Wilde wrote: 'It's a wonder these Manchester misfits manage to make something so massively bright when their imaginations clearly hover on the lunatic fringe.' He called 'Freaky Dancin'' the 'most fucked up piece of dance music ever to exist' and again drew attention to the band's unusual dress sense, particularly their flares. Wilde had spent the entire day with the Mondays in London, interviewing them for what would be a double-page feature in *Sounds*, another valuable piece of publicity. Unlike the *Melody Maker* interview with Mathur, the band opened up to Wilde. They talked about reading Hunter S. Thompson's book *Hell's Angels* and referenced the Kabbalah. In fact, this would be the very last interview with the music press where the band did not put up any sort of front, and came across as naïve, literate, charming, self-aware and comedic.

'We sat around in the forest and discussed how we were going to be and it was chaos,' Shaun told Wilde. 'Someone wanted to be Alex

Chilton, someone Funkadelic, Tibetan folk, heavy metal…and in the end we thought sod it, throw it all together and see what happens. Let's be original and famous.' They described their own music as 'fanciful, fantastic, weird, wacky, real, deluded, bewitched, sort of dizzy, unbalanced, most of all frantic'. Bez said they wanted to be entertained by the audience. Someone mentioned their nightmares about thirty-foot cardboard men. 'Sometimes the music all comes together, clicks like magic,' they said. 'Other times, the best bit is when it falls apart.' Paul said: 'I want to say to my grandchildren I was in this pop group, these are the records, this is what we did.'

The lack of image that had led London Records to turn the band down was now proving to be their greatest asset. The country was deeply divided over Margaret Thatcher who, following victory in the Falklands, had used her second term to take on the unions and pursue a radical agenda of privatisation of state-owned companies such as gas, water, steel and electricity. Her brutal war with the miners was seen as starkly politically divisive, and a defeat for the communities of the working-class north who were being left behind in a wave of home- and share-owning yuppyism – a mood reflected in the mainstream charts, where Chris De Burgh's 'Lady in Red' was number one and Madonna, Whitney Houston and Genesis were all scoring best-selling albums. Unemployment reached a post-war high, at 14.4 per cent, and vast swathes of the north were disproportionately affected with many families stricken by poverty. The council estates of northern England became a sort of dead zone.

The indie music scene, by its nature more politicised than the mainstream, was populated by mostly middle-class, arty, intellectual bands. Any political posturing was hectoring or ersatz, often both. Even The Smiths, who continued to poke a stick at Thatcherism, and had provided a rare voice for the dispossessed, seemed now to be writing at a distance, flushed with their incredible success. In their hooded coats and flares, wearing scruffy goatee beards, speaking in thick Mancunian accents, the pot-smoking and beer-swilling Mondays seemed to arrive in London loaded with a savage romantic image, full of symbolism and deep meaning. Even as Shaun was admitting he was more concerned with 'how words sounded' than what they meant, his lyrics were seen to provide a window into a brutal lifestyle.

'The music press was more into Mondays' attitude than music,' said Dave Harper. The band were interviewed and photographed by *Sounds* in the back of their tour van, where they were using a beer can as a bong. 'The journalist told everyone how frightening they were,' added Harper, 'which was brilliant PR.' Saxe said: 'In the van, PD was shouting at me, Phil, tell them to fuck off, they're smoking our draw.' And it was not just the press who were taking interest in the Mondays in London. There was a rumour that Geoff Travis, head of Rough Trade Records, home of The Smiths, was interested in signing the band. The happening Creation Records, too, home to The Weather Prophets and Jesus and Mary Chain, were smitten via the well-connected and well-liked Jeff Barrett, who while working for Creation was also promoting indie gigs in London. He'd organised the recent Clarendon gig and was eager to bring the Mondays back to London to play again. Barrett said the band were 'mad, exciting and funny – the sound of a revolution'.

'Jeff Barrett loved taking us down to London because we were very, very different to what was happening down there,' said Saxe. Barrett, although not involved with the band in any formal manner, became something of a disciple and threw the Mondays' name about with undiluted praise in the circles he moved in – all the right ones – as the best new band around.

The strong interest and glowing praise they were receiving in London threw into sharp relief their lack of success in their hometown. Here, the Mondays were largely ignored by the media and viewed as a bunch of stoned wasters whose backing by Factory was seen as symptomatic of the decline of the once great label. 'We couldn't get arrested in Manchester,' said Saxe. 'It was the intelligentsia in London, the people who worked in the music papers that really kicked it off. Jeff Barrett was superb, a visionary.'

The Mondays were back down in London in August for a show at Covent Garden's Rock Garden. Nicki Kefalas took influential journalist and ZTT Records co-founder Paul Morley to the gig. 'He was impressed with the madness of it all,' she said. 'You could see

Shaun was a poet and interesting; all the good stuff was obvious but it was just very shambolic.' More often than not this impression of chaos on stage was down to Shaun, who if he was having a bad day or was in that kind of mood would perform churlishly, singing the wrong words on purpose or missing cues. 'Shaun would want to cut this or that song and we'd say no, stick to it,' said Whelan. 'If the third song was "Freaky Dancin'", he'd say no, miss that out and go to "Oasis" and we'd go no. So we'd start "Freaky Dancin'" and he'd sing "Oasis" to it. No one would give in, so you could get times when it was chaos.'

The band was well-rehearsed, less temperamental than their singer, routinely fantastic. And they played music off-kilter and out on a limb from an indie scene dominated by plainly derivative sixties-inspired guitar bands who were lumped together under the 'C86' moniker, named after the *NME* compilation cassette which had rounded many of them up. The way these bands all looked – bowl haircuts, tight black jeans, Cuban-heeled winklepicker boots and leather jackets – only made the Mondays seem more alien. As the band's reputation for drug-taking and drinking spread, in tandem with the impression that they were illiterate council estate hooligans, it seemed astonishing to many commentators that they could play at all, and not just that but when Shaun was on his game and fell into the band's groove they were able to deliver songs whose like had been unheard of before. It seemed easier to suggest it was some sort of haphazard genius at work than contemplate the truth, that they were disciplined and hard-working and that this was the result of their endless hours of rehearsal at The Boardwalk. Derek would tape every gig and on the way back to Manchester the band would listen back to it, picking out faults or good bits and finding room for improvement. Shaun would say he was 'off his nut' for many of these gigs, but the truth was he worked hard and made sure he formed some sort of connection with the audience. He was hungry for success and buoyed by the plaudits the band gathered.

In September, there were more music press interviews. In addition to the features in *Melody Maker* and *Sounds*, the Mondays appeared in *Record Mirror* and as part of a Dave Haslam piece in the *NME* about new Manchester bands, featured alongside new Factory act The Railway Children and The Weeds. Haslam, who was also a DJ at the new 'student night' at The Hacienda, as the club sought desperately to attract punters, described his interview with the Mondays as an hour of stumbled conversation dominated by Saxe. 'There are plenty of bands that live here and one or two are alright but there's no such thing as a Manchester scene,' Paul told Haslam. 'It's the worst ones that need to feel part of a movement or a scene. We don't. We're not part of any scene.' Saxe said he was on 'a moral crusade' with the Mondays: 'It's about making money and securing a job, because otherwise Happy Mondays are on the dole.'

A riot at a show in Blackburn, with The Railway Children, earned the band more press inches. Fighting had erupted between a gang of lads from Blackburn and one from Manchester. 'I was on stage and I saw through the light this pint glass coming through the air,' said Whelan. 'I was thinking this is going to hit me, this is going to hit me, no, no it's not, it's going to hit PD, it's going to hit PD, is it? Yeah. It's hit PD and bounced right off his head.'

'Someone's shouting, "Blackburn Youth, Blackburn Youth"' – the name of Blackburn's football hooligan firm – 'and then you just heard a bang and that was Bez whacking the kid in the head,' said Paul. Deploying his maracas, Bez stepped in just as the police arrived to try and take control of the situation. He was cuffed but soon let loose – after vomiting on a policeman's shoes. 'When the pint pot hit Paul Davis on the head and bounced off,' said Saxe, 'he walked off – I'm not going back out there, Phil, they'll fucking kill me. I had to force him back out.'

The Railway Children were young and good-looking, students who played the sort of straight-ahead melodic indie rock currently popular. Tony Wilson, still looking for the band that would become the next New Order, thought at last he'd found it. Despite the recent publicity, the Mondays remained, in Shaun's words, the 'runts of the litter' at Factory. But it was not just Saxe saying they were something special now, there was a growing chorus of voices in London. The band went back to their Boardwalk rehearsal room to jam, to improve their sound, to write better songs. Saxe continued to organise ad hoc gigs and they played a further clutch of dates throughout October, mostly with the ever-supportive New

Order, their new indie celebrity fans The Weather Prophets or local indie rock band The Bodines, managed by Factory insider Nathan McGough. Alongside 'Kuff Dam', 'Olive Oil', 'Freaky Dancin'', 'Oasis', 'Delightful', 'The Egg' and 'Cob 20', their live set now featured three new songs – 'Desmond', 'Russell' and 'Little Matchstick Owen'; fresh results of the hours spent rehearsing in The Boardwalk. The gigs, often depending on Shaun's mood, would be hit or miss, but they were never routine, never became a smooth act. There was a sense that anything could happen at any moment; it made them captivating, kept the music in the moment, the now. 'It was that teetering on the edge of complete chaos that it was all about – it had a sort of power,' said Saxe. 'It was part of the joy.'

Shaun was not the only one capable of throwing the gigs into disarray. Paul Davis was still lobbing curveballs into the mix. 'PD is an abstract character in real life and that comes across in some of his keyboard playing,' said Paul Ryder. 'That was what was so good about him; you never knew what you were going to get. If he was in a good mood you'd get happy keyboards, if he was in a shit mood you'd get moody, withdrawn…if he was in a split mood, it'd be a split personality on keyboards. He was playing how he felt. It was kind of crazy.' Basically Davis would play whatever he wanted – on one memorable occasion he played the keyboard line to Lisa Lisa & Cult Jam's 'I Wonder If I Take You Home' throughout an entire gig. At another, he stood with his arms folded throughout and at the end of the set pressed just one note, 'ping'. He said he was listening to the set and he thought it sounded alright, so he decided not to interfere.

It was Saxe's job to try and keep some sort of order on the road. It was not easy – often things were barmy – but he was having great fun. 'We were playing at a club in Hull – we're talking about a shithouse, we were doing little clubs, toilets – and there was a load of plastic beer crates on stage,' said Saxe. 'They put PD's keyboards on top. He said, I can't go on there Phil, you won't be able to see my legs, I'll look like a fucking glove puppet. The whole band was laughing at this. Another time, he said, I can't go in there, the floor is sloping.'

On 9 October 1986, the Mondays were back in London to play at the Bay 63 club, an event promoted by their new biggest fan

Jeff Barrett. There were only fifty people present but the gig was reviewed positively in the *NME*, the band's sound described as 'loose scraped back funk', 'awesome grunge-ridden funk', 'insistent and compelling' with 'a demonic dance beat'. The review stated that they'd done a 'cracking version' of 'She's Crafty' by the Beastie Boys. Whelan insisted they were just 'messing about' with the song on stage, but they were big fans of the American rappers – they rarely listened to contemporary indie bands such as REM or Jesus and Mary Chain, preferring hip-hop acts like Run DMC or LL Cool J – and would go to see them on their infamous Licensed to Ill tour. They were present at the Liverpool Royal Court Theatre in May 1987 when the gig was cut short after nine minutes and erupted into a riot.

In Leicester, supporting The Weather Prophets, a member of the band's entourage let off tear gas. Day noted that the band 'blew away' the Creation-signed C86 band The Bodines while supporting them in Rochdale. 'Why aren't we big yet?' he wrote in his diary. The Mondays had begun to attract quite a crew – mainly young lads – to their northern shows. 'We were picking up a lot of New Order fans through doing those gigs with them,' said Paul. 'It was Perry Boys dressed like us getting into the music.' In Malvern, supporting New Order, Bez, Shaun and Whelan joined the headliners on stage for their encore of The Velvet Underground's 'Sister Ray'. Later that night Whelan had to be persuaded down from the roof of the van where he'd been dancing. In Leeds, there was trouble with the crowd before the Mondays went on and a fight broke out. Bez smashed his hand on a beer glass and the wound required twelve stitches. 'He was in a temper, must have been fighting again,' said Day. 'Everyone was there to see us and we weren't the main band either.'

Among those present to see the band at the Leeds show was Vini Reilly of Factory mainstays The Durutti Column. He was being suggested as a possible producer of the Mondays' debut album. The band wanted Bernard Sumner but 'Freaky Dancin''/'The Egg' had marked his temporary retirement from production. New Order had a new album out, *Brotherhood*, which would sell close to one million worldwide, including half a million in America where the band were about to embark on a huge tour. 'At one point Vini was going to do it,' said Paul. 'At the gig in Leeds he was talking a lot to Mark about guitars. I don't know what happened, but the idea of him doing it drifted away, or he drifted away.'

Although Factory had agreed to fund the recording of a Mondays album, many were circumspect, including Tony Wilson who was more taken now by The Railway Children and new signing Miaow. James, Factory's one-time great hope, had taken advantage of their no-contracts relationship with the label to abandon ship and accept a lucrative offer from major label Sire. It was Wilson's suggestion that Reilly, whom he had managed for many years now, should produce the Mondays' album. It was ill thought through, but Wilson hoped the respected and thoughtful guitarist could impose some sort of intellectual rigour on the band. He and Factory had been here many times before; a clutch of good reviews did not guarantee good record sales. So even while many influential people in London were singing the band's praises, Factory was unsure about what the band were trying to do. Only Tracey Donnelly in the office showed true faith. In any case, Vini Reilly was turned off by the band. According to Wilson, after meeting them, Reilly called the band 'scumbags' and 'the worst bastards' he had ever come into contact with. He offered a caveat. 'That guitarist, you know what Tony, has no idea how to play the guitar, no idea what he is doing at all,' Reilly reputedly told Wilson. 'That's the strange thing because what he is doing, or rather what he is trying to do, is potentially the most inventive stuff that anyone has played for at least ten years.'

Saxe made it plain to Wilson that he didn't want Reilly anywhere near the band. He had his own idea for who he wanted to produce the album, someone whose name would silence the band's critics and whose stamp of approval would prove that the Mondays were the special band he, and a growing few, believed they were. He just didn't know how to get him.

9
Cale

John Cale was first and foremost the founder of American underground rock pioneers The Velvet Underground. Since the band, one of the most influential in rock 'n' roll history, infamous for their experimental sound, lurid lyrics and patronage from Andy Warhol, had split up in the early 1970s, Cale, raised in Wales and a trained classical musician, had embarked on a successful and challenging solo career. Phil Saxe was a huge fan and had imagined the Mondays as embodying a similar pioneering spirit and encapsulating at Wilson's Factory in Manchester a scene comparable to Warhol's Factory in late sixties New York. The Mondays were Velvets fans too, with Shaun an admirer of the band's singer Lou Reed.

What now interested Saxe was Cale's reputation as a record producer. He knew that Cale had already produced three iconic first albums by hugely regarded artists: the eponymous debuts by The Stooges and The Modern Lovers, and Patti Smith's *Horses*. Saxe wanted to stitch the Mondays into that lineage, imagined their debut album would become legendary too. It was a great idea. He ran it past his pal Bernard Sumner, who agreed but said that if Saxe suggested it to Wilson himself it would be ignored. Sumner said he would tell Wilson. 'So Bernard said to Tony, I think John Cale would be great for the Mondays. Then Tony came to me and said, I've got a great idea for who we can get to produce the album. I said, Who? He said, John Cale. I said, Oh, that'd be brilliant.'

Wilson approached Cale, who he had featured on his Granada music show *So It Goes* and had invited to play at the recent Festival of the Tenth Summer, and for two weeks in December 1986 he found himself face to face with the band Wilson had described to him – 'so he knew what he was getting into', said Wilson – as 'scum'. The band were understandably excited to be working with Cale, although, not unsurprisingly, Shaun harboured reservations purely because the idea of Cale producing had not been his.

Cale chose to record the album in the Fire House studio in Kentish Town, north-west London, where he was friends with the chief engineer, David Young. During the early 1980s Young had been guitarist in Cale's band and they had recently worked together, as engineer and producer, on Nico's album *Camera Obscura*. Fire House had a remit to serve the local community, particularly disabled artists, and was rented out commercially to fund this. Siouxie and the Banshees, Killing Joke and Tippa Irie had all recently recorded there. Cale, who was then forty-four, had recently gone straight after many years struggling with well-publicised drug and alcohol issues.

Problems arose before recording had even begun. Cale arrived at the studio with a little wooden crate of clementines and a box of extra strong mints. This was his clock and when he'd eaten the last clementine and chomped the last mint he'd go home, end of the session. He didn't even smoke cigarettes. As Whelan said, 'We were just starting [drugs] so it couldn't be worse. For the first two days we just played the songs and you could see he was completely bewildered by it all.' But Cale was impressed by Day's guitar work, though he couldn't make out what he was playing. 'He said to Mark in the control room one day, Where did you get those chords from?' said Whelan. 'And Mark said, I think I got them from Marks & Spencer. Typical Mark. And we went, No, guitar chords, tell him about your guitar, you tit.'

As the band ran through the songs live in the studio, Cale would wander from the control room into the live room to study Day's guitar work more intently – 'as if to say, What the fuck's that?' said Day, who thought the whole thing was a bit weird. 'He'd ask, What you doing that for, why? I'd say, Oh I just like it.' Then Cale would wander off for another clementine. The producer was a distant and authoritative presence. He barked at the band for smoking in the studio but didn't communicate any great musical wisdom. He seemed to be deep in thought most of the time, analysing what the Mondays were all about. Day worried about what he was thinking 'because we were reckless in our approach to everything', and that included music making. Cale intently listened back to the live recordings the band had made. He calmly suggested adjustments to certain key clashes he heard. 'We were all in awe of him,' said Day. 'He was a bit of an icon.'

After a day's recording the band would head back to their accommodation, sharing two rooms in a doss house in Belsize Park, and drink until four or five in the morning, while a sober Cale retired to spend time with his third wife and their newly born daughter in a well-appointed apartment. Still, for the Mondays this was the life, being a proper band, in London, recording their debut album with a bona fide legend. It was an enlivening experience and an excuse to live a little of the rock 'n' roll lifestyle. On top of the beer and marijuana came cheap speed, a pink over-the-counter medicine – Kaolin and morphine – and for the first time in a band situation heroin, supplied by Shaun. Whelan stuck to his weed, and Paul was not impressed with heroin, preferring the rush of speed. 'Heroin wasn't my thing,' he said. 'Take it, puke up, sleep for an hour; a nice sleep but that wasn't my thing at the time, I was into uppers.' Shaun associated heroin with musicians such as Lou Reed and Keith Richards and writers like Baudelaire or Burroughs. Many of his favourite songs had lyrics about heroin and his own lyrics too were scattered with references to the drug. Prodded by Shaun, Mark Day tried heroin for the first time while recording the album, hoping it would put him on the same 'wavelength' as Shaun. 'He thought opiates through the centuries had inspired artists and musicians and if he got me onto heroin, it'd be like that,' Day said. It wasn't. Day did not feel the same euphoria as Shaun. He felt dizzy and nauseous. 'I just thought, I can't work on this in the studio,' said Day, who went back to his 'weed and drink'. He would never take heroin again.

Cale drilled the band relentlessly. They had thought the endless rehearsals had made the songs pin sharp, but Cale's boot-camp attitude made them realise they'd been kidding themselves. 'We'd do the song and he'd say, Do it again, finish the song, do it again, finish the song, do it faster,' said Paul. 'Finish the song, do it faster than that, and it'd be like take twenty-two he'd record. He definitely got us even tighter.' It would benefit the band when they went back out on the road, but this way of working would be something they'd never repeat. The band did not feel as if they could question Cale's directions and were unable to make any real personal connection with him to discuss their own aspirations; they were too shy even to ask him about The Velvet Underground.

The midday starts and early evening finishes did not suit the band and Cale's right-hand man, studio engineer David Young, was often left exasperated. 'They were the kind of band who could be really bad,' he said. 'It was difficult to record them, not least because they wouldn't do the same thing twice, which is what producers and engineers want – some semblance of control – and these guys were shambolic. Paul Davis didn't have the faintest idea what he was up to. The drummer had this drumbeat; a curious sort of hopping beat, bit of a sixteenth note thing as you might find in a galloping beat but only one, not enough to make the whole gallop, sort of lop-sided. He wouldn't hit it on the two and the four like a regular rock drummer – one of them would be offset by a sixteenth note. That was the hallmark of the album. I thought the kid just didn't know how to play drums and had lucked in or had found this thing by accident while trying to play a rock beat. That beat got taken on into the machine era of the band later and the guy sort of maintained that off-centre drumbeat. A lot of people copied it.'

Cale too grew frustrated at what he saw as an 'unruly' and 'sloppy' band. He wanted, at the very least, for them to play in time and in tune, without any mistakes. He could not, however, always keep a straight face. He watched Bez trying to play tambourine on one take, and compared it to 'a building collapsing'. He desperately wanted to impose some sense of order, but even when he felt he had the musicians where he wanted them, Bez and Shaun would walk in and 'unravel whatever kind of cohesion had been going on beforehand'. And yet he felt, like Saxe, that this was a rare music, one that reminded him of the elemental and defiantly raw, almost anti-music, force of the Velvets. And the lyrics were way out, he liked that. But something wasn't right.

If the Mondays thought that the first week of recording was hard, they were in for a shock. At the beginning of week two, Cale brought them back into the recording studio and had them start all over again. He scrapped the live performances for better ones, and while he was clearly working to a plan he was keeping it to himself. But it was working, as the feeling coming from the band was that they were recording an album that sounded like nothing else recorded before. As the rough mixes of the finished songs were played back to the band, Paul began to glow with pride. It had been clear while they recorded that Cale had never come across anyone who played or behaved like Paul Davis before, yet he had placed his keyboard with great delicacy in the mix, so that it complemented and enhanced the songs without being too upfront. 'The keys are great on that album,' said Paul. The guitar work was precise, simplistic sometimes, rhythmic and melodic, with Cale keeping Day's excesses largely in check. It was not the lead melodic force it would become but a bedrock for the songs. Whelan's galloping drumbeat gave the songs a languid fluidity, the perfect foil to Paul's bass which dominated the album. The first instrument of attack, it was loud, springy, slightly off-centre and propulsive, hook heavy and repetitive, hypnotic, narcotic. Paul was still lifting small sections of bass parts from other songs and building his own tunes around them, so that they already sounded somehow familiar. On one song, 'Little Matchstick Owen', the bass carried the melody and Paul admitted he'd ripped the whole thing off from a bass run in 'Got to Give It Up' by Marvin Gaye: 'I'd usually just take snippets but that was too good, I thought I'd have the whole thing.'

Cale put Shaun's vocals up front and clear. It was not just his striking lyrics — in which he often convincingly evoked states of mind relating to the use of acid or heroin — that surprised, but the power and range with which he delivered them. There was real anger in his voice at times and he was becoming increasingly aware of studio technique, rolling words around his mouth to make the most of his limited melodic range. The lyrics were a mix of the darkly comic and the truly absurd — peppered with knowing references to characters in the band's circle of acquaintances. They were, he said, 'a mish-mash of ideas, abstract or surreal', just 'words that sounded good and created a visual image'. It was not all palatable stuff – on top of the frequent allusions to drugs, there was death and disease and madness within the words.

Cale could only guess at what the words meant and had run into a nightmare working with Shaun, since he wrote his lyrics on scraps of paper and once he'd finished singing them he'd screw them up and throw them in the bin. As a result, it was impossible to tell sometimes if they could be improved. His vocal takes were also always full of ad-libs and little tics, which made re-recording individual lines difficult, especially when Shaun would claim to have forgotten what he'd sung. Even the band were in the dark – they had long stopped asking about Shaun's lyrics for fear of turning rehearsals into a full-on ruckus.

The one exception on the album was the lyrics to the track 'Russell', which came from the blurb on the back of astrologer Russell Grant's book, *Your Sun Signs*. Shaun changed a few words around and altered 'what makes the sign tick' to 'what makes the twat tick', but essentially the song lyrics were a direct rip-off. 'It's hilarious and brilliant,' said Whelan. 'We had the song and he had no lyrics for it and he couldn't get any lyrics for it. He picked up the book in The Boardwalk, turned the book over and read it.' On 'Desmond', he sang about 'Eddie the breakdancer' and the vocal melody owed much to The Beatles' song 'Ob-La-Di, Ob-La-Da'. 'I hated "Desmond",' said Whelan. 'It was the last one we recorded and we couldn't get it right. A friend of mine had a friend from school, Eddie, who was a breakdancer on Salford Precinct; the lyric is "Eddie the breakdancer in the precinct square stupid top and stupid shoes" or something. Eddie heard it and was really pissed off.'

The Mondays had recorded much of the material before – 'Kuff Dam', 'Olive Oil', 'Cob 20', 'The Weekend Starts Here' (shortened to 'Weekend S') and 'Oasis' – but Cale had given it an aggressive new focus. The two newer songs were uncompromisingly repetitious musically and lyrically bleak: ''Enery's 'pass your germ' hook could be read as about either sexually transmitted diseases or a friend who had contracted HIV through sharing needles to inject heroin. The lyrics to the almost five-minute, chorus-free onslaught of 'Tart Tart' referenced the recent death of an older woman the band used to score draw from, who 'laid it on'. 'When we didn't have money, she'd say, Oh here's an eighth, give it me when you have the money,' said Whelan. 'Then we went round one day and she'd had a brain haemorrhage and fallen down the stairs and died.'

While at Fire House the Mondays also cut a rap version of 'Little Matchstick Owen' – a track named after skinny Welsh boxer Johnny Owen, nicknamed 'the Merthyr matchstick', who had been knocked out in the twelfth round of a world bantamweight title fight in 1980 and never regained consciousness. Discussions had been held about getting someone to do a rap of the song and Mike Pickering suggested using the upcoming Three Wise Men, who were based in London. At that point, in typical Happy Mondays fashion, the window cleaner, who had been working in the studio, piped up saying that he could rap. No one believed him as he stood there, covered in home-made tattoos, until he started rapping to the tune that was playing at the time, and the decision was made. Cale thought it worked perfectly, although none of the Mondays could decide if it was awful or brilliant. But the story was too good to be true, and the song would feature on the B-side of the band's next single.

The time spent working with Cale was possibly the most harmonious in the recording life of the Mondays, with barely an argument or a fight in the studio, certainly not the stabbing that Shaun would later claim. Each band member respected what the others were doing and didn't interfere. 'We just let each other get on with it, never any criticism,' said Whelan. The one exception was Mark Day, who the tight-knit gang saw as an increasingly separate entity from themselves. 'He'd go in and play some heavy metal stuff and we had to go in and say, C'mon, stop being silly, grow up,' said Whelan. Outside the studio, Day also behaved differently. As the only member of the band still to have a full-time job, he had money, an awkward position when the others had run out of cash in London and were stealing food to survive. When Shaun and Whelan caught him sitting alone in a café with a big fry-up, Shaun 'went ballistic', said Whelan. 'He was shouting, You've never been one of us, you never will be.'

Back at The Hacienda in time for Christmas 1986, with no money for drinks or drugs, the Mondays took to inhaling helium balloons for kicks as they waited for the album to be mixed, mastered and manufactured. In the New Year Shaun moved his new girlfriend into his Boothstown flat, forcing Bez out to his own place in Little Hulton. Meanwhile the rest of the band except Day were still on the dole, often pooling their money for band requirements.

The Mondays played a handful of shows in early 1987, continuing to pick up more glowing live reviews. In London, at another night promoted by Jeff Barrett, *NME* journalist Everett True was among the forty people present. He raved about the gig, writing that the Mondays' 'incorporate despair, swallow it wholesale and spit up multi-hued flames of life'. Shaun vomited and urinated in the van on the way back to Manchester. 'We were all in back of the white van with all the gear in and we'd sprawl out on a mattress,' recalled Mark Day. 'He pissed where he was, then was sick where he was.' The Mondays also played the Rock Garden in Covent Garden for a second time, a show reviewed in *Melody Maker* by Simon Reynolds who mentioned 'granite bass lines and guitars that twinkle', and compared the Mondays to both The Stooges and disco/funk band The Fatback Band. Back in Manchester, they played to 150 people at The Boardwalk, now big enough to have their own support band – the newly formed Inspiral Carpets. But some things didn't change – the *Manchester Evening News* said of the gig that the Mondays were 'an odd band getting odder'.

Factory readied 'Tart Tart' as the first single to be released from the Mondays' upcoming debut album, and the band shot a low-budget video, miming to the song in Strawberry Studios. Shaun would later say that he was high on heroin during his close-ups, in which he mouthed the lyric, while Bez featured heavily jerking about with maracas. As music videos go, it neatly summed up everything that people either liked or disliked about the Mondays. Factory used a shot of the band in the Worsley woods for promotional adverts, and for the occasion Shaun disguised himself in a bucket hat pulled down over his eyes, while Davis sported a black eye.

'Tart Tart' was released in March 1987, and Jonh Wilde, now writing for *Melody Maker*, made it single of the week. 'Far more brusque than last year's primitive funk classic Freaky Dancin',' he wrote. Quoting the line, 'Now maggot sleeps on a desk/He wears a sleeping bag as his vest', he claimed it was 'a perfect pop lyric'. In the *NME*, Steven Wells called the single 'dross'. *Sounds* was similarly unenthusiastic, describing the band as 'dour Manchester lads' and saying of the song, 'God knows what they're singing about.' The 'Tart Tart' video, however, was shown on *The Chart Show*, an ITV Saturday morning video show that included a section devoted to the top ten of the indie charts. It was the band's first national exposure on television, a chance for all their pals and family to tune in and see the progress they were making. 'That really did seem a big step,' said Shaun.

The single made it as high as number five in some indie charts, although the Mondays' progress was put into some perspective by the achievements of The Railway Children. The band's first two singles on Factory had gone to indie number one and so would their debut album. As Factory prepared a career-defining New Order greatest hits package, it was clear the Mondays were still some way down the pecking order at the label. Wilson was keen to push the Cath Carroll-fronted Miaow, who bore similarities to new indie darlings The Sugarcubes, and whose Factory debut had also reached number five in the indie charts. To many he seemed to have a crush on the band's singer. Certainly Phil Saxe and PR Dave Harper could see no other reason for his obsession with the band when he had Happy Mondays and their groundbreaking debut album at hand.

Nationally, indie band The Housemartins, who had seen the Mondays perform in Hull and adopted their look if not their sound, were breaking through into the mainstream. The Smiths continued to dominate the UK indie scene with what would be their final album, and their heir apparent The Wedding Present would pick up the slack. In the mainstream, Stock, Aitken and Waterman began their pop dominance of the decade with Rick Astley and Mel & Kim. U2, Whitney Houston, T'Pau, Michael Jackson and Level 42 scored with best-selling albums. A new indie scene coming from the

Midlands, dubbed Grebo, was being critically lauded. Pop Will Eat Itself and Gaye Bykers on Acid had an eccentric look – dreadlocks, lumberjack shirts and big boots – and were mixing garage rock with slabs of electronic noise. Goth rock, with The Mission and Fields of the Nephilim, also enjoyed a revival and a new wave of aggressive American 'indie bands', such as The Pixies and Dinosaur Jr., was becoming increasingly prominent. But developments in hip-hop made all this pale into insignificance. Public Enemy's debut album was seen as a game-changer and their first step towards stardom.

The Mondays did not fit in anywhere. 'Tart Tart' was followed quickly by the release of their debut album, titled *Squirrel and G-Man Twenty Four Hour Party People Plastic Face Carnt Smile (White Out)*. The title was unwieldy and unhinged – the kindest thing to say about it was it sounded a little like Funkadelic. As with the lyrics, so the title of the album seemed to have no significance beyond stringing together a series of ideas that people liked. Squirrel and G-Man were Paul Davis's nicknames for his mum and dad, Paul Ryder wanted to call it 'White Out', Shaun favoured '24 Hour Party People', the famous phrase coined by Little Mini. Someone liked 'Plastic Face Carnt Smile'. In the end they just put them all together.

The album was issued with a removable transparent PVC liner on which were printed, in large bold graphics, the name of the band and album title. The untitled record sleeve within (a ruse used famously on The Rolling Stones' debut album) featured a 1950s kitsch image of trifles and cakes. The back sleeve featured a tray of fish. Reviewing the album in *Sounds* on 8 April, Ron Rom compared the band to 'Sonic Youth with a Motown swing'. He wrote that the album was 'Full of bitter disdain and sardonic esoteric arrogance, as black and depressing as any rainy Monday evening in Manchester...a bastard funk pop album which spits vitriolic torrents of green phlegm into your face.'

Rom felt the lyrics were some sort of state-of-the-nation address. The idea that the Mondays were somehow representing the angst of the forgotten northern council estates under the Margaret Thatcher-led Conservative government was gaining momentum. 'Of course, they weren't,' said Saxe. 'The Mondays might have liked people to think they lived on council estates and I used to read that

– oh, we come from council estates in Salford – but they didn't. I never said they did.'

In a large *NME* lead album review, Dave Haslam wrote: 'There's a bristle, a comedy, a desire running through these souped up grooves that provides much evidence that there's far more LIFE in this band than almost any of their contemporaries. As a debut album it stands comparison to Television's Marquee Moon.' *Melody Maker* also gave the album a lead review in which, for half a page, Paul Mathur rhapsodised over the band's raggedy existence – 'on the rob down the Arndale', he surmised – and the 'brutal charm' of the album – 'the most shambolically lovable record of the year and just about the only justification for independent music as the decade hobbles into insufferable politeness'. He continued: 'Ten songs of discord and vitriol quite unlike anything else ... a dangerous deeply disturbing record ... never less than captivating.'

The band was delighted with the reviews. They had worried that nobody would like the album, a blow from which they sensed it would have been hard to recover. Instead they found their music being imbued with meaning they never intended and garlanded with musical references they felt misplaced. Still, it was a high point for the band and, said Paul, 'affirmed what we were doing was going the right way'. Even Morrissey, singer with The Smiths, said, 'I really like Happy Mondays, I really like their LP,' and in some indie charts the album went to number one. For Phil Saxe, this was vindication of an almost four-year mission. 'The Boys' had cracked it. The album was unlike any other he'd ever heard, anyone had heard: it had a narcotic, hallucinogenic effect. 'It was more than just music, it was a mood enhancer,' he said. It raised the hairs on the back of his neck. 'I used to get shivers listening to it. It was unbelievable and the lyrics were so strong.'

Andrew Berry called it the most important album since the Sex Pistols' *Never Mind the Bollocks*, but Mancunian praise for the album was otherwise rare. Their hometown still did not share the interest in the band of the London press, did not see them as important. The one person who could truly have swayed the consensus of the Manchester cognoscenti was producer Cale. The Velvet Underground were hallowed in the city. He stayed quiet. And over the years, as this album became subsumed by, and then forgotten under, the growing image of the band as crazy, party-mad jesters, he was one of the few people who could have corrected that tide of opinion. Instead, he only ever offered up soundbites that played along with that caricature.

10
24 Hour Party People

On 9 May 1987, Happy Mondays were on the cover of *Melody Maker* – their first music press front cover. Sorrel Downer, who had championed them ever since meeting them in London the year before, travelled to Manchester and interviewed them at The Boardwalk. 'That was the first time me and Bez were singled out from the rest of the group and treated differently,' said Shaun. 'It was only me and Bez on the cover.' In fact it was just Shaun – wearing his anorak hood up, eyes closed, mouth agape, wispy beard, head back.

Downer called the Mondays' debut album 'the most important independent release in years' and said they didn't sound like 'any other British independent band'. But she struggled to get the 'rare and precious' band to open up – writing of long silences in the conversation. 'Most bands are a million miles away from where we are, in every way,' said Shaun. 'Put it this way, if we weren't in a band we'd be in a bad way, 90 per cent of the people we know are insane.' Asked about the lyrics, Shaun said: 'None of them are meant to be taken seriously – most of them just come from what everyone else says, just loonies that you meet. You hear things, just one-liners that sound good and so the words all come off different things and sort of go together.' Downer suggested the songs on the album were full of 'death, gloom and disease'. 'Some songs might be sick,' said Shaun. 'But they're funny. It just depends what you like to laugh at.'

The same day they appeared on the cover of *Melody Maker*, the Mondays were also the subject of major features in *NME*, *Sounds* and *Record Mirror*, a job well done by Dave Harper at Out Promotions who was selling them as the 'most exciting group in Britain today'. For the *NME*, journalist Dele Fadele started off with a question, referencing album track "Enery', about why the band was so fascinated by venereal diseases. 'Oh yeah, we're obsessed,' said Shaun. 'It's to do with dirty women down Little Arndale: 35-year-old divorcees with two kids who give you warts. In fact I've still got a big one to prove it, it's going down now though.' Shaun continued to talk boorishly throughout the interview with Saxe keenly trying to steer the conversation onto more cultural matters. Fadele told the band they reminded him of a 'white Manchester version of Fela Kuti', which pleased Whelan.

Interviewed over an Indian meal for *Record Mirror*, a drunken Shaun said he'd 'like enough money for a gram of coke' to keep him from falling asleep. He bellowed at Phil for saying Manchester humour was 'a bit different'. 'If you laugh at a cripple with one eye you're not laughing because you come from Manchester,' he said. The band, according to the article, were 'politically unsound but know how to party'. It was claimed that four of them threw up outside the restaurant. *Record Mirror* said the Mondays were 'celebrating the don't-give-a-shit attitude'. Asked if that was correct, Shaun said: 'Well I really don't want to say it but I mean I don't give a shit.'

The band toured small venues through May and into June, their longest sequence of dates so far. They often supported The Weather Prophets, who were promoting their *Mayflower* album, or The Bodines, who had left Creation for a lucrative deal with a major label. Often on these dates, alongside Saxe and Derek, driving the orange Salford Van Hire Transit, was Cressa, a close pal of The Stone Roses who they'd met at The Gallery funk night. The Roses had recorded and then aborted a debut album and lost much of their aggressive edge, but they still favoured leather trousers and mean stares. A new single, 'Sally Cinnamon', saw them change direction musically, to a more melodic 1960s jangle, but they had failed so far to get a foothold on any sort of success. Cressa and his close pal 'Little' Martin Prendergast, who had replaced Andrew Berry to DJ alongside Mike Pickering at The Hacienda on the increasingly popular Friday Nude night, both wore voluminous flares and had a taste for obscure psych rock and cutting-edge American dance music. Cressa – occasionally accompanied by Prendergast – would sometimes appear on stage with the Mondays, dancing and playing percussion, to supplement Bez and create an even more diverting spectacle.

New Order continued to offer the band a platform. On 6 June 1987 the Mondays appeared bottom of the bill in a giant tent in Finsbury Park, London, as part of a Factory package with A Certain Ratio and The Railway Children. Reviewing the show for *Melody Maker*, Paul Mathur said the Mondays 'thrilled with a free-fall ease . . . Bez bobbed wildly [in a cowboy hat], Shaun smiled and you knew if Charles Manson had invented soul music it would have sounded like this.' A sign that they were becoming firm favourites of the music press was that the photograph of Shaun accompanying the review was bigger than the one of New Order's Bernard Sumner.

A few days later the Mondays supported New Order again, at Barrowlands in Glasgow. Day recalled trouble when the bouncers found the Mondays attempting to break into the headliners' dressing room looking for booze. New Order were about to release the single 'True Faith' and the compilation album *Substance*. The single, with its memorable avant-garde video, was a worldwide hit, the band's first Top 40 entry in America and first top five in the UK. The album, which featured the twelve-inch versions of all the band's Factory singles, sold in astonishing quantities, including one million in the US and over 400,000 in the UK. There were no recording costs, and it would earn the band and Factory (who routinely shared profits on a 50/50 basis with its acts) huge amounts. When Factory received its first million-pound cheque from distributor Pinnacle, the sudden influx of cash was a welcome diversion from some serious underlying issues at the label. The Railway Children, whom Wilson had told the press would be the next New Order and Smiths combined, left to sign to Virgin. Miaow relocated to London and then broke up before releasing their promised debut album. Longstanding Factory act A Certain Ratio had already left for A&M. Happy Mondays were one of the few bands left on a roster that now, more than ever, seemed to be operating purely as a platform for New Order.

Wilson did not yet see any real commercial value in Happy Mondays. He claimed Factory had pressed 10,000 copies of the Mondays' debut album, of which just 3,500 had been sold to date. After factoring in recording costs, artwork and manufacturing, Factory had not yet made a profit on the record. And now, the rest of the initial pressing had to be destroyed after a threat of legal action because of the Beatles' melody and lyric that they had ripped off on 'Desmond'. While Saxe claims that they had gained permission over the phone, the ultimate consequence was that they had to hastily record a new track to replace the contentious 'Desmond', allowing Factory to reissue the album and potentially further recoup their costs.

Cale was unavailable, so Saxe asked David Young, engineer on the album, to produce the session at Rochdale's Suite 16 in an effort to give the replacement track some continuity of sound with the rest. It didn't quite work out that way. Without Cale's glowering presence, and with the band on home soil, the easy-going Young allowed the session to turn into a high-spirited party and the band took the opportunity to bash out not only '24 Hour Party People' – a song that had taken shape when Shaun decided the phrase was too good to be 'wasted' on an album title and built a new lyric around it – but a number of new songs they'd been writing for their next album. All this made complete sense to the Mondays but Young was befuddled, especially when he heard the songs and they sounded nothing like the music they'd recorded for their debut.

The band were determined that '24 Hour Party People' would have a disco/funk guitar sound. It was a style, exemplified by Nile Rodgers of Chic, that often sounded simple but was difficult to master: fluid, syncopated and rhythmically intricate. It did not help that many of the funk records the band referred to were alien to Day. 'It was really hard to get Mark to play funk but the irony was when he did do it he was great at it and he'd mix it up with his lead,' said Whelan, whose drumming on the track aimed to imitate an uptempo Motown soul feel. 'We wanted it to be a dirty soul song, a punk soul song.' Saxe was blown away. In the track he heard strong echoes of the Northern Soul tapes he'd made the band listen to. It was danceable and soulful and had a real groove. 'We didn't outright say let's do a Northern Soul number but it just turned into that,' said Paul. With Shaun adding the vocal hook, and counting from one to seven as advised by Saxe, the song started to really swing. 'It was a coming of age,' said Mark Day. Paul Davis, who had recently been hospitalised in a savage attack by a gang in a pub near Little Hulton, added a keyboard hook that was supposed to imitate the brass interludes on soul records but came across as stabbing: basic and brutal, but beautiful. The band loved it – 'keep playing that' they shouted at him – and Davis's keyboards aligned with the band's groove provide the song's elemental pop hook.

In a remarkably productive, and collaborative, session the Mondays also recorded 'Yahoo', 'Wah Wah (Think Tank)' and 'Moving In With'. On the latter Paul hoped with his bass to get across something of the feel of Talking Heads' 'This Must Be the Place'. 'Sounds nothing like it but that's me trying to copy it,' he said. 'I'd get some of it correct and not get the rest of it and turn it into my own thing.' Whelan was playing a drum pattern inspired by Kate Bush's 1985 hit 'Running Up That Hill'. And Shaun took the bulk of the lyrics for the track from a children's fable, that of Henny Penny – the folk tale about a hen who believes the sky is falling in after an acorn falls on her head and sets off on a journey to tell the king, meeting other animals on the way – Cocky Locky, Ducky Lucky, Goosey Loosey and Turkey Lurkey were all name-checked in the song. On 'Yahoo', Davis's keyboard line ripped off the melody of the 1975 disco hit 'The Hustle' by Van McCoy and there were strong hints of disco in the drums and bass on all four tracks, a style of music they not only acknowledged as a massive influence but were now learning to use in their music: not so much copying parts of songs directly but using the tempos, feel and groove. 'We'd grown up with it, hearing it in youth clubs, pubs, fairgrounds,' said Whelan. 'It was always around. It was part of our lives, alongside funk and soul.'

Bez couldn't drink during the session, as he was recovering from hepatitis. He was also having visa problems – the band, along with Derek and Saxe, were due to fly to New York after the recording to play their first American gig, a showcase date organised by Tony Wilson, on 15 July. The *Squirrel* album was being pushed by Factory's small New York office; a press release declared them the 'only unique band in Britain'. 'Kuff Dam' was also the opening track on a new Factory US sampler, *Young, Popular & Sexy*, being released to promote other Factory bands in America following New Order's commercial breakthrough there. Both ACR and The Railway Children featured on the album and it seems likely that if they had not left the label it would have been one of them, not the Mondays, playing at Peter Gatien's infamous Limelight club, located in a deconsecrated church, during the city's annual music industry event, the New Music Seminar, in the hope of attracting labels to license the band's records for America.

The Mondays, including Bez who made the flight with minutes to spare, Saxe and Derek, flew over, arriving late the day before the gig. On landing, they discovered that Wilson had decided that they would be put up in the legendary Chelsea Hotel, where they paid the caretaker $20 to see the room where Sid Vicious had fatally stabbed his girlfriend Nancy Spungen. Their excitement soon turned sour when they saw the rooms that they had been checked into; they were revolting, with lino on the bedroom floors – not that any of them slept for the three days that they were there.

Crack was a solid, smokeable form of cocaine and America was in the grip of an epidemic. It had been a growing problem since the early 1980s when a huge rise in the availability of cocaine powder saw its price drop by eighty per cent. Dealers converted the cocaine to crack, which could be sold in smaller quantities and to more people: it was cheap, simple to produce, ready to use and highly profitable.

Smoking 'rocks' of crack through a pipe was said to be the most addictive form of taking cocaine: a fast euphoric high followed by a powerful crash, anxiety, depression, irritability and an intense craving for more. Its use spread from the west coast, particularly Los Angeles, and had slammed into New York causing widespread moral panic. It was a dangerous drug – cocaine-related hospital emergencies in the country had risen by 110 per cent in 1986. The rise of crack correlated with an unprecedented increase in crime, especially violent crime, and with the social disintegration of many African-American and Latino communities. None of this worried the Mondays, who thought they'd seen it all before, and getting some and trying it was top of Shaun, Bez and Paul's list of things to do in America.

Bez and Shaun went on the search for crack in the Bronx as soon as they arrived. 'Before Shaun and Bez had even got to the hotel room, they got dropped off in Alphabet City,' said Paul. 'There was a park down there they were told they could score in.' When they came back at five o'clock the next morning, the two, who were rarely fazed by anything, said 'We're never doing that again.' Paul was equally naïve: 'I didn't know you had to put it in a pipe,' he said. 'I just sprinkled it in a joint.'

The New York trip quickly descended into familiar chaos, with Shaun and other members of the band quickly falling ill due to substances unknown. Let loose on the city they quickly turned the trip into one long party, culminating when Whelan threw up on stage at the gig. They lasted twenty minutes before Davis lay down on the stage, comatose. Some of the chaos, though, was out of their control. None of the instruments that they had hoped to hire had turned up, and much of the equipment that did arrive was wrong. The result was a performance that they remembered as being 'awful' – though the crack, Paul admitted, might have had something to do with it.

An American review of the show, in *B Side* magazine, called the band 'shambling, odd and weird'. It described how Shaun had only been found fifteen minutes before the show started, and how he kicked Day on stage – an incident that came close to escalating into a fight. The singer then smashed two beer bottles together while Paul Davis gave up his keyboards to shake a tambourine. 'It looked like passing out would be the next logical step for the band,' the review concluded.

The Mondays returned to Manchester, if not with an American record deal, at least with a wealth of stories. Bez would say that on their first attempt to buy crack, he and Shaun had been ripped off, sold polystyrene balls; Shaun claimed they'd been attacked outside a crack den by a 'gang of mad black kids' and threatened with a gun and a broken Budweiser bottle. 'I was a bit startled, when you thought about it afterwards and realised that nobody seemed particularly concerned.'

Margaret Thatcher was re-elected in June 1987 for a third term. Unemployment had fallen below three million for the first time since 1981, and youth unemployment to below one million. The economy was growing at a faster rate than any time since 1963, inflation was at its lowest level for twelve years, taxes were predicted to fall and Labour, led by Neil Kinnock, was mocked as weak for its policy of unilateral nuclear disarmament. Support for the Conservatives was high but increasingly polarised, with most Tory votes coming from the south of England where average living standards had significantly risen.

Shaun, Paul, Bez, Whelan and Paul Davis had contributed to the drop in unemployment figures and finally signed off the dole. Saxe had organised for them to join the Enterprise Allowance Scheme, introduced nationwide in 1983 in an attempt to combat mass unemployment by encouraging individuals to start their own businesses. To qualify for the £40 a week (dole was £27.50 a week) start-up money provided by the government (which would last a year), individuals had to raise £1000 and provide a business plan. It was a popular scheme among struggling musicians and had been used by Creation Records' founder Alan McGee and artist Tracey Emin. Saxe provided £1000 for each member – the same £1000, simply switching it between their bank accounts so it would show on their statements. Shaun thought the scheme was a great idea and was vocal in his support of Thatcher, who had introduced it. 'We had some arguments about that,' said Whelan. 'I despised the woman.'

Saxe had arranged for their first headline UK tour to start on 5 October 1987, and Bobby Gillespie of Primal Scream attended the opening date at Portlands in London. The leather-trousered singer had just overseen the release of his band's psychedelic jangle pop debut album. The gig was given a long and electrifying live review in the *NME* by James Brown, another journalist who was a good friend of Dave Harper, which concluded with: 'I see a band that in the future will come to be spoken of in the same breath as Joy Division and The Fall.'

The band debuted a new track, 'Fat Lady Wrestlers', on the short eleven-date tour alongside the tracks recently recorded in Rochdale; although in places such as Hull and Leicester the Mondays could only attract twenty-five or thirty people, so the feedback on the new material was limited. On the road there were minor misdemeanours – Shaun and Bez robbing Cornettos at service stations or Bez boiling up a hallucinogenic fly agaric toadstool, bright red with spots, in a kettle for everyone to drink, or dissolving a wrap of speed in a bottle of Thunderbird or cup of coffee. The band were being paid up to £180 per gig and sometimes could even afford to stay in hotels – albeit all piled into a couple of rooms.

Tony Wilson never travelled beyond Manchester to watch the Mondays, avoiding the squalor of their existence and their struggle for an audience. He had far more important things to do, and if he was frank, he still couldn't see them becoming anything other than a 'cult' band. Wilson was a socialist but he had many of the trappings of a yuppie. His TV career as anchor of *Granada Reports* brought him £30,000 per year. He was also still involved in Channel 4's defining *After Dark*, which had proved a huge critical success. He wore designer suits, drove a Jaguar, owned a four-bedroom house in the leafy, affluent suburb of Didsbury, and talked enthusiastically about the new CD format. Factory was now comfortably off, with money pouring in from New Order's best-selling *Substance* album, and beside Happy Mondays, the other acts on the label were decidedly yuppie-ish: Kalima – who featured several members of A Certain Ratio – and Jazz Defektors both peddled a northern jazz dance sound, new act To Hell With Burgundy played gentle folk music and Wilson's long-term squeeze Vini Reilly and his band The Durutti Column continued to explore mature areas of modern classical, folk, jazz and electronica. Mexican beer (with a lime in the top of the bottle) excited Wilson and Factory bought a former furniture warehouse in the derelict area of Manchester now known as the Northern Quarter, with the intention of turning it into a designer bar. This project appealed to him far more than Mike Pickering's suggestion that Factory start a dance division. Rob Gretton was keen, but Alan Erasmus was still intent on launching a classical division and Wilson did not see any future in dance records – 'dance music will never happen'. So Pickering left Factory to set up his own dance label, Deconstruction, which would release the records that moved the dance floor. He continued to DJ at The Hacienda, where Nude night was now pulling in large crowds of up to 1600, dancing to cutting-edge tracks imported from the US, largely Chicago House or Detroit techno.

Another project that Wilson was keen for Factory to pursue involved two inexperienced film-makers who had caught his ear, eye and imagination. They had come to his attention after shooting a video for Kalima and would have a key role in changing the course of the Mondays' history. Before shooting the Kalima promo, Keith Jobling and Phil Shotton had run a clothes stall in Manchester's hive of independent stores, Afflecks Palace, supplying retro-style jazz suits and worn Levi's to many of those on the jazz dance/rockabilly scene. As video makers they operated under the name The Bailey Brothers (after the company in the film *It's a Wonderful Life*) and had convinced Wilson to get involved in a 'youth exploitation' movie they had planned called *Mad Fuckers!* The storyline to this music-driven feature film revolved around a gang of wild young tearaway Manchester car thieves, and with Wilson, The Bailey Brothers cooked up starring roles for Factory musicians such as Vini Reilly and Peter Hook.

Wilson was a heavy dope smoker and prone to such flights of fancy. Shaun claimed he and Bez were among his drug suppliers. Wilson still had doubts as to the band's potential, but when he sat down with Shaun for a shared smoke and they talked, he found himself completely captivated. 'He'd be wittering like some kid out of borstal, completely out of his skull, and somehow I knew he was something special,' he said. 'You could just feel it – he had wonderful charisma. Completely, utterly natural.'

Wilson took The Bailey Brothers to see the Mondays play at Manchester University on their spluttering headline tour of the UK with a view to them making the video for the band's new single. Factory had decided that, as well as replacing 'Desmond' on the repackaged and reissued *Squirrel* album, '24 Hour Party People' was the best thing the Mondays had for a new release. The Bailey Brothers enjoyed the Friday night show, which took place in the 450-capacity Solem bar and was virtually sold out, and told Wilson they could do something with the band. 'OK, see you Sunday,' said Wilson. The band and The Bailey Brothers met at 11 a.m. on Sunday morning outside The Hacienda but Wilson — who had planned to direct the video — failed to show. Eventually he appeared, explained there was an emergency at Granada and said they'd all just have to get on with it.

The Bailey Brothers were accompanied by a friend who was driving a giant American Oldsmobile car, while tagging along with the Mondays was Shaun's girlfriend's young nephew, not yet a teen-ager. The Bailey Brothers piled the lot of them into the Oldsmobile and shot them driving around on a patch of wasteland in Ancoats. 'We had the tape playing on the car stereo and they were singing along to the tape,' said Jobling. Later, without the band, The Bailey Brothers shot more footage around Manchester from the point of view of someone riding in the car. When they came to transfer the film to video, the owner of the edit suite looked at the footage of the scally-looking band and the young kid, running across the des-olate wasteland to pile into the car before taking off to the city, and exclaimed, 'Who the fuck are these? Are they car thieves or what?' The Bailey Brothers had found their Mad Fuckers.

'24 Hour Party People' was released in late October 1987 on twelve-inch only, with a seven-inch edit for radio. The Bailey Brothers' video was shown on *The Chart Show*, and further enshrined the band's image as a gang of criminal bad-lad hooligans. The single drew praise in the three leading rock weeklies, *NME*, *Sounds* and *Melody Maker* (where it was named single of the week, the band's third on the bounce in the paper). There followed another flurry of music press features. In *Melody Maker* Paul was asked about the band's sound, which had been described as 'psycho funk' and 'spastic funk'. 'It's not even funk, it's just there's no name for it yet,' he said. 'There will be in ten years' time. But one of the main things with these interviews we've done is that no one can ever put us in a bag or pigeonhole us.' If the music was difficult to describe, in this round of interviews Shaun did his damnedest to give the band an easy-to-understand image. He boasted about stealing handbags with Bez and talked openly of drug dealing and other crimes such as burglary and car theft, painting such actions as the only way he had to survive, explaining that he had no choice 'where he came from'. What other band, he challenged, could say that? The answer was none, and even if such stories were true what would be the advantage of pretending to be an objectionable lout?

'I'd purposefully taken the role of being the bad boy of rock because it helped the image,' Shaun said. 'Everyone has got an image. The Rolling Stones were bad boys. Jagger was Mr Drugs. Johnny Rotten was spitting and sniffing glue or whatever – and we had our theme. It was our image – we used what little we'd been given, learned to exploit it. So as soon as we were given this druggie rock 'n' roll image just for liking a spliff, then straight away we decided to turn it to our advantage.'

Except, for now, it wasn't much of an advantage. The image was a turn-off for many readers of the music press, often students. They were just 'too scummy', said Wilson. '24 Hour Party People' stalled at a disappointing number ten in the indie charts. The re-released *Squirrel* album struggled towards the 5000 sales mark. Wilson had run out of ideas for the Mondays and they were left confused by their lack of success. They were all over the music press, being showered with praise, yet their records did not sell and they were making no money. 'To be in *NME* and *Sounds* all the time, I thought that meant loads of money would come in,' said Shaun. 'But it meant absolutely fuck all. We still had to struggle.'

For Factory, fat on New Order's cash, the failure of the Mondays meant little. They had kept afloat poorer-selling bands for years when they had far less money. Wilson was looking to the future, for something new. He gave a speech to the Factory staff as 1987 came to a close. The company had had a great year financially and things were going well. 'But let's not get too full of ourselves,' he warned. 'There's another musical revolution around the corner. It might not happen in Manchester but keep your eyes open.' Little did he know he was sitting right on top of it; that it was happening right now in his own club.

BOOK TWO

Madchester

11
Nathan

In The Hacienda, in the weeks before Christmas 1987, Bez bumped into a pal who had just returned from Amsterdam. He described how his 'normally shy friend' and his small group of acquaintances were doing a 'helluva funky stomp whenever a top tune came on'. They were also hugging one another and brimming with happiness. Bez was handed a pill and found himself dancing, and dancing, until he dripped with sweat, all the while consumed by a new confidence and feeling of love for himself, for everyone. He had never had a drug like it and wanted to know where to get more, so he could share the experience with the rest of the Mondays. He was introduced to a lively and youthful Mancunian, one of the 'main men' involved in the drug's supply. This was not only the first rush of Ecstasy for Bez but in the UK.

The man Bez quickly befriended was still a teenager, and he and his similarly youthful partner were blaggers, sneak thieves who travelled Europe robbing jewellers' or shop safes. Their base was Amsterdam, where much of the Ecstasy trade originated. The lads had recently returned from a wild summer on the party island of Ibiza, an increasingly popular hotspot for working-class British youth. But this was not a scene of drunken holiday carnage in tacky discos. The two young Mancunians had supplied the Balearic island's three main, open-air, dance floors at the clubs KU, Amnesia and Pacha with Ecstasy, and a new 'loved-up' vibe had been created under the stars and moon. This 'miracle pill', as it was known among converts, made all inhibitions fall away, enabling a whole club to unite in a wave of pure euphoria, dancing and hugging in a beatific state. The drug, developed but shelved in the early twentieth century, had become fashionable in 1970s American therapy circles, some psychiatrists calling it 'penicillin for the soul'. During the early 1980s it had also become hip among clubbers in cities such as Los Angeles and New York, and it was only made illegal in the US in 1985.

Over the summer of 1987, in the plushly appointed clubs of Ibiza, to a backdrop of wildly eclectic music, among a stylised and decadent European crowd, this crowd of young Brits, less than a hundred strong, had started a revolution. The two Mancunians, and a cluster of other British working-class kids, had returned to the UK determined to spread the vibe. In London, a couple of club nights in ad hoc locations emerged aping the affluent Ibiza hippy look: loose-fitting T-shirts, often carrying the soon to be iconic smiley face logo, dungarees, and ethnic jewellery, and a musical mix of modern American dance, electro-pop, rock, hip-hop – anything really, as long as you could dance to it. The style became known as Balearic Beat.

To make the whole thing work, you needed Ecstasy, and in late 1987 the supply of the drug in the UK was extremely limited. Bez's new pals had already made serious money in Ibiza and continued to coin it in – this when the scene was still deeply underground and limited to a few hundred people. The 'main man' drove a brand new BMW 325I, noted Bez, whose car at the time was a decrepit hand-painted white Austin Maxi. An Ecstasy pill that might cost up to £50 on the street (the price would soon settle at around £25) cost pennies to manufacture and was ridiculously cheap to buy in bulk. Smuggling it through customs was easy. The drug was not on the authorities' radar, and the scene was spread by word of mouth and had zero media coverage. Although not named, the complex compound was listed as a Class A drug in the UK, and possession could land you seven years in jail, but it was only now becoming available and the police had absolutely no idea what it looked like, what it was, what it did or what was going on. For the dealers of E, as it became known, it was a perfect storm.

While the scene in London stayed under wraps, happening underground and often illegally (at after-hours all-nighters in regular clubs), in the annexes of gay clubs or even, infamously, in a fitness gym, the spacious and stylised Hacienda was the first club in the UK where Ecstasy use was out in the open. The drug began to noticeably infiltrate The Hacienda in January 1988, although a surge in its use in February and March was initially confined to an area on the left-hand side of the club that naturally became known as 'E corner'. Here, in an alcove protected from prying eyes and fuggy with the smell of weed, could be found a wild scene of people dancing with their arms in the air. 'There'd be fifteen people all E'd off their face and the other people in the club didn't know what was going on,' said Paul. 'They'd be looking at this bunch of people dancing crazily, thinking why are they like that?' When they were told, and then given an E to share, they too were converted, and so it went on until the numbers had spilled into the main area of the club. DJ Mike Pickering said Nude was changed overnight: 'As soon as the Pure Boys could get hold of E, the whole place went berserk. One of the things that made it so special was that it was going on in the ignorance of the authorities. They just thought everyone was in a good mood.' Bez described the atmosphere poetically – 'the clouds of an eternally dismal day had finally parted to let in the most brilliant rays of sunshine'.

All this was taking place under the radar of the media – even The Hacienda's owners didn't know what was going on. But the Mondays were in the thick of it, regulars in E corner. Bez had given the band Ecstasy and they'd all been quickly converted. 'It was like being reborn,' said Whelan. 'It was unbelievable. I'd never chatted a girl up in my life, I came home with about ten phone numbers.' Shaun, said Bez, 'went from being a raging smackhead to a raging E-head in an instant'. It was a great pick-me-up for Shaun, who had been sinking deeper into heroin use, mixing the drug with Valium and booze, following a bad break-up with his girlfriend, who had cheated on him while he was away on tour. Shaun began to embrace life again. He moved out of the Salford suburbs and into the city to share a flat with Bez, who was living with his 21-year-old girlfriend Debs in Fallowfield, south Manchester – an area popular with students – in the basement of a large redbrick Victorian semi that had been subdivided into flats. Central Station Design – Shaun and Paul's cousins Matt and Pat and Pat's partner Karen – lived in the top-floor flat and the other two were occupied by an assortment of friends such as Cressa and Eric Barker. The latter, dubbed by Bez 'the wizard of E', would dance wildly on a podium at The Hacienda, occasionally whistling with his fingers at a musical or drug crescendo – often a simultaneous event – leading to the popularisation of whistles at the club. The house in Fallowfield, said Shaun, was 'where it all changed'. When The Hacienda shut at two in the morning there were always large crowds of people, 'up' on E, who wanted to party all night and they would be guided back to the house, where a plentiful supply of Ecstasy ensured wild nights of excess as inhibitions dissolved.

'Everyone's door was left open so you could go from the top flat to the middle to the bottom seeing different people, most were on Ecstasy,' said Paul. Bez's new pals brought a consignment of 15,000 Ecstasy pills to Manchester and stored them with associates of the band. The size of the batch was staggering: 'Two or three weeks later The Hacienda was flooded with it,' said Paul. 'These people weren't messing about.' There was a lot of money flying about, much more money to be made selling Ecstasy than there was as a member of the Happy Mondays. When another few thousand Es landed, they were put in the Mondays' rehearsal room at The Boardwalk, 'so they'd be locked away at night', said Paul.

Ecstasy would have a huge influence on the Happy Mondays, and not just because Shaun and Bez, in particular, were starting to make money dealing the drug. In The Hacienda, the fashion was changing: all the dancing made you sweat, necessitating looser clothing. Some wore hippyish threads – loose paisley silk pyjamas, or flowing shirts – others dressed down in baggy T-shirts and loose jeans or tracksuit bottoms, with Converse All Stars trainers becoming popular. The relaxed vibe also saw 'The Boys' growing out the popular close-cropped hairstyles; a ponytail was now seen as the thing. Bez's dancing style on stage would change too as he adopted the lolloping trance dance and made it his own.

The music they heard at The Hacienda — chiefly the Chicago House played by Pickering (the work of DJs, producers and acts such as Marshall Jefferson, Frankie Knuckles, Adonis and Fingers, Inc.) — was also having an effect on the band, as Paul sought to emulate the pulsating, computerised bass lines. Strung out on Ecstasy, the band discovered the seminal Mick Jagger film *Performance*. It was an acid-soaked, sex-riddled gangster rock movie and along with E came to have a defining influence on the next stage in the band's career. They watched it again and again. 'It took over,' said Whelan. Shaun, the band's biggest Stones fan, took lyrics directly from the dialogue or was inspired into flights of fancy by the characters. He mixed this with the new slang of the underground E scene to come up with more upbeat lyrics. He was enjoying his new lifestyle, happy, with spare cash, plenty of girls and gangsters as pals. The band had built on the musical progression they'd made at the '24 Hour Party People' session, and with the addition of Ecstasy, their musical horizon shifted radically as they began to select new material for their second album. Whelan imagined the band was making its own soundtrack to *Performance*. If they were already out on a limb from the rest of the indie scene, they were now moving to a new planet, starting to set the tone for their generation, as they became the iconic face of the Ecstasy era.

Two new songs, in particular, stood out. 'Do It Better', originally called simply 'E', was the band's first attempt at a short pop song, built on a catchy guitar pattern and Shaun's heavy repetition of, and ad-libbing around, the phrase 'on one' (meaning high on Ecstasy). In the song he was feeling not just good, but 'double double good'. 'Wrote For Luck', which would become the defining song of the era and one of the band's most famous tunes, was their attempt to try and write a dance song that might be played at The Hacienda on a Friday night. Paul had realised that it was physically impossible to copy the sequenced Chicago House bass lines on a real instrument and was trying, in the band's graffiti-strewn rehearsal room, which now doubled as an after-hours hangout, to put a synth bass line on top of a tune he'd come up with. Paul Davis started trying to play 'Two Tribes' by Frankie Goes to Hollywood and Whelan was making another attempt at Kate Bush's 'Running Up That Hill'. It was

Sunday morning and the three had been up all night. Day would later add a guitar part, and Shaun invented a hook for the song that reflected his own state of mind: 'Higher than high high'. Although he would later say the song was about heroin not Ecstasy, it was the sort of lyric only Shaun could have come up with, describing a good drug hit better than Lou Reed or Mick Jagger.

Phil Saxe did not buy into the 'new' Shaun — the idea of him being a drug dealer seemed laughable. He was pleased with the new songs but did not share the band's fervour for Ecstasy. He would soon be forty, his two children were growing up fast, and he lived in a comfortable house in Bramhall and drove a luxury car. Shaun for his part had outgrown Phil, taken everything he could, and all that remained as he saw it was a nice family man with a small business. He began to think about getting a new manager, someone younger, more in tune with the scene emerging at The Hacienda, someone who saw him for what he was now, a happening frontman with heavy connections, not what he had once been — a postman with dreams.

Above all, Shaun wanted success. He was smart, quick and had learned many lessons about the music business in the past two years. Even though they were struggling to sell records, he knew there was still nothing like the Mondays on the scene and he had had enough of their slow progress. The band had been together for over five years now and they needed something to change or they'd simply burn out. Shaun wanted a manager who was as committed to the band as they were, someone who lived and worked at it full time, who could help take them to the next level. But he was not a bastard and, although he wouldn't say it, he deeply appreciated what Saxe had done for the band. So he challenged Saxe to go full time, to make a commitment, knowing perfectly well Saxe could not support his family on fresh air, or the money the band might make in the future. It was too much to ask, even for the evangelical Saxe who had nurtured the band without pay for two long years.

'That was awful, that period,' said Paul. 'We knew that Phil could only take us so far and for us to take the next step we needed a different manager. Phil gave it everything he had and we wanted more. I still, to this day, feel awful about sacking Phil. He was like our brother.' The band did not know who they would get to replace Saxe, but they had in mind someone with 'no marriage, no day job, someone who worked on music 100 per cent of the time', said Paul. They approached Colin Sinclair, who owned The Boardwalk and managed The Railway Children, but he turned them down. So did New Order's manager Rob Gretton, when Mark Day made the call.

'Rob had problems of his own with New Order and Factory,' Day said. 'He didn't want any more. We got on with Rob but he didn't want to commit.' With little on the table work-wise, they were increasingly desperate to find a manager.

Another name the band talked about was Nathan McGough, the young, handsome Liverpudlian transplanted to Manchester who was manager of The Bodines. McGough was well known to all at Factory, having managed the label's jazz act, Kalima. He was also a good friend of Hacienda DJ Dave Haslam, with whom, from an office on Princess Street in the city centre, he ran an independent label, Play Hard Records, home to acts such as King of the Slums and MC Buzz B. The Mondays knew McGough liked the band, as it was he who had offered them numerous support slots with The Bodines; Paul recalled one such gig in Rochdale when 'we came off stage and he was shouting, "Bring back the Mondays, bring back the Mondays". I thought then, He's good.'

In fact McGough had harboured a desire to manage the Mondays ever since he first saw them supporting New Order in 1985, having been 'instantly' drawn to them by Shaun's charisma and the band's unique sound. That night, he'd even asked Rob Gretton if he could manage them. His further interactions with the band had convinced him Shaun was a star – he spoke admiringly of a blue Pierre Cardin suit the singer had worn: 'just the coolest thing ever'. But he stressed that he had never discussed anything of a business nature with the band while Saxe was managing them: 'It wouldn't have been appropriate. I don't feel I did anything to undermine Phil's position.'

Shaun bumped into McGough on a Saturday night at The Hacienda and made the unilateral decision, there and then, to ask him to replace Saxe. McGough didn't need asking twice and a meeting was set up with the band. 'Nathan came in with this spiel and impressed us — Yeah, OK, we'll give him a shot,' said Day. 'He was colourful but he was on a trial.' McGough knew where the band was coming from and was connected enough to get them where they wanted to go. He was also fashionably 'arty', the result of a bohemian childhood. His mother was Thelma Pickles, a former art student and fashion designer who now worked in TV and had famously dated John Lennon; his stepfather was well-known 'Merseybeat' poet, playwright and author Roger McGough. Unlike Saxe, an outsider and a self-confessed novice in the music business, McGough was born into show business and acted accordingly. He wasn't married, didn't have children and had already gathered a wealth of music business experience. Shaun described the 28-year-old as 'business-like but still young and liked to party — perfect for us, just what we needed'.

The sacking of Saxe and his replacement with McGough came as a shock to many at Factory, who had known him as the jazz-suited manager of Kalima and could not get over his radical change of image as he began imitating the look of 'The Boys' in E corner at The Hacienda. The fit between McGough and the band didn't seem right, while Saxe was highly thought of and uniformly well liked. Tony Wilson knew McGough better than anyone at the label. He had looked out for him since he was fourteen and often referred to him as a 'stepson'. At the age of eighteen McGough had been at the first ever Factory club night and, alongside members of Joy Division, had helped assemble the complex sleeves for Factory Records' first ever release, *A Factory Sample* (December 1978). He had even briefly played bass in The Royal Family & the Poor, a band who were included on Factory double album sampler *A Factory Quartet*, released in December 1980. After moving from Liverpool to Manchester, he lived in Wilson's four-bedroom house in Didsbury.

Before Kalima, who recorded and gigged only sporadically, the first band McGough had managed was Liverpool's influential but problematic The Pale Fountains. He became manager of The Bodines in 1986, when they were an unremarkable local indie band releasing records with Creation, and signed them, for a sizeable advance, to Magnet Records, home to Chris Rea and Bad Manners. But the band failed to achieve any mainstream success and the pressure to do so caused them to split up. Wilson, when he wanted to be cruel, would say that everything McGough touched turned to shit; in this instance, he had been correct.

McGough nevertheless felt he could make a success of the Mondays' 'different and unusual' appeal. He spoke enthusiastically about securing money from various avenues, promised to work around the clock for the band. He was genuinely excited by the opportunity. In contrast, Bez said he disliked McGough from the get-go: 'I found myself constantly embarrassed by my unavoidable association with him.' It was not just Bez who was against McGough. Paul Davis wanted to stick with Saxe and six months down the line would tell McGough 'you're not my manager, I didn't ask you to manage me'. Day was prepared to give him a go but didn't trust him, and Whelan tended at first to agree with Bez. He would soon soften, but Bez's attitude towards McGough would never change. 'Bez was really against having Nathan,' said Whelan. 'We all were, but Shaun got his way; he was really persistent.'

Shaun took control of the situation, and McGough never sensed the deep unease and hostility within the band towards him. It was still Shaun's gang, and as gang leader it was his role to make these decisions. He wanted a young, trendy manager on the journey the band were now embarking on, not a funny old man – he already had his dad to contend with. But it was more than image: although they had now split, Shaun had seen The Bodines come from nowhere to enjoy more success than the Mondays, at least in terms of making money. They'd even shot a video in Los Angeles. He told McGough: 'The Bodines were doing ten times better than our band, but I knew our band was ten times better than The Bodines, therefore the difference had to be you.'

Tony Wilson was aghast. He'd been in Hollywood attempting to raise finances for the *Mad Fuckers!* film, an 'event' celebrated by a badge – 'Factory Goes To Hollywood' – and a Factory catalogue number. There he'd had talks with Warner Brothers, who were interested in putting up money against Factory's assets. He returned to find McGough managing the Mondays and demanding a meeting. The Mondays were one of the label's few viable acts and Wilson sensed McGough would try and sign them to a major for a

significant advance, as he had done with The Bodines. The issue of
Factory's refusal to have contracts with its acts had troubled him
during those high-powered meetings in Los Angeles, when trying
to explain Factory's absurdist rationale was too absurd for even
Wilson to contemplate. He didn't want to lose the Mondays, he'd
talked them up so much in Hollywood that he'd convinced himself
the band had a bright future.

He knew too that the label could not live off the success of New
Order's *Substance* forever. It was a comfortable time at the label, especially as The Hacienda was finally close to breaking even: they had
invested in a bar that was still being built, Alan Erasmus was about
to launch the Factory classical division, spending was within reason,
and New Order had commenced writing for a new album that was
scheduled for later that year, and which would be another money-
spinner. But they had not invested significantly in any new bands.

So, for a £40,000 advance, Happy Mondays would become the first
band to officially sign a contract with Factory. 'It wasn't a massive
record deal but at the time it wasn't bad,' McGough said. In fact the
contract was more than fair; it was heavily skewed in favour of the
artist, with royalties of twenty per cent. 'Factory offered those percentages, it was not like you had to get it out of them.' McGough
took twenty per cent of the band's gross earnings, plus expenses,
although he did not have a management contract, and then the
advance and any future record royalties once the advance was
earned out were split equally between the six members – including Bez, whose role was still completely indefinable since he had
neither written a single lyric nor contributed to any of the tunes.

McGough put the Mondays on £80 a week each, doubling
their money under Saxe, and organised for them to record demos
of the songs for the new album in the Out of the Blue studio in
Ancoats. At that first recording, McGough had a taste of what he
had got himself into when Paul pulled a knife on Shaun. Terrified,
he told them that he was there to manage the band and wanted
no part in this kind of thing. The Mondays largely heeded his
request, although that didn't stop them from openly fighting in
front of him.

McGough, unlike Saxe, sensed that the Ecstasy movement

was going to explode nationwide, and saw how the Mondays could grow with it. The deal he'd secured with Factory had impressed the band and bestowed him with instant gravitas. The Mondays needed direction, needed a full-time manager, but they wouldn't have listened to a straight business head in a suit and tie. McGough, in his dungarees and bandana, with an appetite for hedonism that matched that of the band, was also incredibly keen and fearless. He demanded they match his total commitment to them, and drew up a list of things he wanted to achieve. The bohemian McGough, a Liverpudlian to boot, with his talk of strategies and long-term planning, kicked the band up the arse and made sure they did whatever they had to do in order to succeed. He was unwavering. As Derek said, 'If it had been anybody else they wouldn't have done it.'

12
Martin

By May 1988 flares were out and the Mondays had moved on to baggy jeans with sixteen-inch bottoms as they positioned themselves centre stage of the next generation of Manchester music. 'The Hacienda didn't change the Mondays,' Shaun would later say. 'The Mondays changed The Hacienda.' E was available on a mass scale and the club was going berserk three nights a week, Wednesday, Friday and Saturday, with the Mondays right in the thick of it all. This was the dawn of the 'second summer of love' and throughout it the band rarely took a night – or day – off. Sunday night was maybe the wildest of the lot, at Stuffed Olives, a gay bar that stayed open until four in the morning and became the centre of an Ecstasy maelstrom. And many nights would turn into day at the Kitchen, an illegal party zone in squatted flats in run-down Hulme. Bez and his dealer pals were even spreading the love on Mondays at Spectrum, London's new and biggest Acid House night.

The term Acid House, originally used to describe the style of electronic House records from Chicago that Mike Pickering had been playing at The Hacienda as far back as 1986 (and whose bass lines Paul was keen to try and copy), had now become a catch-all term for the growing Ecstasy scene. Like The Hacienda, Spectrum was packed with 1500 people, all ablaze with Ecstasy, and the night's ringmaster, DJ Paul Oakenfold, would become a key figure in the future of the Mondays.

The band's new album had been written in the heart of this rapidly expanding, deeply subversive scene, and it was music written *for* the scene and the generation discovering themselves in it. McGough was now searching for a producer for the album who would drive home that message. Shaun had been so pleased with the self-produced 'killer demo' the band had recorded at Out of the Blue, he asked Wilson if the band could produce it themselves. Wilson politely insisted the band use a 'name producer'. Shaun suggested Keith Richards. The truth was that very few producers were alive to Acid House. There were British dance acts using innovative electronic sampling, such as KLF, Bomb the Bass and S'Express, but genuine homegrown Acid House tracks were a rarity. Who then to turn to?

Factory founder Alan Erasmus had so far had little input into the Mondays' career. Wilson nevertheless called him the company's 'idealist' and acknowledged that much of what Factory represented as a company conformed to Erasmus's 'masterplan'. Paul agreed: 'Alan was a bit out there. He wasn't much involved with the band but he was there and it wouldn't have been the same without him. Whatever bits he did, and he had some pretty weird ideas, Factory wouldn't have been the same without Alan Erasmus.' Erasmus was moreover a man with a deep conscience, a quality reflected in his suggestion as to who the Mondays should choose as producer. 'When we were discussing who to get to produce the album Alan came round to see us and said, What about Martin Hannett?' said Paul. 'And we thought about it for a minute and said, That's brilliant, we all went for it.'

Mancunian Martin Hannett had produced both the city's best punk acts, Buzzcocks and the poet John Cooper Clarke, before joining Factory as a co-founder. He was by all accounts a genius in the studio; obsessive, idiosyncratic and innovative. He had produced all the early Factory acts, but it was his work with Joy Division for which he would be best remembered. Hannett had been at the controls for both *Unknown Pleasures* and *Closer*, and was responsible for the timeless sound quality of the work considered among the best British rock music ever made. He had produced the first New Order album before splitting with Factory in acrimonious circumstances, having opposed the opening of The Hacienda, arguing that the label should invest instead in a studio and equipment. He had famously pulled a gun on Wilson, who from a safe distance maintained Hannett was a genius. His output, however, over the past five years had been anything but. He had produced The Stone Roses' debut album, *Garage Flower*, in 1985 but the band had been so unhappy with it that they shelved the recordings.

Erasmus had offered an olive branch to Hannett and the two were talking. The once lithe Hannett had serious alcohol problems and his weight had ballooned – it was eventually to reach twenty-six stone. He had long been a heavy user of drugs, notably heroin. Having settled his differences with Factory out of court, the producer, who had a wife and two children to support, was now struggling financially. Erasmus could not let a man who had given Factory so much – more than anyone, truth be told – waste his talent like this. Not that any of this would have dissuaded the Happy Mondays from working with him. Perhaps quite the opposite, given their experience with the clementine-eating workaholic John Cale. In any case, Joy Division was a key musical touchstone for the band and New Order had told them plenty of intriguing stories about their producer. For Hannett this was a chance of redemption.

Despite Wilson's reservations, a deal was struck by McGough for Hannett to produce the new album, and in August 1988 the Mondays and Hannett headed for Slaughterhouse studio in Driffield, a small market town near Bridlington in East Yorkshire, to start work on the new material. It was a brand new 36-track, state-of-the-art, residential studio built in a huge eighteenth-century building with fourteen bedrooms. 'Me and Paul had to pick a hire car up and then go and pick Martin up in Chorlton,' said Whelan. 'We were told Martin was a bit nervous and all he requested was, Don't get a red car or a Ford.' Naturally, when Whelan and Paul went to the car hire company they asked for a red Ford. When they arrived at Hannett's house, he opened the door, looked at the car and burst out laughing, saying, 'Oh, we're going to get on fine.' The overweight Hannett had long hair, habitually wore dark glasses and spoke in a tumbling drugged-out slur that recalled a Mancunian Keith Richards. But the Mondays were in for a rare treat; being produced by Hannett was an experience no band could ever forget.

They arrived in Driffield on market day and slipped into the pub next to the studio, The Norseman, staying there for twelve hours. When they finally turned up at Slaughterhouse, the only thing complete was the studio – the bedrooms weren't ready and there were no catering facilities or private bar as advertised. The band was put up in a nearby terraced house that had once housed the studio itself; they had to squat on mattresses on the floor, while Mark Day set up his bed in the old drum booth. Hannett stayed in another house in the town where his wife Wendy and his kids could stay when they visited. He clearly had his problems, but he had not yet descended into the caricature that would come before his death in three years' time at the age of only forty-two. He was still able to summon up some of the genius that had made Joy Division so potent, and this Mondays album would be his final masterpiece. He had listened closely to the band's demo but drilled them further in the studio, making them run through the songs for hours and hours. 'They're something different,' he said about the Mondays. 'The music is harmonically interesting rather than linearly interesting. It's built onto something that I enjoy very much, which is the dead solid groove they get.'

Not everyone understood where Hannett was coming from or what he was trying to do with the Mondays' new songs. After the first session the young in-house engineer at Slaughterhouse started reporting back to the band that he didn't think Hannett had a clue what he was doing. The band let it go, but the engineer persisted – until the end of the week's first full session when, contrite, he admitted that he had got it completely wrong. 'He's a fucking genius,' he said, before walking out of the room.

Hannett recorded a lot of the album as the band played live, via a unique system of microphone placement. Paul and Whelan were fascinated, and were keen to understand why, for instance, Hannett had set up two mics facing one another, almost touching but crucially with enough room between them to pass a cigarette through. Hannett had once been a bass player, and he and Paul worked for hours on the bass sound, which was fed through an array of digital filters, echo units and a time modulator. But Hannett was most famous for obsessing over the drums, mixing the acoustic sound with a synthesiser to create a bewilderingly heavy thump. Day used one of Hannett's own guitars, a Schecter, on the recording. The band – Shaun really – had bought it from Hannett for £300 as a favour to the skint producer. 'It looked alright and sounded alright,' said Day. 'I didn't want to say it's not my style. I took it because it was Martin's and I had to.' Although Day called his guitar parts on the album simple and repetitive – and they were to some extent – the guitarist was experimenting with the key of songs, odd chordal structures, down-tuning, up-tuning and a capo to get the standout guitar part on 'Do It Better'. There was an almost child-ish freedom and lack of sophistication to the way the band played, focusing in on finding the song's central groove. Hannett would lock in too and started to hear things in the music no one else did – other dimensions of sound or space he could enhance with his studio tools.

Hannett had a complex, highly distinctive way of working and slowly he began to warp the Mondays' sound, so that the songs became a whole living beast and not the separate parts they had been on the demo. The Mondays never questioned what he was doing, allowing Hannett all the freedom he wanted to experiment, and the producer, known for being a dictatorial presence in the studio, began to relax and enjoy himself. 'He was such a great bloke,' said Whelan. 'We really loved him. We used to do lines from Monty Python sketches and he'd finish the lines, he knew them all. He said to me, Do you know who was a big Monty Python fan? I asked, Who? He said, Elvis.'

During the recording Hannett was drinking heavily but he had temporarily kicked heroin, the drug that he said had helped him achieve the sense of alienation in the music on Joy Division's albums. He was taking cocaine with the booze, a mix that kept him on a fairly even keel. But what really started to do it for Hannett, on this record at least, was when the Mondays introduced him to Ecstasy. It put him in a good mood and retuned his ear. 'The E started to affect the music,' said Paul. A close friend of the band during this period, Leon, who was heavily involved in the scene, brought to the studio hundreds of House records that he'd brought back from Ibiza. 'That's what we were listening to while we were making the album,' said Paul. While the Mondays did not intend to try and make a pure House record, the pulse of 'Wrote For Luck', which seemed to stretch into infinity, was enhanced by a sequenced synth bass line not dissimilar to a Chicago House track; to 'keep it going and keep it tight and steady', said Paul.

But, for all the undoubted hard work that went into the studio recording, there was no escaping the hedonism of the Manchester scene, if that had been the idea of recording at Slaughterhouse. Partying pals came up throughout the time they were there, and in a backroom at the studio House music played twenty-four hours a day. Inevitably there was a lot of Ecstasy involved. Tony Wilson had now witnessed first hand the Ecstasy explosion at The Hacienda, with Wednesday night's Ibiza-themed Hot an inferno of 2000 paying customers all seemingly high on E, and the night that he turned up to find half the band missing from the recording studio, he described the scene in the party room as 'a mini-Hacienda'. 'Is this what you've wasted my money on?' he asked rhetorically. 'Fucking great.' He loved things like that.

Wilson brought with him a camera crew to film the band for a programme made by ITV Schools, an educational television service aimed at under-eighteens and broadcast on Channel 4. 'They were making a six-part series about the workplace – printing works, long haulage – and one of them was about the music business,' said McGough. 'The producer had asked my mum and I jumped at it because of the power of television. The film crew followed me a lot because they wanted to cover the business side of it.' The ITV Schools team would film the making and launch of the Mondays' new album. Wilson was in his element and McGough looked handsome and spoke intelligently on camera. The Mondays were unsure. 'We were told but then we were never asked any more about it,' said Whelan. 'Kids at school watched that programme and thought that's what I'm going to do when I leave school,' said Paul. One of those kids, he added, was Bernard Butler, who would go on to form Suede. 'I'd have said the same thing if I'd have been at school and watched that programme – if they can do it I can do it.'

While visiting Driffield, Wilson recalled asking Shaun what he was writing about. 'He just smiled and said he was writing about nothing!' It was typical of Shaun. The lyrics were coming free and easy, as all around him inspired flashes of inspiration and word play. The themes of death and disease of the band's first album were replaced by tales inspired by Ecstasy and his new single lifestyle. He was in a good space, popular with the girls at The Hacienda and the top lads, his £80 a week wage from the band supplemented by the money he got from knocking out a few Es.

As usual in his lyrics he plundered and then bludgeoned into shape across all the ten new tracks references from a variety of sources. He took major inspiration from the film *Performance* and the Stones' film *Gimme Shelter*. On 'Lazyitis', a word he'd got from his nana, he remarkably mixed 'This Little Piggy', Sly & The Family Stone's 'Family Affair' and The Beatles' 'Ticket to Ride'. For 'Bring a Friend' he took a passage from a pornographic magazine (a tale of two sisters and their 'greedy little cunts') and on what was becoming the album's centrepiece, 'Wrote For Luck', he grabbed the line 'you were wet but you're getting drier' from a famous scene in the film *Stardust*. The lyrics to 'Wrote For Luck' were his first cogent effort at writing a whole song about the same thing, albeit a heroin deal gone wrong – exemplified by the line about asking for juice and getting poison. But he'd written it in such a way that it could have been about a woman. He'd surprised himself with how clever he'd been.

The music too was sounding clever. While Cale had insisted the band play faster, Hannett had them play, in his own famous words, 'slower but faster'. The band's grooves were more relaxed but still rolling, and without having to strain to stay on top of the music, Shaun found more melody in his voice. But he was still uncomfortable singing in the studio, the nakedness he felt. 'He wasn't one to work at it,' said Mark Day. 'He wasn't trying to get it perfect, he'd just go and do one or two takes and that was it.'

Driffield was a small town and the Mondays were big characters. During the three weeks they were there, they became something of a local talking point. Not everyone was taken however by their sudden outbreaks of dancing and their E'd-up love vibe. There was a run-in at a local pub with some 'squaddies' from the nearby Royal Air Force base who reacted badly to Bez in particular. A massive fight was averted after Bez turned the soldiers on to Ecstasy. He'd only just returned from a summer trip to Ibiza, where New Order were recording their new album, with a gang that included infamous Hacienda drug dealer Jeff the Chef, and he would not see out the recording as he was arrested back in Manchester for taking a car without consent and possession of marijuana. Bez said that he also had 500 Es confiscated but the police did not know what they were. He was lucky: Jeff the Chef would eventually get five years in prison for possession of E, but in 1988, there were very few arrests for Ecstasy across the country and none in Manchester.

There were however the first rumblings of concern about the uninhibited Acid scene. Paul Oakenfold's club night, Spectrum, was forced to shut down after the *Sun* published a shock story on drug use at the club, reporting on 'pushers plying their evil trade' and 'tiny tabs that blow your mind'. At first the tabloid took the term Acid House literally and mistakenly claimed LSD was the drug that was sending the Spectrum clubbers crazy. It would not be long, however, before Ecstasy was named and the drug became public enemy number one. Bez was at the heart of the storm as Acid House, now feeding off the growing publicity in style and music magazines and the national press, moved beyond the confines of The Hacienda and a handful of London club nights to become an epidemic sweeping the nation. Acid nights were being set up in every major city, smiley face T-shirts (with logos such as Take a Trip) were being sold on the high street and D-Mob's Spectrum-inspired track, 'We Call It Acieed', and Inner City's 'Good Life' were among the first wave of Acid House tunes heading towards the top ten.

At Manchester magistrates' court, Bez argued that the car he'd been driving was a hire car and the stash inside was not his. He was bailed, but the loss of 500 Es did not go down well with the dealers. 'The baddies were after him for a few weeks but I never knew the full story,' said Paul. 'There were now a few really dark people turning up.' As a nation of kids fell in love with the drug and the Acid House scene, so did a growing number of criminals. Everybody wanted E and if you had it, you made big money. These weren't the original lads from Ibiza, the cheeky scamp sneak-thief clubbers who spread the love, but serious organised crime gangs, club bouncers or football hooligan firms. Bez was walking a fine line.

The band returned to Manchester exhausted. Hannett had wrung every last drop out of them. But he wasn't finished, not by any stretch of the imagination. He took the tapes of the band's new material into his favourite recording studio, Strawberry in Stockport, and began to experiment. He called on additional musicians, adding extra percussion from renowned drum teacher Dave Hassell, along with keyboards and piano from his pal Steve Hopkins. The band joined in, suggesting that Shaun and Paul's dad, Derek, add banjo to one of the tracks. They were also keen to add dialogue from *Performance*, with Shaun choosing the excerpts he wanted. Then Hannett the alchemist went to work: he turned tapes backwards to run guitar parts in reverse, processed the music through all manner of machines he'd hooked up together, adding echo, reverb and electronic washes, until there was a swamp of sounds, an indication of what was in Hannett's mind on Ecstasy, a bizarre, claustrophobic, dense and throbbing oneness full of power and volume.

'Wrote For Luck', the longest track at just over six minutes, was the obvious first single. It was the best thing the band had ever recorded and the track most attuned to the burgeoning Acid House scene. Over a hypnotic, hallucinogenic beat and a queasy soup of bass/keyboard and rolling guitar hooks, Shaun had not even sung his 'higher than high high' chorus line; instead he kind of half groaned it. It was off its head, some sort of new music from a band that still sounded steeped in rock history but had somehow gone beyond it towards a new space, yet without using the rudimentary DIY sample-heavy obviousness of pioneering British DJ records by MARRS or Coldcut. The combination of Hannett and the Mondays had been a masterstroke. 'Wrote For Luck' had been written with club or dance music in mind and the end result wasn't too far away from it, described by Paul as 'a band with extras'.

Buoyed by this undoubted masterpiece, McGough suggested creating versions of the song that were even more attuned to the dance floor, more Acid House. The band had been listening

The front room of Shaun's and Paul's parents' home, late 1970s. Their Dad, Derek Ryder, is on upright bass with his musical and comedy partner Barry Seddon on guitar. *Courtesy of Paul Ryder*

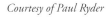

Paul, aged 16, outside the family home in Worsley, with Derek and his first motorbike, a Yamaha FS1E.
Courtesy of Paul Ryder

Paul and Shaun, as youngsters. *Courtesy of Paul Ryder*

A missed album cover opportunity, the pre-teen Shaun modelling his new Manchester United strip.
Courtesy of Paul Ryder

Mark Day, on guitar, and Paul Davis, playing his tiny keyboard with lid, at an early band rehearsal, 1983.
Courtesy of Paul Ryder

Shaun and Paul, a formidable and close-knit pair, early 1980s.
Courtesy of Paul Ryder

Gary Whelan, then fifteen, on drums and Shaun.
Courtesy of Paul Ryder

Mark Day and Shaun, band rehearsal, 1986. *Courtesy of Anthony Young*

Early band shot with Bez, 1986. Left to right: Davis, Shaun, Bez, Paul, Day and Whelan.
Courtesy of Anthony Young

Gary Whelan, on stage, as certain band members tried out a smart new look, 1986.
Courtesy of Anthony Young

Mark 'Bez' Berry, the luckiest man in the world according to band manager Phil Saxe, 1986. *Courtesy of Mark Day*

Paul Ryder and Gary Whelan, blue-eyed and bushy-tailed, 1986. *Courtesy of Mark Day*

Shaun's girlfriend Suzy with Shaun and Mark Day, 1987. *Courtesy of Mark Day*

The inimitable Paul Davis, in tour van, 1986 (Gary Whelan and Bez in background). *Courtesy of Mark Day*

Shaun, on stage becoming
an icon, 1987.
Courtesy of Anthony Young

Gig advert featuring Bez and
Shaun, Mr Happy and Mr Evil
according to second manager
Nathan McGough.
Courtesy of Anthony Young

D.M.P. presents

Happy Mondays

MONDAY NOVEMBER 27
Top Rank Suite, West Street, Brighton

Manager Phil Saxe, the 'Andy Warhol of the Perry Boys' and Whelan, on the band's first visit to America, New York, 1987.
Courtesy of Mark Day

Photo shoot out-take, taken on Mark Day's camera. Whelan was fascinated by Sioux Indians (as seen on his T-shirt).
Courtesy of Mark Day

MADCHESTER

HAPPY MONDAYS
RAVE ON
VIDEO

11 tracks including
'HALLELUJAH', 'CLAP YOUR HANDS', 'W.F.L.'
Available now at £9.99

Temperance CLUB

THURSDAY 12th MAY
HAPPY
MONDAYS
ON STAGE
AT 9·30 PM
ADMISSION £2·50
(£1 AFTER 10 PM)
25% OFF PRICE OF DRINKS

above: Press advert for a Hacienda gig, 1988. Temperance was the club's student night. *Courtesy of Anthony Young*

left: Press advert for 'Rave On' video, featuring popular Madchester logo, 198? *Courtesy of Anthony Young*

Bez, relaxing poolside, America, 1989. *Courtesy of Mark Day*

above: Shaun, in red Kickers, and Paul Davis, America, 1989.
© *Andrew Hardy*

above right: Derek Ryder, 'Horse Man', an ever present for the band's entire career 1982–1993.
© *Andrew Hardy*

right: Paul, Bez and Shaun, on stage in America, 1989.
© *Andrew Hardy*

Backstage with Paul, Whelan, manager Nathan McGough, Mark Day, Bez, Shaun (out of shot) and Shaun's minder Muzzer, at the legendary CBGB club, New York, 1989.
© *Andrew Hardy*

Influential Factory PR man Jeff Barrett, McGough and Factory boss Tony Wilson, 1989.
© *peterjwalsh.com*

The infamous Glastonbury pass that was copied by lads on the firm creating pandemonium backstage, which contributed to the following year's festival being cancelled.
Courtesy of Anthony Young

Advert for gig in Ibiza, the first rock band to play at the celebrated KU club, 1990. *Courtesy of Anthony Young*

left: American advert for *Step On*. The band's US label, Elektra, spent close to $1 million marketing the band. *Courtesy of Mark Day*

bottom left: Gig advert for two dates in Paris, featuring iconic lettering by Central Station Design, 1991. *Courtesy of Anthony Young*

below: European tour itinerary, 1990 – a document made by Factory and distributed to the band and touring crew, featuring Paul Davis on the cover. *Courtesy of Tracey Donnelly*

Gold discs for the *Bummed* album: collected in the top floor of the still unfinished Factory HQ, 1990. Left to right: Davis, Whelan, Paul, Day, Bez, Shaun, McGough & Wilson.

HAPPY MONDAYS

PILLS N THRILLS
AND BELLYACHES

above: The entrance to Blue Wave studio in Barbados, where the band recorded their fifth album in 1992. *Courtesy of Mark Day*

opposite: American poster advert for *Pills 'n' Thrills* album signed by Shaun: the background colours are from the band posing in front of a Central Station painted installation to promote clothing label Gio-Goi. *Courtesy of Christopher Donnelly*

above: Top dog Shaun cocking his leg in Barbados before prescription pills and crack cocaine took hold. *Courtesy of Howard Thompson/Elektra*

left: Advert for a European tour that was abandoned as the band disintegrated. *Courtesy of Anthony Young*

happy mondays

live 92 — yes please!

Mi. 2.12. Hamburg - Große Freiheit
Do. 3.12. Berlin - Neue Welt
So. 6.12. München - Nachtwerk
Mi. 16.12. Köln - Live Music Hall

Mixing the *Yes Please!* album in New York. Left to right: Wilson, Shaun, Elektra A&R man Howard Thompson, Chris Frantz (seated), Tina Weymouth, Paul and McGough.

Courtesy of Howard Thompson/Elektra

non-stop to a twelve-inch called 'Jibaro', made by Paul Oakenfold under the alias Electra, and in keeping with the sound of the record McGough suggested stripping Hannett's 'Wrote For Luck' back to basics, adding a basic electronic beat pattern and building a vibe around Shaun's vocal hook, while various parts of the song were faded in and out. It was the Mondays' first attempt at a 'club mix', but McGough was no Oakenfold. Nor was Laurence Diana, Hannett's engineer at Strawberry, who also attempted a 'dance mix' of the song.

It was a novel idea, a first for a rock band, but crudely executed. In the coming months McGough and Wilson would return to the idea and reshape the British musical landscape. For now though, the unfathomable Hannett sound was what would propel the Mondays forward.

13
The Bailey Brothers

To promote 'Wrote For Luck', McGough used his contacts to arrange for the Mondays to tour the UK supporting James, for which they would be paid a fee of £100 to £150 a night. Since leaving Factory in 1985, James had built a loyal fan base despite having failed to make the leap to mainstream success. The grass, it turned out, was not greener with Sire, who they had recently quit after two flop albums. The band was interested in rejoining Factory but Tony Wilson was as hostile to that idea as he was to the Mondays supporting them. But McGough was adamant, knowing that James' gigs regularly sold out around the UK and this was a ready-made tour, where at every show the Mondays would play to 800 or 1000 people who had never heard them before. It was either that or they could go out and do their own headline tour, playing to 150 a night. There was a huge fight between Wilson and McGough over it, but McGough stood his ground and got his way.

Wilson had his own ideas for promoting the Mondays. They included the band accompanying him and Granada's TV cameras on a visit to the office of Joe Bloggs, a local clothing firm famed for their voluminous jeans and heavily logo'd T-shirts and sweatshirts, which were growing popular with Acid House clubbers. Wilson had arranged for Bloggs to sponsor the Mondays. It essentially meant free clothes in exchange for publicity for the company: the visit would be shown on Wilson's new late-night Granada music and arts programme, *The Other Side of Midnight*.

The resulting piece makes for uncomfortable viewing, especially for the band members. Wilson described Bloggs as 'casual wear', while the Mondays, he said, were 'as casual as it gets'. The band was filmed flicking through clothes rails as Wilson asked Shaun: 'Is this the sort of stuff you'd normally go and buy?' Shaun pointed to the Bloggs logo on a long-sleeved T-shirt and said, 'We probably wouldn't have that on it, would we?' Paul can be heard saying that he 'usually just wears Marks and Spencer stuff'. The band members were then filmed awkwardly modelling Bloggs. Shaun, in red leather Converse trainers, looked seriously unhappy. He would list labels such as Hugo Boss, Armani, Paul Smith, D&G, Versace and Ralph Lauren as favourites, 'the looser bits of gear', and say he was getting into a 'designer hippy vibe'. The Bloggs episode was as excruciating as it sounded, and, thankfully, most viewers seem to have forgotten it the moment it was aired, despite Bloggs going on to become the era's most profitable and ubiquitous street fashion label.

Ecstasy-drenched parties studded the James tour. On 8 October the band were with Wilson, The Stone Roses — who were developing a new sound and look, taking many of their moves from the Mondays — an unknown Noel Gallagher and New Order at Manchester's first illegal Acid House 'warehouse' party, Sweat It Out, organised by Anthony and Christopher Donnelly; the brothers had stayed on the periphery of the band since they were introduced through Tracey, who still worked at Factory. It took place in a railway arch near the city centre and was part of a wider movement, inspired by Ecstasy, of illegal all-night warehouse parties that was spreading across the UK. It was edgy, full of raw energy and emotion — and an unforgettable bonding experience. Many of the same faces travelled by coach to Box studios in Bath, where New Order were completing the album they'd started in Ibiza, and set about a hedonistic night of Acid House madness that some who were there claim was the wildest party of all time.

Despite the band being asked to step up to new levels of professionalism on the James tour, things were spiralling almost out of control. After a sold-out show at the 1500-capacity Ritz in Manchester, Shaun went missing and, with a gig in Newcastle requiring an early start in the band hire van, could not be found the next day. He was eventually located and the van set off from Manchester three hours late. When the Mondays finally arrived in Newcastle and began to unload their gear they were asked what they were doing, and after they explained were told, 'This is Simply Red, you're at the wrong gig.' Shaun and Bez had already dashed into the venue and bundled on stage, staring perplexed at the band they found already there. They would laugh about it later but when they all finally turned up at the right venue, they'd missed their slot, and arguments exploded.

In Scotland, James' singer Tim Booth recalled a show where 'Shaun was so out of it he came off after twenty minutes thinking he'd been on for hours'. More commonly the band delivered on stage, continuing to pick up glowing live reviews (which often failed to mention the headline act) in the music press, but the mayhem on the road continued apace. 'They were like a cartoon,' said James bassist Jim Glennie, who recalled coming off stage one night to find that all the beer on their rider – four crates – had been stolen. He said there was security on the door, 'so they must have got in through the window'. The band had a party to go back to in Manchester that night. 'There were quite a few sneak thieves hanging around with us at this time,' said Paul, who recalled Liverpool University being relieved of its entire stock of rugby shirts on the tour. The Mondays' guest list regularly stretched to forty people, a few of whom 'probably wouldn't have been into the music'. Many were younger than the band, still teenagers, and wilder, and for them crime and drugs really was a way of life. 'They could see us having a good time and were thinking I want some of that. They enjoyed hanging around with us – we could get them in The Hacienda for free. Friendships were forged.'

The hardcore partying continued in Manchester, on 19 October, with an Ecstasy-fuelled carnival during the video shoot for 'Wrote For Luck'. Wilson had again enlisted The Bailey Bothers, Jobling and Shotton – dubbed by the Mondays Tyne and Wear, since they were both Newcastle-born – to direct the video. The possibility of making the *Mad Fuckers!* film still dominated their thinking and they hoped to shoot scenes around the band while making the video. Shaun, particularly, loved the idea of making a movie and shared with Jobling a love of rare cult films. Despite Shaun's burgeoning self-portrayal as a drug-crazed criminal, he had a keen intelligence and deep cultural knowledge. The Bailey Brothers had a simple idea for the video – to film the band in the context of a full-on club night, hoping to capture some of the spirit of the time. They hired the city's Legend club, which was now hosting a packed Acid House night with an atmosphere to rival The Hacienda and had one of the most impressive lighting systems of any club in the world.

The shooting of the video was to take place on Sunday afternoon but the party rolled over from Saturday night. 'There was no difference between day and night-time then with us,' said Whelan. As the Mondays' entourage started to roll in, The Bailey Brothers shot the band members acting out what were supposed to look like drug deals, 'pushing the doormen away, picking up parcels', said Paul. When the music started blasting out, the lights started to flash, the party kicked in. 'I think we had three or four murderers who came along to take part,' said Jobling. 'But they were on E so it's not a problem, they were kissing and cuddling you as they came in.' According to Bez 'half of Manchester turned up in full party spirit, raring to show the world and his grandma what was going down on our plot'.

The scene was bonkers, and The Bailey Brothers shot the band off their heads, dancing in the middle of the writhing mass of people. Shaun was seen dancing playfully with Paul, the brothers close to hugging, before turning to camera to voice the drug-drenched words of the song. These images would come to define the era and frame Shaun as the poster boy for the blissed-out euphoria of Ecstasy. Paul Oakenfold would say the video captured the early days of Acid House perfectly: 'That video sums the whole thing up.' But it was not exactly the sort of video you could play on *The Chart Show* or MTV, a bombed-out band in the middle of an obviously E-fuelled party, writhing and sweating, with strobe lighting flashing to the pulse of the beat.

The drug was no longer an underground secret. The *Sun* was now running a series of articles on the 'evils of Ecstasy'. There was a 'good chance', it posited, that taking the drug would see you end up in a mental institution for life or suffer sexual assault. A wave of hysteria drowned out any sensible debate on the long-term effects of Ecstasy use. Smiley face T-shirts were banned from Top Shop, *Top of the Pops* banned songs with the word 'acid' in them and MPs eagerly came forward to condemn the drug. The moral panic stepped up a gear when a young girl died after taking two Es at a party. The police were suddenly very interested in the 'danger drug sweeping discos and ruining lives', as the *Sun* would have it.

Not one media outlet would show the 'Wrote For Luck' video, and in an era before YouTube that was not a good thing. The single was released on 31 October 1988, the same day The Stone Roses released 'Elephant Stone' − a track that borrowed heavily from Mark Day's 'wah-wah' guitar sound and started the Roses' achingly slow rise to prominence. The Central Station sleeve for 'Wrote For Luck', their first post-Ecstasy cover, was a blast of bright colours, with the Mondays' name spelled out large and in distinct cartoon lettering − a design that would adorn posters, badges and T-shirts as Factory gave the band significant promotional support. 'Matt, Pat and Karen were kind of part of the band,' said Whelan. 'They had a blank canvas from us.' The sleeve was different to their earlier fumbling work for the band, which had lacked a clear identity. And it was a giant leap away from the usual Factory aesthetic, as defined by Peter Saville's clean and controlled graphics, evidenced that summer as the label put a Joy Division singles compilation into the top ten and a single, 'Atmosphere', into the Top 40 and to number one in the indie charts. The two events seemed intertwined, the closing of one chapter at Factory and the beginning of another. Tony Wilson asserted that the design team's Happy Mondays logo marked the beginning of a new era at the label. 'The second half of the Factory story,' Wilson said, 'is best summed up by the painterly eccentricity of Central Station.'

Reviews of 'Wrote For Luck' were mixed. 'You used to speak the truth but now you're clever' was named 'one liner of the week' in *NME* and the single praised for its 'near blistering hypno rhythm', but the review − remembering Shaun's outbursts during the promotion of '24 Hour Party People' − concluded that 'yobbos are never cool'. The indie scene and music press were way behind the Mondays in adopting Acid House styles, not because of the drug outrage, but because it was seen as a little too close to working-class disco with no real stars to get behind: just a bunch of – often instrumental – records by faceless American DJs. British acts that did break through into the mainstream from the dance scene, such as S'Express and Yazz, seemed to have stripped the music of any sense of illicit excitement – certainly their videos were shiny and bright, and did not represent the actuality in the way that 'Wrote For Luck' did.

The most popular new indie acts, House of Love and My Bloody Valentine (both signed to Creation Records), and mainstays The Wedding Present and The Sugarcubes were all welded to their guitars and to rock. Stock, Aitken and Waterman continued to dominate the UK charts with Kylie Minogue, a new superstar to rival boy band Bros. The Mondays were nowhere. Factory's radio and TV plugger, Nicki Kefalas, could not get the band on daytime radio, for although several programmers found their music interesting none would stick their neck out. 'The Mondays were still seen as left-field, a bit weird and people were a bit cautious about the drugs and the lifestyle,' she said. 'And they all found Shaun's vocals very difficult to cope with.'

As a result, though the single came in a variety of formats, including 'club' and 'dance' mixes, 'Wrote For Luck' stalled at number seven in the indie charts – better than 'Elephant Stone' but still a major disappointment. 'I thought "Wrote For Luck" was going to be the one that broke through,' said Paul. Factory had been predicting the single would reach the top twenty, but according to Wilson it sold a paltry 1500 copies. Neither McGough's nor Laurence Diana's remixes of the track were hits in the clubs; in fact they went largely unnoticed.

Despite the odd mixed review, the one place the Mondays were guaranteed success was with the UK's weekly music press. Dave Harper, who had introduced the band to the medium, largely defined their message and established key relationships with individual journalists eager to help the band, had recently quit Out Promotions to become the head of press at major label RCA. He left the Mondays and Factory with a more than able replacement: well-connected and long-time Mondays fan Jeff Barrett, who had recently set up his own PR company, Capersville, representing Creation acts such as Primal Scream and My Bloody Valentine. He was determined to convert all in his path to the cause of the Mondays, a crucial injection of enthusiasm just when the band needed it. 'When Harper gave me the job, New Order should have been the big attraction,' said Barrett. 'But it was the Mondays who really got me. I knew from the start that group had a shot.'

Barrett, who the Mondays dubbed Foxhead or Lionman because of his long flaming hair, called the band's new Hannett-produced album 'mind-blowing'. He distributed preview copies to the press. The opening track was listed as 'Some Cunt from Preston' and the album was called *Bummed* – the latter title at least designed to be deliberately offensive. That was Shaun's idea. 'It was a saying at the time,' said Whelan. 'Shaun used to say he was out all night and he bummed her all night, a slang word for sex. I didn't even know what the album was called until it came out.' The album cover, again designed by Central Station, featured an image that would become as iconic as their new Mondays logo: a photograph of Shaun's face, painted over in garish colours so he appeared smeared in eye make-up, blusher and lipstick. It was a technique Central Station was applying to a range of celebrities for an art exhibition.

The skill and impact of the design was somewhat negated by the inclusion of two twelve-inch pornographic images of the same mature, reclining, large-breasted fully nude woman with a shaved fanny. Taken from a period porno magazine, they weren't exactly pretty, but they caused some heated debate, with local journalists accusing the band of misogyny. Like Shaun's title, it was intended as a cheap shock and done to amuse the band. 'I burst out laughing when I saw that,' said Paul. 'It was typical of Matt and Pat to do something like that.' It gave the record a tinge of illicit thrill, with many young teenage boys forced to hide the record from their parents – 'kind of cool' said Paul. But, like the video for 'Wrote For Luck' which no one would play, the porno image backfired. Many record stores refused to stock the album and its Japanese release was delayed indefinitely as the artwork was impounded at customs.

Factory was still operating with only a handful of staff and these problems were not easily sorted.

The reviews of the album in the UK music press nevertheless put fresh wind in the band's sails. Large, lead reviews, they were nothing less than sensational. Jeff Barrett acted quickly to get the band prominent interviews in each of the three leading papers, *NME*, *Sounds* and *Melody Maker*; in the latter *Bummed* was called 'towering' and 'phenomenal' and described as the band's 'dole age revisionism of psychedelia'. The photo of the band accompanying the paper's double-page spread featured both Cressa and the Mondays' new soundman, the tall dreadlocked Si Machan, who had previously worked in the same role for The Stone Roses. Cressa, one of the few who had continued to wear flares after the Mondays abandoned them, went in the opposite direction, acting as a sort of ersatz Bez on stage with the Roses, who began to pick up a slew of glowing live reviews and whose trousers started to grow wider until they were the voluminous flares of legend. 'We taught Cressa all he knows,' said Shaun. But there was no sense of rivalry between the bands. Ian Brown openly acknowledged that the Mondays 'were the best band in Manchester'.

McGough, who sat in on the interviews but only to stop the band saying anything too stupid, was shocked at how Shaun presented himself, especially when it came to his lyrics, which had drawn considerable praise: 'Shaun turned around and said, Listen, they're just nursery rhymes, I just make them up and they sound good and that's it. He was not accepting of himself as an artist.' What became apparent in all the interviews to promote *Bummed* was Shaun's contradictory attitude. He wanted the band and their music to be taken seriously, yet claimed he didn't, insisting he was 'just in this for the money'. The best thing about being in the Mondays, he said, facetiously, was 'The trilby, trilby hat, twat, pussy'. He glibly confessed to taking heroin – but only because, he said, it was 'cheaper than water-skiing or hang-gliding'. He was unrelenting in the image he was trying to portray, as a new bad boy of rock, even though it had as yet brought limited success.

The rest of the band was less than impressed, when they read the supposed 'band' interviews, to see how Shaun's comments dominated. 'It was not long after that I fell away from interviews,' said Paul. 'I had nothing to say. I just wanted them to listen to the music. They just wanted more crazy stories from Shaun.' It would become a minor but niggling annoyance within the band that the only opinion ever in print seemed to come from Shaun and was often bullshit. But he was hardly to blame. The Mondays had no media training and Shaun was simply thrown in at the deep end, under pressure to be the frontman, an entertainer. He may even have been intimidated by the situation – music journalists were for the most part university-, even Oxbridge-educated – and laying it on thick was a defence mechanism. Whatever the reason, Shaun started 'to lie and bullshit', said Paul, 'to make things up and make them sound glamorous'. The band certainly weren't yobs as they were being portrayed, but no one else wanted to do the interviews, had the skill or will to correct the impression. 'It was up to Shaun,' said Paul.

Supporting Shaun was Jeff Barrett. He relentlessly promoted the band's links, and those of *Bummed,* to the Acid House scene and Ecstasy. This in the face of the first heavy-handed jail sentence – ten years – passed down to a promoter of a London party 'where drugs were supplied', an indication of how seriously the police were beginning to treat Acid House. Many illegal warehouse parties – for one of which 3000 tickets had been sold – were besieged by riot police and the tabloid press were relentless in their damnation of the scene. Barrett's promotional efforts also went against all received wisdom, as the Mondays' current sound would never find a place at any Acid House night. Barrett seemed to be wishing the link into existence. An Ecstasy convert but also a connoisseur of rock 'n' roll, he felt that Acid House had legs, was a story that would run and run, could have the same impact as the anti-establishment punk movement. The descriptions of all night-partying, sex, drugs and crazy music were quintessentially rock 'n' roll, and after a decade of Thatcher rule, the switched-on Barrett was willing to proselytise a profound political edge to the communal experience of Acid House, to depict it as a fight-back by the disenfranchised. If Shaun wanted to characterise himself as a drug dealer, then so what? So many people were now doing drugs it was almost normalised; criminality was democratised.

Many of these thoughts would soon be echoed by Tony Wilson and given greater relevance, but it was clear Barrett was a brilliant addition to the team. He understood the make-up of the music press and knew he could bring something of this vision to print. 'They had been searching for a band to represent this incredible new youth culture,' he said. 'The Mondays were so naturally right it was incredible. Had I not been involved with them I might have wondered if at least a little of it was contrived.' The band's lifestyle was absolutely genuine: 'We are in this band all day and all night,' said Paul. 'This is it, this is how we live and we live like this all the time.' But it was Barrett, who had been around the best indie music for the past five years, who saw it as something sensational. He was hyping the lifestyle as much as the music.

Despite the band's lack of commercial success, Wilson too now joined the revolution happening on his doorstep. Propped up at the bar in his designer suits, holding forth on topics of great artistic significance, Wilson was everything that Acid House was out to slay. But this dinosaur had quickly now got with the programme. He arranged for the Mondays to record two tracks from the new album – 'Performance' and 'Do It Better' – in the Granada 2 studio for a slot on *The Other Side of Midnight*. Shaun had chosen the tracks and the Mondays recorded them live; they were then edited for transmission a few days later, although in the end only 'Performance' was aired. Wilson introduced the band with, 'I work with them but this isn't nepotism, it is a profound devotion to the cause, the cause of Happy Mondays.' It was Sunday, the studio was all white and Bez hadn't slept – his frenetic, vacant dancing, framed in this way, was as shocking as any rock 'n' roll moment ever. The whole band and its music seemed to revolve around him. There was no doubt he was inhabiting some other space, had locked into the band's groove and wouldn't let go. Shaun shook maracas around him and looked cool in a pair of over-sized tinted dark glasses that he'd borrowed from Phil Saxe – who, remarkably, was now working as head of A&R at Factory.

It was this TV moment, the band felt, when their fortunes finally started to turn. For the first time a mass audience had a chance to see them live and the impact was resoundingly positive. 'It gave us a bigger fan base overnight and acceptability in Manchester,' said Whelan. 'There was a change in the air after that. Tony's intro-duction was fantastic and we delivered.' After they had finished recording the show, they were interviewed by *NME* in the Granada canteen. Jeff Barrett had convinced journalist Stuart Maconie that the Mondays were the 'next big thing', and in his article, Maconie was to quote Tony Wilson's bold comparison: 'I've got two things to say about the Happy Mondays. One's sex and the other one's pistols.' Wilson had the bit between his teeth. Elsewhere he would call Shaun 'the Johnny Rotten of Acid House'. He was now con-vinced Acid House was the new punk rock. The Mondays did not consider themselves anything like the Sex Pistols, but accepted Wilson's grandiose claims as all part of the game. 'He knows how to sell it,' said Whelan. 'We just went along with it.'

Maconie bought it wholesale. He called *Bummed* 'an explosive collision of two cultures – the traditional value of rock meets the ethic of the dance underground'. He wrote that the Mondays were 'prime movers and luminaries in the city's Acid scene' as well as 'providers of much of the scene's impetus'. The inference was obvious: the band were E dealers, and the article was awash with drug innuendo – E was referred to, awkwardly, as 'sweeties'. Maconie made it clear that the Mondays were a 'drug band' and asked them if drugs were essential to make great music. Shaun's answer drew on figures as disparate as a jazz master and a figure from the legends of Robin Hood: 'Of course, it goes without saying. Count Basie was a skaghead. Alan-a-Dale did mushrooms. That's how he got all those great tunes on his lute.' Ecstasy was now reaching sectors of the British population who had not danced in a club before, and alongside the youngsters a swathe of people in their mid-twenties and beyond were joining in, just like the Mondays a year ago. Despite police pressure, the number of warehouse parties increased, Acid House nights becoming commonplace as a new mood spread, evinced by the ever brighter, baggier and freakier moves in club and street fashion. Being a drug dealer in these circumstances was no longer 'scummy' but cool, loaded with an outlaw chic as recreational drug use increased exponentially; the 'chemical generation' was the term coined by author Irvine Welsh.

In the same issue of the *NME* as Maconie's article, *Bummed* was given a long and frothing nine out of ten review by James Brown who, like Maconie, would be a key future ally for the Mondays at the paper. Brown called the album shockingly original, the songs 'drug lullabies', and described the Mondays as 'The only band in Manchester to absorb the full influence of Joy Division, New Order, The Fall, A Certain Ratio and James without letting it soak their sounds or drown their character.' The rave review concluded: 'If you love the energy of Acid and the awkward aggression of good independent rock but want your music to be scarred with the character of Dennis Hopper, Charlie Bukowski, Hunter S. Thompson and Johnny Rotten, you can stop looking to the past and taking these pleasures separately by getting *Bummed* for a truly stimulating contemporary sensory thrashing.'

Shaun was still essentially talking himself and the band up as an unpleasant and petty-criminal hooligan gang who made careless but brilliant music on the side, and both Barrett and Wilson were now pushing the same message – that of drug-dealing petty criminals made good. And the weekly music press were lapping it up. 'We were built on bullshit,' said Whelan. 'Shaun doesn't let the truth get in the way of a good story and that's what a lot of rock 'n' roll is built on . . . Tony [Wilson] told me once, Nothing is ever what it seems.' Drugs, drugs and more drugs was the common theme of every article written about *Bummed* and the band encouraged it. In the same issue of *Sounds* where the album received a glowing four-star review, calling the band geniuses and comparing them to The Doors, the band listed their own 'Top ten' songs, choosing such titles as 'Lucy in the Sky with Diamonds' by The Beatles, 'Cocaine in My Brain' by Dillinger, 'Sex and Drugs and Rock and Roll' by Ian Dury, 'Heroin' by The Velvet Underground and 'King Heroin' by James Brown.

In Manchester, Factory had a novel approach to promoting the album. The company had recently purchased a huge, ramshackle two-storey building on Charles Street, directly behind what was then the BBC's northern studio, with plans to turn it into a new headquarters. The building needed complete renovation, including significant structural work, and Alan Erasmus, whose idea it had been to buy it, decided to make use of it in the meantime as a giant billboard. The city centre location was perfect and the entire façade of the building was covered in multiple posters of *Bummed*'s lurid sleeve. It was classic Factory: unconventional, artistic, a statement. On a smaller scale, multiple *Bummed* posters were used to line the walls of the walkway into the launch party for the album that took place in central London, in the Star Bar at Heaven nightclub, on 28 November. The music press, corralled by Barrett with help from Dave Harper, and Factory industry contacts were confronted with bacchanalian scenes as hundreds of Manchester's maddest party crowd were transported to the venue on coaches organised by Factory.

The event, scheduled for early evening, was another ruse by Barrett to cement the link between the Mondays and Acid House in the eyes of the media. Heaven had been home to pioneering Acid night Spectrum, and DJ Paul Oakenfold was now running a new and equally wild Acid night at the same club; in fact it would be taking place later the same night as the Mondays' album launch, which the band were to follow with a gig at a more traditional indie rock venue, Dingwalls in Camden. The band and their entourage had E available at the launch should any journalist wish to join in the fun. 'Probably they made more money that night selling Es than they did from getting paid for the gig at Dingwalls,' said McGough. For many in London this was their first sight of the now infamous Hacienda/Mondays crowd and they were not disappointed. The gig at Dingwalls was simply an extension of the party, the small stage packed with pals dancing beside the band. 'Everyone in the place was on E,' said Shaun. A review of the night in *Melody Maker* suggested that the Mondays were 'the most exciting thing in years'. In the *NME*, Bez's pupils were said to be 'dilated wide enough to drive a stretch limo through'. Afterwards the Mondays, journalists and scores of dancing Mancunians headed back to Heaven to enjoy Oakenfold's Acid night and then continued the party until the morning at the infamous rock 'n' roll Columbia Hotel in Lancaster Gate, where the band had rooms. They were subsequently barred from staying at the hotel.

This glut of publicity, organised by Barrett, helped *Bummed* perform significantly better than 'Wrote For Luck'. It reached number two in the indie charts and fifty-nine in the national charts. Yet privately, Factory were disappointed. They had invested around £50,000 in recording the album and initial sales had not enabled the company to recoup the money, never mind turn a profit. Wilson called it a 'flop' and despaired. He and McGough wondered how they could transmit the Mondays' 'genius', as Wilson called it, to a wider audience. 'Tony loved the band,' said McGough. 'He had a really strong feeling for the band and their relevance – it was unwavering.' The Mondays were lucky to be on Factory at this time. Poor sales had seen many bands thrown on the scrap heap, however much promise and PR they had.

Finally realising Erasmus's dream, Factory Classical began to release a series of albums, largely featuring contemporary British composers. It was a brave project, exciting, time-consuming and ultimately commercially doomed. Pursuing the Classical project, however, meant Factory had not signed any new acts (To Hell With Burgundy had come and gone with a whimper) and other than New Order and The Durutti Column, the Mondays were the label's only band. Again, it was New Order's commercial success that allowed Wilson the money to indulge in the Mondays in the hope that one day they would come good. New Order's new album performed even better worldwide than *Substance* and was their first UK number one. With *Technique*, part recorded in Ibiza and smoothly incorporating many Acid House musical moves, the band had stolen a lead on the Mondays. When performing the album's lead single, 'Fine Time', on *Top of the Pops*, singer Bernard Sumner had even copied Bez's dance, commenting afterwards, 'He's a very influential lad.'

New Order had at the same time opened the door to Happy Mondays' future success. In December they played in front of 10,000 fans at G-Mex in Manchester and it was noticeable that there had been a sea-change in their audience – gone were all the long-coated Joy Division fans, to be replaced by a young, brightly coloured, baggy, Ecstasy-fuelled crowd, including large numbers of football lads turned party heads. Happy Mondays were supporting that night, to appreciative applause but nothing like the fervour reserved for New Order. It was obvious to the band and all those around them that they too would find their audience among this crowd. It was out there waiting for them — all they had to do was win them over. Next year would see the band gigging relentlessly; hard work, one thing not often associated with the Mondays, not hype, being the key to future success.

14
Money

In early 1989 Happy Mondays signed a publishing contract in London with FFRR Music, the publishing arm of London Records. McGough had used the publicity surrounding the band to generate several offers from publishing companies, convincing them that the Mondays had the potential to be the band that would define the Acid House generation and be as successful as their Factory label mates New Order. FFRR was chosen, it was said, as they were the only label whose representative had been bothered to come to see them in Swinton all those years ago, but each band member also walked away with £2000 in cash, which would have persuaded most musicians whose largest cheque in five years had been their weekly £80 wage. They immediately descended on Covent Garden to go clothes shopping, Paul Davis and Shaun both coincidentally buying exactly the same leather jacket, to Shaun's evident annoyance.

For the first time Bez found himself sidelined over a financial stake in the band. He would receive a sixth of the £69,000 advance, but not a share in the copyright on the songs placed with FFRR. Once the advance was earned out, any future publishing royalties – from performance-related payments such as plays on the radio – would be split equally between Shaun, Paul, Day, Whelan and Davis, twenty per cent each. It was difficult to understand why Bez should receive *any* money from the FFRR deal: he didn't write any of the songs or play on the records, and there was concern among the band about the other income streams in which he had an equal share.

The Mondays were also due a generous sixty per cent share of a US deal worth $120,000 from the renowned Elektra Records, owned by the Warner Music Group. Factory held worldwide rights to the Mondays' records and licensed them to a range of world territories. On the strength of the 'Wrote For Luck' video and an animated sales pitch, Wilson had convinced Elektra to hand over the sum as an advance to license the group's records in America. 'We were made up to fuck about being on the same label as Love and The Doors,' said Bez, as the band talked excitedly about touring the States in the near future. Factory also cut minor European licensing deals for the Mondays' records, notably with Rough Trade in Germany, where the band were due to tour next. For the first time since they had been together there was a decent amount of money coming in; nine months after signing up with McGough, the band were financially provided for, with what appeared to be an organised and structured plan for the future.

In January 1989, the Mondays tore into a cluster of dates in Germany – their first ever European trip. Although they forgot important bits of equipment such as a bass drum pedal and guitar effects, the band, plus McGough, Derek and new soundman Si Machan, travelled in relative luxury on a twelve-seater minibus with a TV, video, sound system and fridge. And while they didn't always have the equipment they needed – or, when they turned up at the venue, the sound systems they expected – they were determined to enjoy their first proper road trip. Although they were now consistently delivering entertaining performances, the lifestyle became more important than the music; perhaps inevitably, the money ran out towards the end of the tour and a few hastily arranged gigs were added so the band could afford to get home. And their reputation for attracting a chaotic whirlwind of hangers-on was maintained, with Mancunian grafters working in Europe – Paul described them as 'a mini Salford crime wave' – ever-present at the dates. When he returned to the UK, Shaun gleefully reported to the enthralled journalists stories of theft and break-ins on the tour, embellishing the details with each telling.

The band were back in London for a show at the University of London on 10 February 1989. In attendance was Howard Thompson, head of A&R at Elektra, eager to meet the band, check out his investment in the flesh and hear more about the Acid House scene he hoped to import to America. The band introduced him to Ecstasy. 'Needless to say, about halfway through, everything seemed quite *nice*,' Thompson said. The show was a 'big success' with 'everyone grooving mightily'. Afterwards, Wilson took him, along with Bez, out clubbing. Thompson said: 'Tony rolled joints on the bar, Bez did his loping, goggle-eyed Bez-dance for the next two hours and I floated about the place, trying to get to grips with House music.' Whatever Thompson had hoped to get out of the meeting is lost in the smoke of another Mondays vortex.

On 21 February the band recorded a second Peel session at the BBC studios, playing three tracks. 'Tart Tart' was dominated by Paul Davis's keyboards and all the better for it – this is the best recorded version of the song. The band's sound was now benefiting from the introduction of samplers and sequencers, a hesitant process as the equipment was delicate to use and prone to breaking down. Davis utilised the new technology to approximate the 'woo woos' from the Stones' 'Sympathy for the Devil' and repeated them throughout on 'Mad Cyril', a song from *Bummed* named after a character in the film *Performance*. Shaun also sampled the lyrics from 'Sympathy for the Devil', using them as ad libs during the song. The instantly propulsive 'Do It Better' again benefited from some dramatic keyboard flourishes. This was the Mondays' most 'pop' song and with its 'on one, do one, on one' chant referencing E and Shaun's 'double double good' lyrical sentiment, it seemed very much of the moment. As the Acid House scene continued to grow, it was the band's choice for their next single.

The Mondays continued to promote *Bummed* on the road. Strobe lighting was now a distinct feature of the live show and in union with the driving bass sequencer the band had introduced to their sound on 'Wrote For Luck' and the E'd-up crowds, the Mondays were creating an Acid House vibe in rock venues. In Manchester they played the 2000-capacity International II, supported by 808 State and MC Buzz B. Three years after Tracey Donnelly had proclaimed them the next New Order, it appeared that Mondays had finally arrived, the mood of the nation and the shift in the music and club scene providing the ideal environment for their amalgam of dance and rock.

If there was one band that defined the eye-popping menace of a Britain breaking apart under a Thatcher government, it was Happy Mondays. Suddenly they were not only leading a cult sub-genre in a washed-out Hacienda but tapping into a national mood. Ecstasy culture threatened to overwhelm the authorities, one illegal Acid party in an aircraft hangar attracting 6000 kids. The Thatcher ideology, summed up in the phrase most commonly attributed to her, 'There is no such thing as Society', had divided the country, promoting the interests of the individual above the collective and privatisation over nationalisation. Acid House was a communal, all-inclusive experience, a movement that not only flouted many of the government's current licensing laws but also rejected ten years of Thatcherite values. Swathes of the British working class had been downtrodden again and again in that time and they were still dancing. Acid House was freedom from oppression, liberalisation, and the image of scores of riot police confronting smiling, brightly dressed party-goers was a powerful one.

In London, at the 2000-capacity Astoria, the Mondays were filmed for BBC2's indie music show *Snub TV*. Their electrifying performance of 'Do It Better' was introduced on the show with the words: 'Happy Mondays, with their manic and dynamic live shows and eccentric and original musical fusions, currently have audiences in ecstasy up and down the country.' Elsewhere in the UK, they played universities or polytechnics with capacities between 500 and 1000. Wherever the band went, so too did an entourage of party people, happy to share their drug stashes. For many, a Mondays show was their first taste of the Acid experience. And the band, even on their most punishing tour to date, where crowds were now expecting to hear the music as well as revel in the debauchery of the performance, showed no signs of slowing down.

In Birmingham Whelan and Davis got stuck behind a curtain after the soundcheck, and by the time they escaped the venue was full and everyone was laughing. In Sheffield, the band all took acid before going on. 'It was the first time I'd done acid on stage,' said Day. 'It's not good to play on acid, your fingers get bigger and your guitar neck warps.' When it came time in the set to do 'Wrote For Luck', all Davis had to do was press any key on his keyboard to set the bass sequence going. But, tripping wildly, he was incapable of doing any such thing. Shaun started to scream at him and, without thinking, Day, who was also falling apart from the trip, hit Davis in the face, causing him to fall backwards in slow motion over his monitor, kicking his keyboard on the way down. This triggered the start of the song, at which point Day was about to start playing when Davis came up behind him and hit him back. Meanwhile the crowd looked on in astonishment, Paul frothing at the mouth from a bad trip, and the set ended in chaos. The next day it was all over the press, the *Sun* and the *Daily Mirror* describing the 'crazy Acid House band fighting on stage'. In fact it turned out to be great PR for the Mondays.

The touring continued with the band's first visit to Ireland to play Belfast and Dublin. But before they left, Bez was arrested at Manchester airport by his dad. He was remanded in Strangeways for a breach of bail conditions relating to his arrest during the making of *Bummed*, having already missed four court dates. When he again failed to appear at Manchester magistrates' court to face the charges of taking a car without consent and possession of marijuana, a warrant for his arrest – and that of his guarantor, Tony Wilson – was issued. They both appeared in court later that day. 'Wilson played an absolute blinder,' said Bez. 'Giving me a sterling character reference.' He pleaded guilty to the charges and escaped with a fine of £700, while an old friend named Andrew McKean (Macca), who'd worked on Saxe's stalls in the Arndale, stood in for Bez on stage on both Irish dates.

Bez was back with the band as they hit France for dates supporting indie guitar noise darlings My Bloody Valentine. Here they were accused of wrecking a hotel in Grenoble and then cancelling a date in Paris without telling the promoter. At a second Paris date, the band's pal Anthony Murray (Muzzer), a Mancunian grafter described by Bez as 'big, streetwise and young', who was now acting as tour manager, let off tear gas in the venue, causing complete chaos. In Rennes, Muzzer was involved in a mass brawl that enveloped the band and as a result he and Macca spent the night in jail; the band, waiting for them to be released, missed the final date of the tour. The mass brawl was reported with much amusement in the *NME*, with the band said to be facing a 'nationwide ban in France'. The French saw it differently, the tour promoter describing them as the most dangerous band he had come across in twenty years of working in the music business.

The positive effect of the recent touring was evident in the increased sales of *Bummed*, which had now sold around 15,000 copies – allowing Factory finally to declare a profit on the band. The Mondays still largely appealed to a section of New Order's fan base, and Wilson and McGough were convinced they could sell more copies of the album to a wider audience; the question was, how?

The Acid House phenomenon was now undoubtedly the biggest thing to have happened to youth culture since punk, and, with its own distinct sound, dress style, even language, and the controversy of the drug around which it all seemed to revolve, was tailor made for media dissection. Although the music press identified the Mondays as a part of it, Wilson and McGough needed to find a way to position the band at the heart of the movement in the eyes of the national press and national radio – and of the tens of thousands of kids going to Acid House parties who didn't read the music papers and had never heard of Factory Records or Joy Division, let alone Happy Mondays. 'We decided what we needed was a big club mix of one of the tracks off the album,' said McGough. 'It was a very specific exercise to bring all the Ecstasy kids into our world.' McGough called Pete Tong, who ran FFRR Records and had a dance music show on Capital Radio, for advice on who to approach. Tong recommended Paul Oakenfold, the man Bez had been telling the band they should be working with for the past six months.

When he wasn't hanging out with the Mondays, Bez was still partying around the country and was often out with Oakenfold's crowd. It was a source of frustration to him that his reputation, and behaviour, meant his better ideas were not always listened to. Oakenfold, he'd been telling them, was not just the most popular and groundbreaking British DJ on the Acid House scene – mixing in all manner of weird and wonderful music, sometimes even indie rock, in his crowd-pleasing house sets – but was looking for tracks he could remix.

With McGough, the band and Bez all now behind the idea, and Oakenfold keen to try his hand, the DJ took a master tape of 'Wrote For Luck' and was given carte blanche to transform it. The band were keen to hear what he would come up with: they liked his ethos as a DJ, said Paul, of 'mixing indie stuff with dance stuff'. Oakenfold was a wild card choice and McGough quizzed the band as to who else might remix the track. Paul made an unusual suggestion – Vince Clarke, the founder of Depeche Mode, Yazoo and more lately high-energy synthpop duo chart stars Erasure, a band one would not normally associate with the Mondays. True, they had started out with a camp, poppy Depeche Mode cover version seven years ago, but the music had taken a wildly divergent direction since then. Paul, however, was the one band member who continued to appreciate catchy pure pop music and Clarke was one of Britain's most skilled writers – he was the man behind hits such as 'Just Can't Get Enough', 'Only You' and 'A Little Respect'. Paul hoped that some of Clarke's pop magic would be transferred to the Mondays. McGough met Clarke in London. 'He said, I've never done a remix before, no one's ever asked me,' said McGough. Did Clarke want to have a go? Yes, he said, he'd love to.

Before either mix was completed, Shaun and Bez flew to New York to promote the upcoming US release of *Bummed* and generate publicity for a forthcoming July tour supporting their Elektra label mates, influential alternative rock band The Pixies, whose recent single 'Monkey Gone to Heaven' had reached indie number one in the UK. McGough's decision to send only Shaun and Bez was an early sign of real division in the band. It was true that the media naturally gravitated towards a band's frontman, lyricist and voice. But why send Bez? He didn't write any of the music or lyrics, so why was he doing the interviews? 'You play to the strength of the band,' said McGough. 'They were a good double act and their repartee was good.' For the media, he explained, they were the two characters – Mr Happy (Bez) and Mr Evil (Shaun). He argued that interviews were about something other than the music-making process – they were designed to inform people about the band's lifestyle, motivations, character and personality. Bez was good in this situation; always trying to raise a laugh, he often succeeded, if sometimes inadvertently.

McGough admitted, however, that neither Shaun nor Bez could probably tell an interviewer how the band's records were made. That was the domain of the band, relieved in one respect to be free of media duties to concentrate on making new music, but also feeling strangely sidelined by McGough's new PR strategy – which, on this occasion, spectacularly backfired. Bez and Shaun's visit was even more chaotic than the Mondays' first visit to the US in 1987, which had seen them play a disastrous show and was best recalled for being a crack cocaine orgy. This time McGough had called ahead, already managing to freak out Elektra's Howard Thompson: 'He said that they'd need an ounce of draw, eight hits of E and a couple of grams [of cocaine] at the hotel or he couldn't guarantee their complete co-operation.' Shaun and Bez would only be in New York for two nights, and Thompson felt the request was 'somewhat excessive', but McGough insisted it was necessary and, said Thompson, 'he wasn't joking'. As McGough put it, 'They're not going to sit in Elektra's offices all day without a smoke or something to do in the evening.'

Shaun and Bez's first evening in New York turned into an all-nighter involving strip clubs, cocaine and hookers, with Thompson swept up in the fun. The following day, at around noon, having already had to cancel two scheduled appointments with journalists, Elektra's head of publicity, Sherry Ring, began panicking. Shaun and Bez hadn't shown up yet and no one was answering the phone in their hotel room. When they finally did appear, the day was almost over and according to Thompson, 'most of the journalists scheduled to interview them had left'. Shaun and Bez flew back the next morning having still not slept, but Thompson, if not Ring, had found the behaviour endearing and exhilarating, proper rock 'n' roll.

Though the band were less than enthusiastic – Shaun described it as a 'shit song with shit words, every melody in it is stolen' – Factory had now decided that 'Lazyitis', the track from *Bummed* that borrowed heavily from Sly & The Family Stone and The Beatles, and not the more immediate 'Do It Better', was going to be the Mondays' next single. Lessons had seemingly not been learned from the brouhaha surrounding 'Desmond' on the band's debut album.

Even more annoying for Shaun was that he would have to re-record the vocal as a duet with 58-year-old Karl Denver, who'd had a run of yodelling-based hits – most famously 'Wimoweh' – in the early 1960s. The idea had come from The Bailey Brothers; they had cast Denver, who was based in Manchester, in the *Mad Fuckers!* film and planned to use the duet as a theme for the movie. It was a classic example of why Factory never made sense financially: for a start, since Wilson had failed to raise the $2 million needed, there was no budget for a film like this. Factory, however, revelled in their scattergun ethos. It was a refreshing antidote to a business swamped by faceless men holding endless marketing meetings, and many, like Keith Jobling, loved the idea of these 'Situationists' living for the moment and not worrying about the consequences. But when combined with the habitual anarchy that the Mondays brought to anything that they did, such an approach made for a potent cocktail.

What interested Wilson, however, was not the accumulation of money but art, and the attempt to leave behind something of cultural value. It made little sense, but Wilson loved 'Lazyitis', and was keen on the idea of promoting it via a duet with a dusty relic best recalled for a novelty hit and now a fixture on the cabaret circuit. Shaun didn't see it – what had this got to do with Acid House? But a deal was struck between him and Wilson, and Shaun, for once agreeing to back down, did as Wilson requested.

The duet between Shaun and Denver was recorded at Square One studio in Bury, and produced by Hannett. It was a chaotic session during which a lot of drugs and booze were consumed. To a song already featuring borrowed words, which would make the attribution of publishing monies difficult, Shaun now added lyrics from David Essex's 'Gonna Make You a Star'. On 21 April 1989, the Mondays, Denver and The Bailey Brothers shot the video for the track – or part of *Mad Fuckers!*, or both, no one could explain – on waste ground under the Mancunian Way flyover. The band were dressed in prison clothes smuggled out of Strangeways, and played football as if in the prison yard. Big Les, who used to drive the band's equipment about and was over seven foot tall, was filmed walking around a perimeter fence with an Alsatian dog. The Bailey Brothers wanted rain, but because they were filming under the flyover had to hire a rain machine. Water poured down on the action, the artificial rain much colder than real rain. Filming stopped when Denver could no longer mime the words because his teeth were chattering too much.

On 4 May, after a gig in London at the Kilburn National Ballroom, Shaun travelled to Jersey to do an interview with the *NME* to promote 'Lazyitis'. Karl Denver often played a residency in a cabaret club on the island, but the Mondays had paid for him to go there to recover from the flu he'd caught filming the 'Lazyitis' video. The idea was for the *NME* to interview the duet-tists together, but on arrival at Jersey airport, Shaun was arrested after being found with a small polythene bag containing traces of cocaine. He was charged with importation and possession of the drug – an offence that could result in a three-year sentence. Blood tests revealed he also had cocaine in his system. 'I was out there with him,' said McGough. 'We were due up before the beak at four on Friday afternoon. There was a bank holiday weekend coming up and the customs officers were applying to have him detained on the island until trial – which was a six-month lie down. So I got five grand wired over from the mainland to the lawyers.' McGough asked the barrister to pay Shaun a visit but he came back saying Shaun had refused to see him. McGough asked him to try again, but he kept coming back saying Shaun didn't want to see an advocate.

'So we're up in Jersey Royal Court, guy in a white wig, red coat, Friday afternoon, four o'clock. We had a Hillsborough disaster fund-raising show coming up at The Hacienda and we'd already raised fifteen grand. The barrister argued if they detained Shaun on the island this money would be lost and the bond we were offer-ing of £5000 was substantial enough to bring him back.' The judge, who Shaun maintained was Roman Catholic and, recognising him as a fellow Catholic, was therefore willing to show him some leni-ency, allowed him to leave the island. On the plane back Shaun asked McGough, 'Why the fuck did you leave me sat in the cell all day, why didn't you get a brief sorted?'

'The brief was down there every hour asking to see you,' said McGough, 'and you wouldn't see him.'

Shaun said, 'Fucking hell, they never asked me if I wanted to see a brief, they kept asking me do you want an advocaat? I said to them no, I'll have a cup of tea. They never asked me if I wanted a brief.'

McGough said, 'Advocaat? You mean advocate. An advocate is a brief.'

'I thought that was bit weird,' said Shaun – 'my nana used to give me that at Christmas.'

The bust made the national press, and while it enhanced his reputation as a bad boy it left Shaun shaken. He'd never been in prison before and although people were saying it wouldn't come to that, there was a three-year sentence hanging over his head. The publicity didn't even help 'Lazyitis', although it was another single of the week in *Melody Maker*: 'The lunatics have taken over the Hacienda.' For all Wilson's buoyancy over the potential, and reports that it was currently the favourite single of America's newest hip-hop stars, De La Soul, it was a commercial flop, peaking at six in the indie charts and not troubling the national charts. The video, centred on football, was not shown by British media outlets in view of the recent tragedy at Sheffield's Hillsborough stadium, when ninety-six people lost their lives during an FA Cup semi-final featuring Liverpool and Nottingham Forest.

The show Shaun had been allowed back from Jersey to perform at – one of the first benefit shows for victims of the disaster – took place at The Hacienda on 8 May. The cause and the band were so popular in Manchester – despite the footballing rivalries – that the Mondays played The Hacienda again the following night, raising even more money for the Hillsborough fund.

They then headed to Pink Museum studios in Liverpool hoping to record new songs, including 'Clap Your Hands' – 'an anthem for thieves', said Shaun. Again, they had chosen Martin Hannett as producer. But the recording went badly. Hannett was drinking heavily and back on heroin. During a break in the recording he went out for fresh air. Derek found him three hours later sitting in the corner of a nearby pub. He walked up to Hannett, who said, 'Fucking hell, Hiya Derek, what you doing round here?'

'What?' said Derek. 'What do you mean, around here? We're in the studio, Pink Museum, everybody's been waiting for you. He said, Fucking hell. He thought he was at home in his local pub.'

Back at the studio things got worse. Earlier in the day both Hannett and Paul Davis had bought replica guns from a fishing tackle shop. Davis let off shots in the studio. 'As soon as he did it Hannett went right, let's go home, session ended,' said Paul. 'He couldn't hear anything. There was nowhere for the sound to go, it just stayed in the room and bounced in and out of our eardrums.' It didn't end there either. As the band grumbled and moaned, Hannett pulled out his gun and fired six shots – one at each member of the Mondays.

A sense that things had begun to unravel followed the band to Spain for an all-night summer festival show in Valencia on 15 June. Bez was missing, occupied elsewhere in Europe with a well-known crew of Mancunian pop concert bootleggers. When they stopped off in Barcelona for interviews with the Spanish media, Shaun fell asleep outside and got badly sunburned, leaving him in agony for the gig. The band was due on stage at a dangerous-sounding 6 a.m. and as soon as they arrived in Valencia asked around for Ecstasy. A Spanish guy called Juan said he could get some but he would have to drive to Barcelona, and it would be a couple of hours' wait. The band told him to hurry, they'd cover his costs. He arrived back at four in the morning, 'clicking his fingers, big smile on his face', said Whelan. 'He said, Ecstasy yes, we have Ecstasy. We were like great, where is it? We all sat down, he put it on the table and there was one tablet. We all went, what's that? He said it's your Ecstasy. He'd driven all the way to Barcelona to bring back one Ecstasy!'

The gig was a complete shambles, the band scowling and snapping at one another on stage. Whelan was so drunk he fell off the stage and the band carried on, doing a couple of songs without him. In total they managed just four songs, lasting just ten minutes. A photograph of Shaun at the gig, clearly holding a joint, was printed in the British music press.

Back in Manchester, Shaun tried to unwrap the bandages he'd used to cover his sunburnt legs and found his blistered skin had stuck to them. He claimed it was the pain that caused an increased reliance on heroin, a habit that was now costing him more than £40 a day. McGough noticed for the first time that Shaun might have a problem with the drug but thought he was taking it to escape from the worry of the cocaine charges hanging over his head.

A second attempt to record new material with Hannett at Pink Museum went no better than the first. Shaun, who would always ask for the music in the studio to be turned up so loud the sound started to distort, blew the speakers and the recording was abandoned early. The only thing the band came away with was a bill for £3000 to replace the speakers.

Wilson gave the band another helpful push in July, recording them live for what would be the final episode of *The Other Side of Midnight*, 'a Party edition' filmed in a giant Granada studio. Factory hipsters were out in force, the Mondays invited hundreds of their own entourage and some of the growing army of Mondays fans sneaked in. Mike Pickering's new act, T-Coy, with their Latino-tinged club hit 'Carino', played first. Pickering was still DJing on Friday nights at The Hacienda, while his label, Deconstruction, was picking up the tracks he'd hoped to push through a Factory dance label. He had snapped up the summer's biggest underground Acid party track, 'Ride on Time' by Black Box, which was now on its way to number one in the UK charts; it would be the best-selling single of the year. Factory's decision to ignore pure dance records also infuriated Rob Gretton, who – while New Order pursued solo projects – started his own label, Rob's Records, to release dance material.

Even local Acid House artists were being passed over. The best of them, A Guy Called Gerald, played after T-Coy at Wilson's TV special. The lad behind the name, Gerald Simpson, had created 'Voodoo Ray' in his bedroom, and it was a longstanding Hacienda classic that had just gone top twenty. From Moss Side, the former McDonald's burger flipper also started an Acid House band, 808 State, whose track 'Pacific State' was another Mancunian Acid classic (and would be a top ten hit later in the year). They too were ignored by Factory as the label persisted with its avant-garde classical release schedule.

Finally came the Mondays, who Wilson introduced as his 'favourite group in the whole world'. Bez was still missing – said to be in a police cell in the south of France having burgled a caravan. The band had spent their own money hiring a huge sound system and from the first note the audience were theirs, dancing as if this was an Acid party and the band the DJ. Shaun, his hair grown into a centre parting, smoked a joint and the band was joined on stage by ten to fifteen pals either dancing or playing percussion. Shaun changed the words to 'Mad Cyril', adding a call-out to 'Mad Tony', and Paul's bass line became a physical force inside the room. When the sequencer pattern to 'Wrote For Luck' kicked in, the excitement reached a crescendo, with a cacophony of hoots, piercing whistles and swirling hands; heads rolled, hips gyrated, and the scene grew more chaotic as, over a remarkable seven minutes, the stage was swamped by dancers, including Shaun and Paul's father Derek, a couple of pre-teen kids and two of the band's pals, stripped to the waist, writhing on top of huge speaker stacks.

It was four o'clock in the afternoon, but this was the Mondays and time meant nothing. It was always now. The band had never sounded better, their increasing confidence in using sequencers and samplers a huge boon to their live sound, giving them a contemporary dance edge. They were the greatest rock 'n' roll band in the UK, of that there was no doubt now. The Ecstasy kids were going to get their Sex Pistols, Rolling Stones, Funkadelic and Velvet Underground rolled into one.

Acid House and Ecstasy culture exploded over the summer of 1989. A heatwave brought an explosion of massive outdoor parties: 11,000 at an airstrip in Berkshire, 20,000 in a field in Surrey and 17,000 in Buckinghamshire. Meanwhile the tabloid exposés of 'evil' drug-crazed nights continued. In an editorial, the *Daily Mail* called Acid House 'a façade for dealing drugs of the worst sort on a massive scale'. Home Secretary Douglas Hurd ordered an inquiry into unlicensed parties and a series of giant events were interrupted by thousands of police with dogs and tactical aid units, the chaos featured on national news bulletins. A newly formed police squad began using undercover technology to try and bust the party organisers, but the police were logging around 400 parties per month and admitted they were struggling to control the phenomenon. The band watched with fascination as the hedonistic movement they'd helped start grew increasingly political. 'Watching the evening news and seeing these police helicopters, police roadblocks, police dog patrols, trying to shut down the parties, stopping people from moving around the country,' said Paul, 'I was like, You can't do this, you can't stop us moving around the country of our own free will.'

In Manchester the Mondays' pals, the Donnelly Brothers, Anthony and Christopher, organised the north's biggest illegal rave for 20,000 people on farmland near Rochdale. It was an audacious coup given the level of police surveillance. But the popularity of Acid House inevitably meant the original atmosphere was diluted. 'A load of idiots in smiley T-shirts had ruined it,' said Paul, who observed the movement across the country 'dying and growing at the same time'. The same could be applied to Factory, certainly The Hacienda. Though the club continued to enjoy a boom, making a good profit, full almost every night of the week with punters unrecognisable from those who'd started the revolution in early 1988, New Order's Bernard Sumner said this 'straight crowd' (even though many were E'd up) had 'spoiled' the scene. Even Wilson said Acid House was now ruining the club, and expressed regret at the introduction of the interchangeable banging dance nights that attracted an identikit crowd, saying he preferred The Hacienda's former eccentric individuality. The Mondays had cut back on their attendance and Paul, now twenty-five and celebrating the birth of his second child with his partner Alison, stopped going altogether, preferring the comfort of his local pub.

The Hacienda's success also brought more serious problems. There was an armed robbery at the club and an attempt to take over the door, the latter the first warning shot of a ferocious war that would be played out over control of the drug trade in the city centre clubs. A drive-by shooting of doormen took place at another of the city's popular Acid clubs, Thunderdome. In Manchester, among those who had been there at the start, there was a sense that 'the good times were over', said Paul. This was compounded by the death of a teenager who had collapsed in The Hacienda after taking Ecstasy. Greater Manchester Police, led by Chief Constable James Anderton, who had become known as 'God's Cop' for his assertion that he had a direct line to the Almighty, launched 'Operation Clubwatch' to crack down on Acid House in the city, moving undercover officers into The Hacienda. It wasn't just the Mondays who were getting increasingly out of control.

15
Oakenfold / Osborne

Things were getting so crazy on the Acid scene that its most recognisable face, Paul Oakenfold, had decided to back out from behind the decks. He and his long-time but unsung partner, Ian St Paul, had been the driving forces who got the movement off the ground in London in late 1987. They'd run club nights together since the early 1980s and Oakenfold had been heavily involved in the early hip-hop scene in London, promoting records by Run DMC and the Beastie Boys. He and St Paul were part of the crew who'd discovered in 1987 that the mix of Ecstasy and Ibiza club tunes created some new piece of heaven.

The pair had tried unsuccessfully to introduce an Ibiza-influenced night in London as far back as 1985, mixing fast-paced indie with Europop, early American House music and many obscure rock oddities. Back in London after the summer of 1987, they tried again and with the addition of Ecstasy found their nights were a success, a radical departure from the then predominant soul or jazz-funk nights, where hipsters sipped expensive drinks in flash suits. The dancing, the sweating, the baggy clothes and the unpretentious mix of music became an underground sensation in the capital, similar to what was happening at The Hacienda at the same time. When, in early 1988, Oakenfold and St Paul started Spectrum at Heaven, the scene exploded. It was where Bez first recognised Oakenfold, who soon found himself on the front page of music magazines, explaining all about the

'Balearic Beat', as the music he conducted from behind the decks was then known.

As the scene developed into Acid House, Spectrum was the first club night to be forced to close by lurid tabloid headlines about drugs. Although Oakenfold and St Paul reopened the night under a new name, their success – like that of The Hacienda – attracted gangsters and heavies trying to control the drug traffic in the club. St Paul was said to have been almost blinded during a deal involving 12,000 Es and relocated to Los Angeles, where in due course he'd start up Acid nights, and where the Mondays would catch up with him again.

Oakenfold had DJed at some of the country's biggest Acid House parties and his name on a flyer was always a key attraction, even if he was not booked to play. But, like the Mondays, he too felt the scene was becoming a monster out of control. His reworking of Ibiza club staple 'Jibaro', a 1974 track by Colombians Elkin and Nelson Marin, had been an underground hit in 1988 when released by FFRR Records and he'd been fishing around for more studio work ever since. But remix culture was in its infancy and being known as the country's leading Acid House DJ was not the calling card it ought to have been to the paymasters at major labels: one of the hit Acid tracks of the summer, E-Zee Possee's 'Everything Starts with an E', had been banned by Radio 1 and all TV outlets.

When McGough handed Oakenfold 'Wrote For Luck' to remix it was the first time anyone had given him a piece of professional paid studio work. Oakenfold had recently hooked up with studio engineer Steve Osborne, who like Oakenfold was twenty-five and eager to prove himself musically. What was to become a hugely successful partnership began when Osborne created a sync track by taking a pulse off Whelan's bass drum and running a drum machine to that. Oakenfold then suggested adding a sequencer part from a remix of 'Zobi La Mouche', a track by Les Negresses Vertes. Osborne, a musician himself, added new keyboard and bass parts in the studio. After a day in the programming room they took the material to the mix room; there they would build the remix around Shaun's 'higher than high high' vocal hook, which they were both in awe of. Even though they were working in one of London's top studios, the pre-digital equipment was basic; as Osborne mixed the track down to tape for a final time, Oakenfold spun in samples live on a record deck, adding parts from NWA's 'Express Yourself' and Prince's 'The Future'. It was high-wire stuff and something that would be unheard of today.

White label copies of the Osborne and Oakenfold remix of 'Wrote For Luck', titled the 'Think About the Future' mix, were circulated in select London clubs and the response was immediate. There were whoops and dancing, whistles and dancing, arms aloft and dancing as the seven-minute track unfurled to shake the dance floor. Factory PR Jeff Barrett saw the response and was going crazy for it too. The white label got the same response at The Hacienda and Factory decided to couple the track with the more poppy Vince Clarke remix as the band's next single.

Meanwhile the Mondays were in America, playing dates on their first major tour, with the original version of 'Wrote For Luck' picking up good radio support and *Bummed* just released. But the tour got off to a predictably uproarious start when someone in the entourage stole a selection of random suitcases and bags off the luggage carousel at New York's JFK airport, ripping them open and plundering them at the band's hotel. It was also claimed that Shaun stole a $1000 leather jacket from duty free at the airport and that he missed a gig because he'd overdosed and was having his stomach pumped. The truth, as ever, was somewhere in between; it turned out that Shaun was in hospital to have shots for 'the clap' after an incident that involved acid and a lap dancer.

The tour mainly took in small if established alternative clubs — with some noteworthy venues along the way, including The Fillmore in San Francisco and The Ritz and CBGB in New York. The Pixies, who the Mondays were supporting on most of the dates, had just released their acclaimed second album *Doolittle* and were breaking across modern rock radio in the US as well as college stations.

'We got on really well with the Pixies,' said Whelan. In Seattle, the first gig of the tour, he went out front to watch them play.

A girl approached him and said, 'Hey, can you sell me some X?' Es were known as X in the States at the time, and it was strongly rumoured that the Mondays were willing to supply them. When Whelan said no, she said, 'Don't you guys sell drugs? I've got my friend here, he's a singer and he wants some.' She introduced him to a small, very quiet man with long ginger hair and a bandana. 'No mate, can't help you, sorry,' said Whelan. He went backstage and the guy turned up again. 'Someone said, Oh, it's Axl Rose.' It was the lead singer of hard rock band Guns N' Roses, who had taken the US by storm with their debut album *Appetite For Destruction*.

The band also crossed paths with David Bowie, after he had seen them play in Los Angeles, as well as the Beastie Boys. While they were understandably star-struck by meeting Bowie, the band gained a clear sense that their time in the US had finally arrived, that something was really happening, for all the falling about that had gone on in getting to this point. The energy of the band was at its peak, and – even though they were still consuming titanic quantities of drugs – the sets they played were tight and strong, whipping up the crowds and the media in a way that had not happened on either of their previous visits. The *New York Times* review of the Ritz gig described the music as 'somewhere between disco, dance-rock and punk', and while the Acid House movement had thus far made little impact in America, everyone who saw them play felt the tour was a huge success.

In fact it went to their heads a little. Shaun had his prima donna moments. At one gig he felt the sound was below par, whinge-ing throughout to Derek – who was still handling the band's onstage set-up – that he couldn't hear Paul's bass in his monitors. Shaun sang to the bass, not the guitar, keyboards or drums, and already during the soundcheck Derek had done his best to try and improve the sound. It was something he took great pride in, but the venues they were playing did not always have the greatest of sound systems. Shaun threw a hissy fit and hurled his tambourine at Derek's head. His dad walked out to the stage, grabbed his son around the neck and wrestled him to the ground. 'I wanted to kill him,' he said. 'When you're doing your best for somebody and they don't realise it...I lost it.' Muzzer had to try and pull him off but he refused to let go. The audience cheered, thinking it was part of the show.

Offstage, too, it didn't all go their own way. The band ran into trouble in Harlem over an Ecstasy deal, although they quickly brushed it off as being 'no different than Salford'. There was trouble in Cleveland as another drug deal went wrong and they were attacked with baseball bats; they came back to the hotel with every window of the people carrier smashed in, something they were less used to. Others were responsible for matters like getting them to the venue and on stage at the right time – American venues, and American fans, were used to bands adhering to start and finish times. The Mondays' US agent Marc Geiger, a pal of Wilson's and responsible for US tours by The Smiths and New Order, despaired at the band's work ethic, especially compared to that of The Pixies, though he also admired what he called the band's 'wonderfully insular' mindset – in other words, they didn't give a shit. But on stage they were routinely, mind-blowingly good and Geiger noted that it was a shame that Bez's crazed image and the band's reputation for drug-taking crowded out the more serious appreciation of their 'magical' music – as it had done for some time in the UK.

Triumphant but shattered – they'd been partying hard for a year and a half now – the Mondays arrived back in Manchester in late August 1989 for a first hearing of the Oakenfold/Osborne mix of 'Wrote For Luck', and they were blown away by it. It was, they said later, exactly the sound they had been looking for all along. Advance copies of the Factory double A-side had already created a huge buzz in clubs across the UK. It was crowned dance record of the year by *NME* and went to number one on the indie charts as well as reaching sixty-eight on the national charts, selling over 2000 copies a week well into the autumn. 'It hit all the targets that we wanted,' said McGough. 'It absolutely kicked it. I loved Vince's mix, but Paul's mix was special, really beautiful and epic. It was the first mix of an indie band that had entered that [Acid House] world.' It also reignited the sales of *Bummed*; the album was to go gold in the UK the following year. Not only did the single start to bring in much-needed cash, it also put the band – and Factory – in a new space culturally.

Jack Barron interviewed Shaun for an *NME* feature in Dry, the Factory designer bar that had opened in the city's Northern Quarter while the Mondays were in America. Shaun regaled Barron with tall tales from the recent American tour: acid scored from the Grateful Dead, strong Mexican weed gifted to them by heavyweight gangsters, knife fights in bars with pink-suited Puerto Ricans. He also mentioned the hallucinogenic drug PCP (Angel Dust). 'It's alright but it's dangerous gear,' Shaun said, claiming that it had sent him a bit mad – attempting to lift up cars and walking down the street trying to snatch the gold off black kids. While hard to tell how much of that was true, it was entirely conceivable that he had been shot at, as he claimed.

For the first time Shaun gave an in-depth description of his childhood, one supposedly spent blowing up mice, nicking cars, committing burglaries, and taking acid aged thirteen on 'a council estate in Swinton'. 'We've all been in nick for this and that, so what?' he said. 'Where I come from it's just part of living.' Rather than talking up the music and the success of America, he reverted to type, to the annoyance of the band, calling the Mondays 'one big fucking blag'. While this was the image he had long been projecting, it is hard not to think in hindsight that after all the work they had put in, both in the studio and on tour, it was time to rebuild people's perception of them now that they were on the verge of going mainstream. But at a time when Stock, Aitken and Waterman's finest, Kylie, Jason Donovan and Sonia, were launching their careers, managed by PR machines to script answers that would help them on their journey to stardom, there was something almost gloriously unreconstructed about the Mondays. And *NME*, like the rest of the music press, lapped it up, even if they still didn't quite know what to make of it. They found it hard to do anything other than write down what Shaun said and print it verbatim.

It wouldn't have helped that Barron also encountered Bez, who had a huge gash on his hand from falling through a window trying to break into his own flat after losing his keys, and Wilson who alighted from his Jaguar in a Yamamoto suit. Barron wrote that Shaun had called Wilson 'Fat Willy' before vomiting and falling to the ground in a drunken stupor. 'Sometimes I like being dead nice and sometimes I like being a real cunt,' Shaun said. 'I get a good buzz out of both.' Shaun was nothing if not good copy.

Dry itself was a further sign of the cultural renaissance in Manchester that had started at The Hacienda. Alongside the chart-topping New Order, the hip Mondays, and the homegrown Acid tracks by A Guy Called Gerald and 808 State, both The Stone Roses and Inspiral Carpets were becoming increasingly popular. The Inspirals, a psychedelic band with a distinct organ-driven sound, who had adopted much of the Mondays' 'laddish' style, had scored two indie chart number ones on their own Cow record label and their 'Cool As Fuck' T-shirts were hugely popular. The Roses had actually reached the Top 40 with their single 'She Bangs the Drums' and their eponymous album. The band's cartoon image, voluminous flares, bucket hats and baggy T-shirts and zipped-up outdoor coats — a look long abandoned by the Mondays — their easy-on-the-ear, melodic guitar sound and pretty-boy looks made them the favourite of many for superstardom.

Such a powerful musical wave was impossible to ignore. The narrative of a city that was finally leaving behind its post-industrial malaise was compounded by the vitality and energy of the Acid House scene; not only The Hacienda but Thunderdome and new club Konspiracy were packed every night. The Acid look had been a boon to companies like Joe Bloggs, clothes shops like Geese and the now buzzing Afflecks Palace emporium, where band T-shirts were flying out the window. For the first time since Joy Division in the late seventies, when the city could boast The Fall and Buzzcocks and a host of other post-punk pioneers, Manchester was the UK's musical and cultural hotspot with the media. And at the heart of everything was Factory and the Mondays.

The band's touring schedule had been constant for the past year and finding time to write new songs was difficult. Shaun's input at band rehearsals, already minimal, was now virtually zero. Having aborted their previous two recording sessions, the Mondays and Martin Hannett finally got down to work at the end of September at The Manor, Richard Branson's expensive residential studios in Oxfordshire. The idea was for the band to spend a week away from the distractions of Manchester and record material for a new single that would finally push them into the Top 40. Factory were feeling good about the band and were prepared to back them financially. 'When you're hustling genius, no expense spared,' declared Wilson. They arrived with three songs, 'Hallelujah', 'Holy Ghost' and 'Clap Your Hands', and by the time they started recording they had a good bass line around which to build a further song; they just needed the lyrics. Although Shaun had previously dismissed the notion he'd ever consider writing a love song, the phrases 'you're a walking miracle' and 'been lonely for so long' that peppered this new track seemed inspired by his new eighteen-year-old girlfriend Patricia (Trisha) McNamara, who had previously dated McGough. Shaun, as ever, wouldn't commit to explaining what, if any, meaning the song might have.

The *Daily Telegraph* visited the band in the studio to interview them. The interview was scheduled for a morning, and since Shaun was a notoriously late riser it was Whelan and Paul who spoke to the paper. 'We were really hung over, listening to records,' said Whelan. 'The journalist asked what we were recording and we played them some rough tapes of what we'd been doing. We played them the new song but it didn't have a title.' The journalist asked what it was called. Paul had been flicking through a selection of records and he stopped on a Buddy Holly album that included the track 'Rave On'. That, he said, was the title of the new song. The journalist, not realising that Paul had lifted it straight from the album cover, went on to explain at length in his article that 'Rave On' was so called in homage to the Acid House 'raves' that were sweeping the nation at the time, even though no one called them that. The term, however, caught on and raves, raving, rave music and ravers would begin to replace Acid House as the term applied to the growing movement.

Although outwardly brimming with confidence, the band was feeling the pressure. Their first two albums had been written in a spirit of carefree abandon, with little thought about chart positions or sales figures. The spirit of togetherness and collective support evident in previous sessions began to fade as everyone became a self-appointed expert. On 'Rave On', Day had recorded a guitar part on just one chord, hypnotic and repetitive. 'That's what the drugs did to me,' he said. 'Put me in a trance.' He wanted to try something different but the band insisted he couldn't, that was their favourite take. He had to play the same again. 'My attitude was, if you don't try something else you'll never know,' he said. 'It pissed me off being told what to do.'

Once the best of pals, Shaun and Bez almost came to blows during the session. Bez had offered an opinion on a track, to be met by a volley of abuse from Shaun, the idea that he was the band's tastemaker now clearly a thing of the past: 'What the fuck do you know about anything being right or wrong?' Bez resisted the urge to attack Shaun and went about smashing up his room at the studio before being packed off home, fearing he would be sacked from the band.

Paul Davis and Shaun had long stopped seeing eye to eye. On the road, Shaun had grown dismayed by Davis's individualistic attitude to the songs, playing his parts when and how he felt, and gigs would be peppered with Shaun shouting at him, 'You should be in here, you should be in here.' Shaun had taken to calling him 'knobhead', even in print. Davis had retaliated by nicknaming Shaun 'Penis' and now Shaun was calling Davis 'Penis'. At the start of 'Rave On'. Shaun can be heard calling out, 'Penis, Penis, you should be in here, you should be in here.' To some extent it was banter, but Davis would never stop referring to Shaun as 'Penis' and had developed a deep-seated dislike of the singer.

The band's small taste of fame was clearly affecting Davis. 'In photographs he always tried to stand next to Shaun – usually on his toes – because people said if you stand next to the singer you'll always get in the pictures,' said Whelan. The irony of Ecstasy for the Happy Mondays was that while it appeared to be bringing a generation together on the dance floor, and to some extent had triggered the success they were currently enjoying, it had driven them apart as individuals. Shaun and Day were both almost twenty-eight, Paul had two children, and Whelan and Davis were no longer the same kids who had joined the band at fifteen. The idea of the band as a gang was over, at least privately. 'We all found our own group of friends and went off on our own individual trips,' Whelan said. 'We got girlfriends and everyone had their own thing going on.'

Despite the fractures in the band, not to mention Hannett's deteriorating physical state as his addictions overtook him, the music the band recorded at The Manor was their best yet: machine driven, experimental and heavy, combining Shaun's sleazy lyrics, drenched in drug references and gangster speak, with deep bass, thunderous drums, crazed keyboard flashes and beautifully fluid guitar melodies. Both 'Rave On' and 'Hallelujah' were six minutes long, strung out, too far out for a single. 'Holy Ghost' was a glorious avant-garde cacophony. Only 'Clap Your Hands' could be considered a vaguely normal song. The work surpassed *Bummed*; it was fresh, aggressive and supremely counter-cultural. It was not the compact three-minute pop of the Roses or Inspirals, nor did it have the clean synth sound of the European Acid House records that were now hitting the charts, such as 'Ride on Time' or 'Pump Up the Jam' by Technotronic. It did not take Wilson long to get over his disappointment and recognise that the band and Hannett had delivered music from a new dimension, something to be proud of, of great cultural importance. He planned to release all four tracks on an EP. The band in the end simply didn't care about chart positions and were pleased with what they had achieved, happy to put out such a strong collection of material.

The Mondays decided to call the EP *Rave On* but Wilson had an epiphany. The *Mad Fuckers!* idea was still being kicked about at Factory, the thought of making a feature film starring the Happy Mondays too seductive to let go. With real-life gangsters now becoming increasingly involved in the scene around The Hacienda, The Bailey Brothers had wisely decided to alter their script. They did not want anyone to be offended by their humorous tale of a daft gang of Manchester criminals, car thieves and drug dealers. Wilson visited their office, which was in the same run-down building as Central Station Design, intending to ask them to shoot videos to edits of 'Hallelujah' and 'Clap Your Hands' in order to promote the EP. Jobling had misspelt 'Manchester' one day, inserting a 'd' for the 'n', and had become stuck on the result, Madchester – what better place to set a film called *Mad Fuckers!*

He mentioned this to Wilson, and Wilson, said Jobling, 'went ballistic'. Wilson suddenly saw the whole thing clearly. This was bigger than just the Mondays, this summed up everything that was going on in Manchester. The ultra-proud regionalist was going to rebrand the city as Madchester: Madchester United, the University of Madchester, Madchester Piccadilly railway station. They already had the best club in the world, the best bands in the world, and now – he saw it all – with this one perfect word he would sell the city to the world. 'He basically stole our word and ran off with it, used it as a marketing tool,' said Jobling. And the first thing he did was make the Mondays use it as the title of their new EP, which would now be called *Madchester Rave On*. They would sell the brand and the brand would sell them.

The band were unhappy to have someone else naming their work, but Wilson told them it was too late – the single had gone into production. It hadn't, but he made Central Station keep quiet about it as they dreamed up the Madchester logo. 'We got told, It's Madchester in small letters,' said Paul. 'And it came out and Madchester was spelt out massive, right across the front of the sleeve, so everyone was a little bit pissed off at first.' But they had to admit the cartoon-style lettering was a winner. What they felt most uneasy about was that it was clear Wilson was trying to brand a scene, when they had never considered themselves similar to any of the other Manchester bands. 'I never wanted to be in a band that was in a scene because they didn't last very long once the scene was gone,' said Paul.

As with 'Wrote For Luck', the EP was handed to Oakenfold and Osborne in the hope that club versions of the tracks would continue to help the band's crossover success with the Acid House crowd. The result was an excellent collection of tight club remixes which were critically acclaimed and commercially successful. These were released by Factory alongside a plethora of other formats of the EP, a ploy Factory hoped would help gain them their highest chart position yet. To be sure Wilson wanted a radio edit of 'Hallelujah' that could be played on daytime Radio 1. The Hannett sound and the Oakenfold remixes were too left-field, and Wilson wanted someone who could add a commercial edge to the track. Paul suggested Steve Lillywhite, who had produced Talking Heads and U2 and whom he'd long admired. Lillywhite was perfect. He cut the track to two minutes thirty-nine seconds and added the honeyed vocals of his wife, Kirsty MacColl. Everyone involved thought they now had what they needed to finally crack the charts.

16
Top of the Pops

In late October 1989, Shaun and Bez posed in front of Central Station's distinctive Madchester logo for the front cover of *Sounds*, the Mondays' first press cover for two and a half years since Shaun had appeared on the front of *Melody Maker* in May 1987. The pose this time was far from studied: Bez was wearing a straw hat with a marigold glove draped over it. *Sounds* called the band a 'howl of innovation' and 'purveyors of the non-stop party spirit', who had 'lit the touchpaper on the smouldering Manchester scene'. Local journalist John Robb wrote that 'the Mondays' spirit permeates the city' and 'everyone is loosening up – including the Roses'. In the same issue of *Sounds*, *Madchester Rave On* was single of the week. 'Clap Your Hands' was called a 'giant of a disco song'.

The EP was officially released on 13 November, the same day The Stone Roses released their new single, their iconic 'Fools Gold', built on a dance groove that marked a departure for the band. While the timing wasn't ideal – although McGough tried to put a positive spin on it, suggesting that people buying 'Fools Gold' would then buy the Mondays single – Factory radio and TV plugger Nicki Kefalas finally got the Mondays on Radio 1's daytime playlist with the Lillywhite edit of 'Hallelujah'. This was of much greater importance, and would make the band accessible to up to ten million listeners, more than they had ever been exposed to before. Meanwhile, The Bailey Brothers had filmed a slick black and white video of the band miming to the track with Shaun, Bez and Mark Day showing off their groovy moves under a downpour of feathers. There was now talk, with 'Hallelujah' blaring out from the radio, of *Madchester Rave On* making the Top 40, of perhaps even appearing on *Top of the Pops*.

'We didn't expect it because there was no one like us in the charts,' said Whelan. 'There was the odd indie band on the show but very rarely.' The first time he thought it was possible was when they did a gig in Newcastle and 808 State were on there doing 'Pacific State'. 'They were the first [of the 'Madchester'-associated acts] to go on it.' The gig in Newcastle, on 16 November, was the second date of a four-week tour of the UK to support the EP's release. That night Paul Ryder set fire to the bed in his hotel room when his cigarette butt fell onto the mattress and remained smouldering as he slept. He woke up in the morning to a fog of smoke and news that *Madchester Rave On* was number fifteen in the midweek charts, and that the band were wanted on *Top of the Pops* — something that even Wilson, for all his love of what the Mondays represented, had only ever dreamed of.

First the band played Manchester's 2000-capacity Free Trade Hall — the same night that The Stone Roses were playing to a crowd of 7500 at Alexandra Palace in London, a sign that Madchester was steadily reaching the masses. The Mondays' request to have the venue's seating removed had been denied and Shaun said before the gig that he hoped the audience would rip the seats out. At the start of the evening a large gang of lads rushed the door in a show of strength, forcing their way past the doormen, and there were fights out front between ticket touts, merchandisers and bootleggers. None of this was new to the Mondays, but it was on a different scale to what they had been accustomed to, and they revelled in the madness. Bez said he couldn't get stoned enough to cope with the excitement before the gig. Then he hit the stage. 'I knew as soon as the music started up that I'd taken too many drugs,' he said. 'By the third tune I'd completely lost my body — something bigger than me had taken over control of my arms and legs.' By contrast Shaun frequently sat down on the drum riser looking bored, a pose that Liam Gallagher would come to adopt, and the crowd loved it.

The Mondays cancelled their next gig in Leeds on 21 November as they headed to London to record *Top of the Pops*. *Madchester Rave On* had entered the charts at number thirty; meanwhile, 'Fools Gold', which The Stone Roses would be performing on the same edition of *Top of the Pops*, was at thirteen. The battle was truly on, although there was never any animosity between the bands themselves.

Most of the Mondays had grown up watching *Top of the Pops*, and even after five years of touring, for the first time they were really nervous. The Roses too were nervous. They had wanted to pull out of the show, fearing they wouldn't be allowed amps on stage to make their miming look vaguely real. They arrived at BBC Television Centre with a warning from their manager to be careful around the Mondays; they might try to spike their drinks!

Although the Roses were being linked to Acid House, they had not been around The Hacienda at the start of the movement and the Mondays had never hung out with them as a band. While the Mondays had stayed essentially the same since the two bands emerged on the Manchester scene almost simultaneously in 1985, the Roses had chopped and changed styles and line-ups and looks. They weren't close friends but there was now a deep respect between the two acts. And the Mondays had been listening to the Roses' debut album on their tour bus, seriously impressed. With the two bands having also shared soundman Si Machan and scenester/ roadie/dancer Cressa, there was a sense as they exchanged hellos in rehearsals for the show that this was Manchester against the world. Both bands had been shopping for new clothes to wear on the show, and if there was any rivalry between the two it was over who had the best gear. As it happened, both Gary Whelan and Ian Brown were wearing the same new Jean-Paul Gaultier jacket. 'We pointed at each other and started laughing,' said Whelan. They tossed a coin to see who would wear it on the show and Brown won.

With both bands oozing anti-establishment vibes, it wasn't long before they hatched plans to make mischief. In one rehearsal, Roses bassist Mani played drums for the Mondays while Whelan played bass for the Roses. They planned to do the same when they came to be filmed for the show. But someone had evidently noticed and threatened to pull both bands' performances if they didn't stop acting up. 'So we never ended up doing it,' said Whelan.

The Roses played 'Fools Gold' in their voluminous jeans and colourful tops, looking pretty and pop perfect. Ian Brown radiated insouciance, mouthing the words and doing his monkey dance, shaking the microphone above his head. The Mondays, by contrast, were smartly dressed like top lads on a night out. Shaun was all in black, his shoulder-length hair freshly washed. Bez was in black too, strangely subdued but doing his groove, as was Paul. Kirsty MacColl, who the band had never met before this moment, mimed her backing vocals in a matching light denim oversized shirt-and-jeans combo.

Shaun oozed a deviant charisma, lost for moments in his own euphoria. He smirked and mimed smoking heroin to the lyric 'Shaun William Ryder will lie down beside you and fill you full of junk'. For anyone who had grown up through the indie scene and watched the birth and burnout of the previous decade's bands before they had made it into the mainstream, it would have been a mesmerising experience to see Happy Mondays and The Stone Roses on the same show. But what the moment really brought into sharp relief was Madchester. For the Ecstasy generation, here were two bands that clearly were like them, in dress and attitude. For the indie kids who had read about the bands but never seen them it was a perfect introduction: here were two bands of the now. The closest equivalent would have been something akin to the Sex Pistols following The Doors, such was its wider significance as a cultural weather vane for the new decade in Britain.

After the show Tony Wilson turned up backstage laden with champagne. While Whelan ran around the BBC naked, as was his wont when drunk, Mark Day excused himself to go home. For all the excitement, the band was still not making enough money to live on and he had his Post Office round the next morning.

It was clear that the Roses had the much easier look to identify with, the more rave-friendly and easy to copy. Their sound too was more crystalline and – crucially, it was felt, in the search for super-stardom – they were the prettier group. Plus there were four of them, each member easy to recall, whereas there were six Mondays;

music was entertainment, not a memory test. There was a growing sentiment that the Roses were destined to become the bigger of the two bands. Even the Mondays felt that way. The studied Roses gave little away but the Mondays just weren't bothered; they would have felt embarrassed to speak, like Brown, of being the best band on the planet and wanting to be the bigger than The Beatles. Good luck to them and watch your heads.

Wilson saw it differently; in terms of Madchester the rise of the Roses was perfect. He framed it in terms of a battle, just like The Beatles versus the Stones, a war of the bands that defined who you were. It was clear he felt Happy Mondays were the Stones. But there was no war; instead there was a growing respect between the two acts. This was not the battle that would ensue between Britpop bands Oasis and Blur, both deeply influenced by Madchester, when the animosity was transparent. In contrast there were never any but kind words for one another in the press from both the Mondays and the Roses. Wilson was left to stir things up. Backstage at *Top of the Pops*, he ridiculed the Roses' recent poor-sounding Ally Pally show, claiming the band couldn't handle their drugs. When it came to clothes, well, the Roses were plainly wearing the Mondays' cast-offs. He passed comment on the Whelan/Brown jacket issue. 'Gaz is only the drummer and he dresses as good as their singer,' he crowed. Live, where it counted, 'the Roses couldn't even begin to compete' with the 'untouchable, dirty, funky, sexy Mondays'. Then there was the question of originality: musically, 'no one else was doing what the Mondays were', he said. 'If there was a group like Happy Mondays in Britain and they were on another label then I'd be terribly upset.'

Wilson's war of the bands was a good publicity stunt and a marketing tool to promote the cause of Madchester and the Mondays, but it never really caught on. Although it was true he'd disliked the Roses for many years, disparagingly calling them a Goth band, at the start of 1989 he'd had them play on *The Other Side of Midnight*, an appearance that had set their rise in motion, admitting in his introduction that he'd been wrong about them. Instead of being seen at war, over the next year the Mondays and Roses were often seen as a two-headed beast, the twin focal points of the Madchester era. As it happened, from this moment the Roses were to head backwards, towards nullifying court cases, creative collapse and management problems, releasing just one single – the disappointing 'One Love' – in the coming years. The Mondays, by contrast, were heading towards their biggest and best music.

Wilson saw the moment as a vindication. He'd been slow to come round to Happy Mondays but had backed them without question for the past year. In three months he'd be forty, an event he celebrated, he said, by taking eleven different drugs on a wild rampage involving the Mondays. Despite his commitments to TV – he was, after all, still the respectable face of Granada's evening news show – Wilson seemed committed to the Madchester lifestyle. In fact, at Factory his behaviour was a cause for concern. Erasmus had a massive row with him, telling him to sort himself out. Rob Gretton had his own label now and New Order's solo projects were being pursued amid rumours they might split up. When he did visit the office he called Wilson a 'cunt'. Peter Saville was in London, watching his friend become increasingly dictatorial and autocratic.

Blame often fell on the Mondays for leading Wilson astray, their success a catalyst for his loss of focus. The new offices, still incomplete, were over estimate to the tune of hundreds of thousands of pounds, but instead of taking a close look at the state of the label's finances, in the face of warnings that they were less healthy than he believed, he preferred to fly to Los Angeles to pursue the loss leader of the *Mad Fuckers!* film. Meanwhile, although it would be some time before the news became public, he was embarking on a relationship with 21-year-old Yvette Livesey, a former Miss UK. He felt good. Finally, after ten years, he felt he had a band that could be as big as Joy Division/New Order. No more listening to Gretton calling him a cunt, and running the label around him. Now he had his own New Order, but better – figureheads of a culture that he was going to sell to the world, the saviour not just of music but a city: Madchester.

Wilson felt even better when he saw the 3 December 1989 issue of the *NME*. He was on the cover, and no one could recall when any other record label boss had been on the cover of the *NME*. Wilson was depicted alongside Shaun, posing in front of the Madchester logo. The headline read: 'Manchester so much to answer for' and inside, 'Mad mad Madchester'. Manchester had now reasserted itself as the UK's 'musical capital', declared the *NME*. 'Where rock meets dance,' said Wilson in the article. He also told the story about how he'd described the Mondays to John Cale as 'scum' and said gleefully: 'My psychiatrist asked me whether my immaturity bothers me. I told him in this industry it was an asset.' There was talk of a rock revolution, and of Madchester as part of the 'death pangs' of Thatcherism, even of the wider uprisings taking place in El Salvador, in China and in Berlin, where the wall had just come down. Shaun, in the same interview, remained more prosaic. 'Wilson goes over the top, always has done,' he said. 'This is real for us, it's our way out.'

The Mondays had the utmost respect for Wilson. They'd take the piss, but only in the same way they did with one another. 'No way were we running circles round him,' said Paul, responding to the way some saw it. Wilson had kept faith in the Mondays, invested money in them when others at the label had told him he shouldn't. Now his belief was borne out. 'It was his belief that powered it through,' said McGough. 'My job was just to make it work. Tony financed it all.'

The *Madchester Rave On* EP peaked in the UK at number nineteen in early December and sold well in January. The joint Mondays/Roses *Top of the Pops* sparked a fevered interest in all things Madchester. The same day as the Shaun/Wilson *NME* front cover, the band was also on the cover of *Melody Maker*, and the Roses too were on the cover of *NME* and *Melody Maker* that month. Programmes from *Panorama* to *Blue Peter* clamoured for a piece of Madchester. Acid House raves were being slowly strangled by new laws passing through Parliament that increased penalties for organisers and allowed confiscation of 'criminal proceeds from illegal parties' – in Norfolk 10,000 ticket holders were turned away from a massive Acid party that had run into licensing problems and the scene looked dead. The Madchester scene offered a ready-made alternative.

In Manchester, indeed, the party never stopped. In addition to The Hacienda, Konspiracy and Thunderdome, new nights at clubs like Isadora's packed them in with a mix of Madchester rock, sixties psychedelia and dance music. The Dry bar was a beacon for small businesses which began to spring up around the previously derelict Northern Quarter, where cheap rents and creativity gave it the feel of a new Haight-Ashbury. Wilson was delighted. Madchester fashion was everywhere you looked; the city was full of flares, bucket hats and vibrant band T-shirts, or more generic city-proud T-shirts declaring 'Madchester, Just Say No to London', or famously, '...AND ON THE SIXTH DAY, GOD CREATED MANchester'. Local clothing firms began to turn over big money. Joe Bloggs made £60 million as the fashion spread around the UK and Identity in Afflecks Palace became a Mecca. Entrepreneurs (read borderline bootleggers) sold improvised T-shirts, posters, postcards and live bootlegs of bands such as the Mondays and Roses. Record stores such as Piccadilly and the dance-orientated Eastern Bloc thrived, becoming a hub of gossip amid talk of the new bands that were emerging.

With Manchester bands becoming the hottest properties in the business, A&R men from major labels descended on the city, the rumour being that they had been told not to return to London until they had signed a native. Inspiral Carpets, James (for a second time) and 808 State were three of the big beasts to be snapped up, all signing big-money deals, and a wave of sub-Roses/Mondays bands were formed, signed and celebrated in record time, the first being The Charlatans. Manchester University became the most sought-after destination for university applicants in the UK.

And 'Madchester' did sum up very precisely an atmosphere in the city at the dawn of the new decade. The city was steeped in marijuana — the Northern Quarter stank of the stuff, smoke billowing out of the doors of clothes shops and record stores. There was a sense of lawlessness about the city, of opportunity and hedonism. It had gone a bit mad and it was genuinely exciting, a very vivid, intense period. The genie was out of the lamp.

The final dates of Happy Mondays' Madchester tour in early December took the scene to cities such as Leeds, Sheffield, Liverpool and Glasgow, and the gigs were triumphant and chaotic as demand for the band swelled. In Liverpool they were filmed for a second feature on *Snub TV*, introduced on the show as the 'top band of

1989' who had 'captured the manic spirit of the year as no one else quite managed'. They were shown playing 'Hallelujah' and 'Wrote For Luck' to a packed audience with a swarm of people dancing on stage. For all the bravado that he didn't care about the music, that the band was just a 'blag', Shaun was as delighted as the rest with their reception, and they gave the crowds some of their most assured performances to date, even if behind the scenes the door stayed open to 'the lads' — the bootleggers, the drug dealers, the touts, the party animals, the liggers, gangsters and hooligans — and McGough struggled to control the strong personalities in and around the band.

Of all the people at the centre of the storm as Madchester crashed into 1990, Bez was the one who offered some genuine perspective. Through the haze he would remember that the feeding frenzy around the band now 'moved up a notch' as the hangers-on clambered for their piece of the cake. Whereas before the band's 'entourage' had included thirty or forty close, if dubious members, now when they played there might be over a hundred people, some barely known to the band but with terrifying reputations, all off their heads as cocaine rather than LSD became the drug to mix with Ecstasy and Madchester became currency.

The tour had lasted just under a month, the Mondays' longest stretch of dates yet, and during that time Shaun, who had always been somewhat aloof from the band, became further estranged as stardom grew and heroin took hold of him. Happy Mondays were not just music press darlings now; *Top of the Pops* had propelled them to new levels of recognition. As the band's frontman, Shaun was hassled on the street, his picture used whenever Madchester featured in the mainstream media. He was being elevated above the band; everyone wanted to speak to him, wanted a piece of him. And if they didn't want Shaun, they wanted Bez. The tabloids, especially given the Mondays' colourful background, saw good copy to be had from the pair. The band, of course, were pleased — with all the publicity, their back catalogue had started to sell and there was talk of bigger, more lucrative gigs ahead — but they could not help but notice that whenever their name was mentioned, there was a picture of Shaun or Bez and description of the Madchester scene was not far behind. A large feature in the *Daily Mirror* in early January 1990 was typical. 'The whole world', the article said, was 'raving at a new hot spot...the hottest place in Britain, the place where it's all happening'. Overwhelmed Factory PR Jeff Barrett, who had seen the Mondays phenomenon blow up beyond his wildest dreams, was quoted in the article, sounding as if he was catching his breath. 'The Hacienda is at the core of it all,' he said. 'These bands are really different. They're building up a huge following and believe it or not it's only just beginning.'

Happy Mondays had not played by the rules most bands follow in order to become successful. They hadn't compromised in any way, and they had broken into the mainstream as radicals and rebels with a sound and look that was unique. But they were not immune from the consequences of fame and success. This was no longer the tight gang of *Squirrel* or *Bummed*, and the pressure of the spotlight would force them even further apart. They called Shaun names behind his back: 'vandal twat', and worse. To some extent the musicians were left even more bewildered by what was happening than Shaun, who had heroin as a comfort blanket. They were not in charge any more, the band's world had suddenly exploded in a way they'd never expected, and in the eye of the Madchester storm they had a third album to write and not a great deal of level-headed input from the fast-living Wilson, partying McGough or a singer whose moods changed in tune with the supply of drugs. One minute he was high and everything was cool; then, coming down off heroin, he'd be argumentative and unpleasant – 'a worst nightmare', said Day. Other drugs too – chiefly cocaine, but also acid, with booze and spliff ever-present – fractured the band's inner dynamic. The days of Ecstasy euphoria and non-stop laughs in endless rehearsals were over: they were quitting The Boardwalk, too big for it now (the years' accumulation of detritus required a visit from the city council's sanitation department), and looking for a place they could call their own.

Some adapted to the regime more easily than others. Day, in particular, was growing increasingly disillusioned and withdrawn. 'I would get mega pissed off about everything,' he said. 'It felt like Nathan only wanted to manage Shaun; that the band don't matter, who gives a fuck about that band, they're replaceable.' He had stopped talking to Shaun. 'He wasn't going to listen to my point of view because he said to me, You don't know nothing. I wanted us to work as a team, but all I was good at was playing guitar – that's what Shaun thought of me. Fair enough,' he thought, 'I'll just play guitar.' Paul Davis and Shaun had not had a conversation in months, maybe years. Only the bond between Whelan and Paul Ryder remained strong. The band knew this was their time but there was a sense they were charging straight over the edge. Feelings of triumphalism mixed with trepidation at what lay ahead.

They would not let this chance slip, though. Eight years it had taken them to get here. There was a resolve among the six that was rarely acknowledged in public. Even Shaun seemed to accept a level of responsibility, spending early 1990 in rehab at The Priory in Altrincham. He had moved into a city centre flat with Trisha, the charges against him for importation and possession of cocaine had been dropped after a judge ruled that the amount of cocaine wasn't enough to warrant a guilty verdict, and there was plenty to look forward to now Madchester had opened a world of opportunity. 'I always said the better we got there was no way we'd be wasting our time on drugs,' he said. 'I'm looking to take me more seriously.'

But kicking heroin addiction was no easy task and the scene that his band were at the centre of was too hedonistic to simply step out of. He smuggled whisky and cans of Guinness into The Priory, argued with the staff, and then discharged himself. Shaun had problems, doubts, deep down inside about his own worth as a singer, writer and artist – and about the band. He'd talked himself into believing they were a blag and his words were just thrown together carelessly. It was difficult for the band to get close to him, difficult for anyone to see the smiling, handsome, sharply dressed Shaun with the attractive young Trish on his arm, cruising the Manchester hotspots, and think he was troubled by words and singing and music and the constant demand to perform, to be the Shaun Ryder he'd created in the eye of the media. And heroin took it all away; on heroin the pressure lifted, the super-confident Shaun Ryder came back for a few hours. 'I had no empathy or anything toward him simply because I didn't know,' said Paul. It was only going to get worse, as Wilson expected the band to turn the world on to whatever it was they had in their possession. But maybe there was a chance it would all get better too?

17
Step On

In February 1990, the president of Elektra Records, Bob Krasnow, was busy finalising a deluxe double album to celebrate the fortieth anniversary of the label in May that year. On it, acts from Elektra's current artist roster would cover songs that had made the label famous. The Gipsy Kings were doing a version of The Eagles' 'Hotel California', The Cure covered The Doors' 'Hello I Love You' and Metallica took on Queen's 'Stone Cold Crazy'. Head of A&R at Elektra, Howard Thompson, belatedly called Wilson to invite Happy Mondays to be a part of the project. There was a song from the Elektra catalogue he loved, 'He's Gonna Step On You Again' by South African John Kongos; a minor hit in America in 1971, it had done better in the UK, where it reached number four in the charts. 'I really wanted someone to cover the song,' Thompson said. 'So I threw the tune and another Kongos hit, "Tokoloshe Man", on a cassette and sent it to Nathan.'

'He's Gonna Step On You Again' was a protest song about the white man's appropriation of native territory in Africa, and was built around a drum beat lifted from an African tribal dance that was cited by the *Guinness Book of Records* as the first ever sample used on a record. A cover version of the song by The Party Boys had been a number one hit in Australia in 1987. It wasn't exactly the most obvious song for the Mondays, but it was all that was left. McGough was given $1500 and told to 'get it sorted'.

'The songs were awful,' said Paul. 'Why couldn't we have a Doors song? With "He's Gonna Step On You Again" there was this kind of rhythmic drum thing going on and I thought if we could sample that and loop it we'd got the basis of the song. That was it – that's all the thought we gave it.' McGough asked remixers Oakenfold and Osborne to produce the track, an unusual but visionary step – they'd never produced a record before – but one he felt comfortable making because 'there was no risk', the track was only destined for an American compilation album.

The recording took place in late February at Eden Studios, where Oakenfold/Osborne had remixed 'Wrote For Luck'. Here the band met Osborne and Oakenfold properly for the first time, and having been out the night before in London, arrived at the studio with a coterie of pals. 'Initially I was a bit scared because there were so many people,' said Osborne. The Mondays had still not given the recording any great thought and there was confusion over which track they were doing, symptomatic of the chaos around the band but also the lack of communication among themselves. Whelan thought they were going to record 'Tokoloshe Man' but Day had spent the past two weeks at home working on parts for 'He's Gonna Step On You Again'. 'We were doing "Tokoloshe Man" and when it came to Mark's part, he starts playing and we go, What the fuck are you doing?' said Whelan. Day adapted and they cut a rough version of 'Tokoloshe Man'. Wilson arrived at the studio in the evening to hear Day, sat in the control room, still playing around with the lick he'd worked out for 'He's Gonna Step On You Again'. Wilson asked, 'What's that? It's great.' Day explained and, said Whelan, 'Tony went, So why don't you record that as well and see?'

Day had listened to the guitar fuzz of the original, stripped it back, lifted the main melody and then honed that to its 'bare necessities', he said. It was a brilliant guitar hook and now a long way from the original. It triggered in Whelan memories of a particular horn section from a Northern Soul record. When he went in to record the drum groove for the track, the first element in recording the song, he kept that record in mind and 'just slowed it down'. Osborne programmed a drum loop to go with Whelan's drums and then Paul recorded his bass part. 'Just with the drums and bass you could tell this was going to be great,' said Osborne. 'There was a key point for me when I had a line of blokes on the back wall of the studio all dancing to the drums and the bass – it was just a really great feel. Tony Wilson said, This is going to be massive.' Day laid down his guitar lines and then threw on some 'mega power chords', said Paul. 'I just went, Stop, stop, stop, this is way too good to give away to Elektra. That moment was pivotal. The whole feel and vibe of the record, it sounded up, you could groove along to it.'

'We were all in the control room – me, Paul and Tony Wilson, listening to Mark doing his guitar and it was mind-blowing,' said Whelan. 'We all liked Mark, he was a very nice guy, but he just wasn't like us and he didn't want to be. I said, You know what, we're unfair to Mark, we call him this and that, give him stick and he's great really, he's an artist. We all started bigging him up, saying how creative he was, and he finished with long feedback, amazing, and we were all sat there ready to congratulate him as he came back in the control room. He popped his head in and said, Back in a minute, just going for a big shit. We all looked at one another and went, No, we're right.'

The guitar part didn't sound like the original. It was better. Next, Davis put a piano intro of his own making on the track – again it was nothing like the original, and provided another giant hook for the song. Then it was Shaun's turn. 'Me and Paul [Oakenfold] were like, What the fuck's going to happen now,' Osborne said. 'The first thing he did was "You're twisting my melon man", all that stuff, "Call the cops", and we're like, Fuck, this is amazing. I've never had a moment that beats that. Where did that come from? We had no idea he was going to do it.' Finally, with the band back at home and none the wiser, Oakenfold and Osborne added backing vocals from Mancunian session singer Rowetta Satchell, who McGough had tracked down in Manchester and ferried to London. The band heard her sing before they met her. 'When we heard her vocals on the track, it was whooaa, this thing just gets better and better,' said Paul.

'It was pretty obvious we had something special,' said McGough. He called Howard Thompson in New York and told him the track sounded amazing. 'It's so good,' he said, 'we're going to release it here in the UK as a single.' When Thompson told him it was intended exclusively for the compilation, McGough insisted it had to be a single. Thompson's response was, 'No, we gave you the money, it has to be for our compilation.'

'Howard, I'm sending you the money back,' said McGough. 'I sent him back the money so that we could release it as a single.'

'Step On' was the first giant song of the Madchester revolution. It was almost too good to be true, a pop moment that captured the grooves of the new decade with timeless hooks. It was immediately placed on Radio 1's A-list and was played repeatedly. As their most pop moment began its rise to the status of a national anthem, the delighted band went back on the road. They'd only had two months off since the final date of their previous UK tour, and now they were heading to Europe where a series of dates, promotional appearances and interviews had been arranged in the hope of spreading the Madchester vibe to Germany, Spain, France and Holland, countries where the Acid House phenomenon had not yet caught hold. In these countries, the Mondays were still an underground indie band and Factory's control of its European licensees was not tight, so the trip had an exploratory feel, buoyed by the fact the band knew they had their next hit in the bag and this was what they had always dreamed about, travelling the world in style. Factory hoped the short tour would help sell the *Madchester Rave On* EP, raise awareness of the new single and pave the way to the band playing bigger gigs in Europe.

On 1 March 1990 the Mondays left The Hacienda at 2 a.m. in a coach heading for Harwich to catch the ferry to Hamburg, where they were to start the tour in a club in the heart of the red light district. The band had been booked into clubs that held between 500 and 1000 people. For the most part the crowds just stood and watched and the venues were often ill-equipped. When two of the next four gigs were cancelled, it suited Factory for the British press to report that the cancellations were the result of some chaotic incident involving Shaun, even that the bad boy band simply couldn't be bothered. In fact they were always up for the gigs, and enjoyed being on the road where every day felt like a new beginning. The gigs were cancelled because they had so swelled their live sound, with the addition of samples and sequencers, that they needed a forty-channel mixing desk, as per the specifications sent ahead. They simply found the small venues' rudimentary set-up impossible to work with. In future the band would carry their own PA system, at huge expense to themselves.

In Valencia, they ate all the food, had a shower, drank the rider, put the rest on the bus, took the money and drove to Barcelona for the next gig. Here, at the 500-capacity Ars Studio, there was a scare with the police. 'The dressing room got raided twice,' said Paul. 'The police came and made us all sit down, empty our pockets and give them all our drugs and the money. Once they'd gone we went to the bus where there was more drugs and more money and carried on. An hour later the same two coppers came back and did it again – just confiscated the drugs and money. No one got charged. I don't think they could be arsed with the paperwork.'

There were two days off after the Barcelona show before the tour moved on to France, and the band stayed on in the city as The Bailey Brothers flew over to film a video for 'Step On'. There was no plan, but Shaun suggested the video be shot on the roof of a hotel in Sitges, a coastal town close to Barcelona known as 'Ibiza in min- iature' – a flash holiday resort with a thriving gay scene. 'We arrived there on Saturday night,' said Whelan. 'The video was scheduled for early Sunday, they wanted to film when the sun was rising.' The Mondays immediately went into party mode. The *NME* journalist who'd come to interview the band, Jack Barron, feared he would be killed as a van in which he and McGough were travelling smashed into a parked car. The band's coach driver, a veteran of countless band tours, flew home complaining of drug behaviour the like of which he'd never seen before.

The Bailey Brothers finally rounded the band up and got them all on the roof. 'How we used to treat the Mondays was like wildlife documentary makers,' said Keith Jobling. 'We used to get them to be completely natural and try and get as far away from them as we could, on a long lens, and film them like they were a pride of lions on the Serengeti – don't disturb them, just let them do their own thing. They never had a camera shoved in their face until quite late in the process.' No permission to film was sought, of course. The damage included Shaun snapping off part of the E from the giant 'HOTEL' sign as he clambered up on it, while the sign's L vanished completely. The upmarket hotel was left with a sign that read 'HOT'.

The band travelled to Paris, where many UK fans had made the trip to see them at the 1000-capacity Bataclan club and the Madchester vibe was back. The gig was being covered for *Q* magazine by Chris Heath, who wrote that while the Roses had fans, the Mondays were 'simply at the centre of a major party and for the Paris trip the whole party came along'. Heath had trouble getting to speak to the band and recalled McGough fending off French journalists at the venue, all of whom had similarly been promised 'exclusives'. Finally Shaun told Heath he'd have to do the interview there and then on the floor of the venue as fans poured in, and as he went to work on a fan who had abused him. Even by Shaun's standards this was an extreme setting and odd behaviour for an interview with a leading music journalist.

In Amsterdam the band was supposed to be interviewed for a cover story by *Sounds* journalist Mary Anne Hobbs. It never happened as a familiar chaos descended. The European press were treated even less seriously: interviews impossible to rearrange were blown out or treated as huge jokes, much to Factory's despair. But not that of Tony Wilson, who enjoyed such behaviour. The Mondays travelled back to the UK and then flew to Iceland from London for the final date of the tour at Reykjavik University. Here their behaviour and that of the tight coterie of lads who travelled with them tumbled from lovable and roguish to over-the-top and tinged with nastiness. A clothes shop was robbed and the hosts' hospitality abused. The concept of a warehouse party had been misconstrued and an after-gig party had been arranged in a shoe warehouse – which was also robbed. There was a fight on the plane home when Muzzer reportedly head-butted a London clubber. *The Face* called their 'all lads together' vibe 'sad'. Of course, the band took no notice, had not even registered much of what was going on. They were over the edge and being sustained by forward momentum alone.

Back in Manchester, a pair of bootleggers and ticket touts had organised their biggest ever shows – two sold-out nights (24 and 25 March) at the 10,000-capacity G-Mex Centre, with the strapline 'The rave is on'. The pair, John 'the phone' Kenyon and Jimmy Sherlock, aka Muffin, were also now handling the band's official merchandise. McGough had reasoned that if he gave the bootleggers the 'in' – legitimate merchandise sold inside the venue – they would cut the band in on the 'out' – the bootleg merchandise sold outside. Kenyon and Sherlock thought all their Christmases had come at once, and had taken the opportunity and run with it. The band thought Sherlock and Kenyon had been lunatics in trying to organise the one night first advertised at G-Mex, and had no conception of how Madchester was now being received around the country, pumped up by regular blasts on the radio of 'Step On'. The pair had sold many of the tickets to coach companies around the UK who organised packages to all the big shows, and much to the band's disbelief quickly added a second night – which followed the first and sold out. 'That jump from your regular club to a night in G-Mex, the biggest venue in town, was enormous,' said Paul. 'I thought it was madness,' said Whelan. 'It was weird.'

Even weirder to look out from the stage and see a sea of young fans in the band's T-shirts, baggy jeans, many of them copying Shaun's 'curtains', his long centre-parted hair (which he referred to as his David Cassidy haircut). 'We just thought it was a fashion change, not the influence of the bands,' said Whelan. 'We didn't feel part of a movement.'

In the venue the band had spent time and money installing a vast sound system, one of the biggest ever put together, and a lighting rig. Even on stage they had installed a full-sized PA system because, said Paul, 'we had to be able to feel it and hear it quite loud for us to get into it'. The atmosphere in the venue was rapturous. 'I took a lot of drink and drugs before we went on,' said Paul. 'I used to have four pint-pots each half full of vodka topped up with grapefruit juice, so that's two pints of vodka, and I'd do that during the show. So I was drinking quite a lot – and the cocaine was quite a lot. I used to make myself sick so I could get more alcohol down. I got to the point of feeling invincible.' The second night was filmed and would be shown on Channel 4 and released on VHS as *The Happy Mondays Party*. There was a sense of unreality surrounding the band. Both nights saw them play their longest sets ever, each song welcomed as a favourite with cheers and non-stop dancing. New Order's Bernard Sumner made a guest appearance with support act 808 State, who were now in the top ten with a new single, 'The Only Rhyme that Bites', featuring MC Tunes: now New Order were supporting Happy Mondays! The band brought the two-day party to a climax with a twelve-minute version of 'Wrote For Luck'. Bez, dripping with sweat, stripped down to his boxer shorts on stage as Shaun swigged from bottles of champagne and Paul, all in white, staggered off unsteadily. He missed the aftershow at The Midland Hotel, where the band's out-of-control entourage caused them more hassles: mirrors and glass doors smashed and jewellery robbed. The party made the *Sun* — 'invasion of fans left trail of destruction' — and the *Daily Mirror* — 'Hooligan Happys' hotel riot' — as 'Step On' continued its dominance of the airwaves. 'The whole city seemed like a cartoon,' said Shaun. The fact that well-known young blaggers were organising the band's highly lucrative merchandising and the almost a quarter of a million pounds' worth of ticket sales generated by the G-Mex shows certainly fitted that evaluation.

'"Step On" was the one that went stratospheric,' said Factory's radio and TV plugger, Nicki Kefalas. 'The video was great too, very popular.' The song was made record of the week on Radio 1's breakfast show and it was a longstanding tradition for the person who held that coveted spot to phone the show on the Monday at 7 a.m., for a chat to be repeated through the show. 'It was stressful because if you didn't phone up and do the interview you lost the slot,' explained Kefalas. Shaun did it. 'They were strangely professional amid all the chaos,' she added.

Happy Mondays were now in demand across the UK media, and all over the UK music press. In his *NME* cover story on the band, written on his recent trip to Europe with them, Jack Barron called them the 'least macho band you could come across on stage. There isn't a single rock 'n' roll clichéd groin thrust in sight.' Shaun was on the front cover, wrapped round the giant letter E from the video shoot in Sitges, and also appeared on the covers of *Melody Maker*, *Sounds* and *Record Mirror*. He continued to peddle the line he thought they wanted to hear — that his lyrics meant 'fuck all', the band was a blag, Manchester was built on drugs — and then out came the exaggerated bad-boy posturing, that money not art was his driving motivation, tales of an impoverished background and bad jokes about wanting to 'corrupt' girls with drugs and daft claims, such as that at the age of eight 'someone took me to a garage and pulled down my knickers'. He told *Sounds*: 'I know it sounds bad and everything but I like money. I always have done.' He professed a philosophy of looking after number one: 'This is just what we do for a couple of years and that's it. I just want to be able to go where I want, do what I want, spend what I want, buy what I want, when I want and how I want.'

In interviews with teen magazines *Smash Hits* and *Blue Jeans* and fashion magazine *Elle*, he continued to talk about the band in relation to money, expensive designer clothes, watches and cars. It was clear from this glut of covers, routinely featuring Shaun and not the band, that the Mondays were becoming increasingly, in the public eye, Shaun's band and what he was saying spoke for them all. It wasn't and he didn't, but it was a perception he made no attempt to correct. Whelan, for instance, had become a vegan and had a growing interest in Eastern philosophies. Perhaps Shaun just felt he was being 'honest'.

To some extent the band were glad to be excused media interviews; the fewer distractions the better as they locked themselves away in a new rehearsal room in Stretford working hard on putting together songs for their next album. But understandably, they would have liked some credit, and it was annoying to read Shaun talk about the new songs he was writing when the band knew that his contribution to them was minimal. 'He wasn't there when we wrote the other songs,' said Whelan. 'He wasn't really interested in the songs that much but he knew how to work the press like Tony did.'

It wasn't even a question, for Whelan, of getting his face on the front covers – that had never interested him – but he shared with the rest of the band a feeling that it was 'growing into a monster', where the band was perceived as just Shaun, or Shaun and Bez. 'Shaun always played it down, saying he hated all the attention, but had to do it,' said Whelan. 'I'm not sure he did hate it.' For his brother, the lies were closer to home, and arguments flared: 'I'd be annoyed at his bullshitting in the press.' Shaun could not explain that while they felt the pressure of putting the new songs together, he felt the burden of being the public face of the band, that being consistently photographed and doing fifteen interviews a day – not only with the UK press but often now with European or American publications – brought its own pressure. Why else would he be making up this bullshit?

Factory released 'Step On' in multiple formats, all featuring just the one song in a myriad of mixes by Oakenfold and Osborne with names such as 'Stuff It In', 'One Louder' and 'Twistin' My Melon'. Central Station had been filmed making the artwork for the cover of the single for a Granada documentary *Madchester – Sound of the North*, for which the band had recently filmed a segment in Amsterdam. The documentary attempted to contextualise the 'musical capital of the world' in terms of the Acid House scene and featured a deeper look at the city's creative spirit, including pirate radio stations, rappers, fanzine writers and clothes shops. Of course, with Wilson still being a Granada bigwig, Factory, The Hacienda and the Mondays took centre stage and there was a prominent slot for Phil Saxe's first signing for the label, Northside – a new, young working-class inner-city four-piece whose debut, 'Shall We Take a Trip', would see them quickly elevated to the cover of the *NME*. The documentary was indicative of the wider perception that Manchester, as a cultural hotbed, had moved beyond music and drugs into a social phenomenon that was causing waves across the country.

When Tony Blair, six years later, invited the Britpop royalty to Downing Street he was riding on a wave of cultural change that had begun in 1990, the face of which was the decidedly un-photo-genic (for politicians) Shaun Ryder. History is silent on whether Ryder was ever invited to the Downing Street party. At the time, however, Madchester was seen as another kick against the rule of Margaret Thatcher, whose position was looking increasingly weak following the Poll Tax riots. Although unemployment was down, there were fears of another recession, and Labour's standing in the opinion polls had risen dramatically. Thatcher would be gone by the end of the year.

'Step On' was single of the week in both *NME* and *Sounds*. The *NME* called it 'edgy and splendid', proof that 'good sex still exists on vinyl'. *Sounds* said the band had struck gold dust: 'Isn't it amazing how these bozos can spend every waking hour either high or blotto and still find time to make extraordinary music.' At Factory Phil Saxe, who had stayed close to the band despite the breaking of relations, predicted that in five years they would be as big as The Rolling Stones. The band filmed their second appearance on *Top of the Pops*, this time without The Stone Roses present. Mark Day wore a large Gatsby cap and dark glasses. Guest vocalist Rowetta was in kinky boots, Lycra and leather bodice, showing off generous cleavage. Bez danced convincingly. In the centre of it all, however, Shaun appeared tired; he stood still, seemed ghostly, the effects of heroin addiction catching up with him. On his striped Hugo Boss jumper, Shaun wore a Flowered Up badge in alliance with a new, upcoming band often said to be the London version of the Mondays.

'Step On' climbed to number five in the UK charts and would be one of the top fifty best-selling singles of 1990. Mark Day did not have to rush back to his Post Office job after this second *Top of the Pops*. McGough had put the band's wages up to £150 per week – equalling Day's Post Office pay – and even he now saw a solid future ahead for the band and finally quit his job. His mum also kicked him out of the house, deciding that she'd had enough of him living off her at home, although at almost twenty-nine it was probably about time he moved out anyway. Some things didn't change though. He still took the bus to rehearsals and queued at venues like everyone else. Shaun meanwhile was busy disappearing into the next chapter of his fantasy, the ending to which no one knew.

On 7 April the Mondays played a sold-out show at 12,500-capacity Wembley Arena in London, by far the biggest crowd they had ever appeared before in the capital. Tickets were £15 and the band was being paid a reputed £30,000 for the show, with the Adrian Sherwood Sound System and Paul Oakenfold supporting. There had not been a huge Madchester event in the capital since the Roses' appearance at Alexandra Palace five months ago. In that time, what had been seen as a curiosity by most people outside the music world had exploded and there was huge expectation. The legions of fans were all dressed in the distinct 'baggy' look that had come to define the new lad culture of the decade, and before the Mondays came on, Oakenfold had cranked it up to an unbearable pitch. When the Mondays took to the stage, the front section of the huge crowd exploded into their Bez-dance groove.

'Shaun started a song and then turned round and told the band to stop and start again,' said Oakenfold. 'The crowd went mental . . . it was his mistake but he made it seem cool. The Mondays had a special vibe that no one else got near.' As a stage effect, there was a giant 'E' that lit up brightly and dad Derek rushed to the front to brandish a large cardboard cutout of a number 1. Derek seemed more excited about the gig than the band. For them it held none of the euphoria of the G-Mex shows. They had none of Wilson's regionalism about them, didn't see themselves as proud Mancunians taking on the capital. They had felt more nerves playing in small clubs at the beginning of their career, when they were fighting for an audience. The crowd at Wembley had turned up to see the band because they already liked them. 'As soon as you walk out you're on a winner,' said Derek. Shaun made a few cockney quips but projected little enthusiasm as Bez and the band retrod the G-Mex set. The band's crew had worked hard to create a booming sound and the lights pulsed but it was a gig none of the band could recall later, one that simply passed by.

The drink, drugs, girls, and professional backslappers around the band were astonishing to see, even for seasoned London liggers. The party moved on from backstage to the band's hotel, but before they left Wembley they needed to find Derek. 'When everybody had gone we found him on this flight case asleep, too much champagne, and we had to push him to the back door of the venue, so we could get him into the transport,' said Paul. 'He was celebrating; his lads had just played Wembley.' It was a rare moment that briefly reminded them of where they'd come from; a moment, almost humbling, of unity amid the chaos, quickly gone as, back at the hotel, they all split up and pursued their own ways.

The *Daily Star* reported that the Mondays had incurred a £10,000 bill for playing forty minutes over their allotted time at Wembley, an irony since one of the criticisms that fans and critics levelled at them over the years was that their sets were far too short for the ticket price. Reviewing the gig in the *NME*, Barbara Ellen argued that it was 'not what they do here but the fact they are here' that mattered. The band, she wrote, were 'a noisy totally addictive sprawl'. In *Sounds*, Mary Anne Hobbs wrote: 'The 90s belong to this band, nobody else can touch them.'

The band who sounded like no one else had inspired a slew of imitators. Their influence was apparent not just on the Roses, New Order and James but The Charlatans, Inspiral Carpets, Flowered Up, Northside, and now Primal Scream – whose single 'Loaded' had marked a radical departure for them – and The Farm, back from oblivion with a 'baggy beat'. Then came a slew of new Manchester bands, such as The Paris Angels and The Mock Turtles, and across the country bands like Blur, EMF and Jesus Jones. Tony Wilson paraphrased the *Daily Telegraph* review of the Wembley show – 'before we go on about the madness, the anarchy and the drug hysteria, which is all wonderful, let's not forget that the drummer and bass player of this group have changed British music forever'.

Wilson was on top of the world. His paw prints were all over a very unlikely Factory release: New Order's new single, 'World in Motion' (originally titled 'E for England'), was the official England team song for the Italia 1990 World Cup and would be the band's only ever number one single. It was worth falling out with Peter Saville about. The graphic designer, an influence at Factory for twelve years, disapproved of Wilson's hedonism, did not share his uncritical admiration for Happy Mondays and compared Factory now to a 'coven'. He had been late with the artwork for 'World in Motion' and Wilson excommunicated him: 'Hannett rerun,' he said. Rob Gretton's strong influence over Wilson and Factory had weakened, as had the man's health. The New Order single (which he did not appear to be fully behind) was a one-off, and Gretton was involved neither in Bernard Sumner's solo project with Johnny Marr, a 'supergroup' called Electronic, nor Peter Hook's new group Revenge. Both bands were being released via Factory with Electronic taking their debut single, 'Getting Away With It', into the top twenty. The only other person able to influence Wilson at Factory was Alan Erasmus and he was being increasingly sidelined.

Wilson now had grand plans to take Madchester to America, lining up a tour there for the Mondays and The Hacienda. 'If you're in the lead in youth culture, you are in the lead in the thing that leads,' he said. His city was brimming with self-confidence and a sense of global style – and so was he. Manchester kids, he said, had the best record collections, were brighter, cooler and better dressed than anywhere else in the world. And he had been right about the most important group in this culture, Happy Mondays. No one at Factory could argue with him, and if they did he didn't listen. 'Mr Manchester', as he was being called, was in control.

18
America

Happy Mondays appeared unstoppable. The band were announced as headliners of the coming summer's Glastonbury festival, with a tour of America soon to start. It was true that Shaun had, to some extent, allowed fame to affect him and had drifted away from the band, his incessant talking up of a solo single that would fail to materialise just one of the more harmless examples. More pressingly, his drug habit was becoming burdensome, making him unreliable. He'd recently refused to get out of bed to fly to Paris for promotional work because, he would later admit, he didn't have any heroin. But the band had cracked the top five and the songs they were writing for the new album were among their best yet, even though Shaun was largely absent from band rehearsals, his whereabouts frequently unknown and his absence increasingly unmentioned. The Mondays had also made efforts to get their business affairs in order.

The band's first meeting with their new accountant was a sobering one — but not for Shaun, who wasn't there. McGough had engaged London-based Eric Longley from the music division at Ernst & Young, a huge multinational money management firm, to handle the band's finances. Longley would soon move to Manchester to become the Mondays' full-time business manager. Madchester was not about tax, PAYE and National Insurance, but these were the things the Mondays were being asked to consider as Longley organised their affairs. They became a dry-sounding business partnership, the six band members owning equal shares in a limited company through which all band money was channelled. The Mondays attempted to avoid thinking about the seriousness, perhaps the mundaneness, of such things by calling this limited company Wabash, their own slang for a 'nosh', meaning blow job.

Longley drew up a set of figures that showed exactly what the band had earned up to the end of the tax year, April 1990. They had grossed £427,000, chiefly from touring, publishing and recording advances and royalties. It sounded impressive as many of the sales of 'Step On' fell into the following tax year. But their expenditure in the same period had been £385,000 – touring fees, recording costs, legal fees, accountancy, tax, management costs, agency fees and artwork – and they still had a further £39,000 in outstanding debts, including £11,000 owing to McGough Management and £15,000 to Ernst & Young. At present, the band's balance stood at a measly £26,000. It was from this they were drawing their weekly £150 wage. They were so far from living the high life that they were still nicking equipment.

In the UK, the Madchester scene that so far the Mondays had failed to turn into cash continued to dominate the indie charts and pepper the mainstream. Popular non-Madchester indie guitar bands such as Ride and My Bloody Valentine, both on Creation, were outnumbered and outsold. The Inspiral Carpets' debut album, *Life*, reached number two. The Charlatans went to number one with their debut album. The Stone Roses' 1989 debut had risen again to make the top ten. Wilson had forbidden The Bailey Brothers to film the video for the Roses' belated follow-up to 'Fools Gold', the limp single 'One Love' (which nevertheless reached number four in the UK), insisting it was 'not right for the story' of the war of the bands that only existed in his head. Although they had stalled creatively and would not release another record for over four years, in May 1990 the Roses played to a remarkable 40,000 people at Spike Island, near Widnes, a town between Liverpool and Manchester.

For all Wilson's bombast, the only things that Factory had to show from the Madchester boom were the single by Electronic (a band whose rights the label had only for the UK), New Order's World Cup number one (in which major label MCA had an interest and only sold in the UK) and 'Step On'. Revenge, Northside and a new Phil Saxe signing, The Wendys — a Scottish band who had supported the Mondays and fitted the scene — all struggled to find an audience. The classical line continued in its own idiosyncratic way. Wilson was still apparently infatuated with Miaow singer Cath Carroll, and offered her a fresh opportunity to record for the label. What Factory had failed to produce, since New Order's *Technique* in January 1989, was a best-selling album. The label borrowed money, although all major economists were predicting a recession, to finalise the redevelopment and design of the new offices and to buy the building in which they had opened The Hacienda. It put them in debt to the tune of at least £1.5 million.

The Hacienda had been turning a solid profit for the past two years, grossing almost £1 million a year. Although Wilson found the club nights too pedestrian for his liking, the clampdown on illegal Acid House parties, outdoor raves and the closure of Manchester clubs such as The Gallery, Thunderdome and Konspiracy, meant they were more popular than ever. New police powers and hastily introduced laws had seen club owners and rave organisers losing their battles with the authorities nationwide. The craze that had been dodging the law for the past year had run out of luck. The *Sun*, which had celebrated the wildest fringes of the party at its height, in an unashamed volte-face had run a gleeful front page that read: 'Ecstasy! The Party's Over!' Not at The Hacienda. The club played host to the occasional Madchester band, indie dance night or rare Factory classical night, but it was still best loved for the wild Ecstasy-fuelled dance nights. People travelled from far and wide to attend the most happening club in the world, Britain's most famous, by car and coach from all over the UK, while limousines pulled up with parties flown in from private jets from Miami. There was much money in the club, much champagne, but not much of the original soul. A sort of psychosis and paranoia from the consumption of too many drugs now hung over the place.

The Hacienda had also become a bear pit for local gangs. DJs Dave Haslam and Mike Pickering both claimed to have had guns pulled on them near the DJ booth. Bez claimed that while he'd been partying with a gang of lads, they got involved in a fight with a doorman, as a result of which 'another firm' had been 'shouted up to come and wipe them out'. He was fortunate, he said, to escape with a cauliflower ear from a savage boot to the head in the ensuing fight, which involved knives and machetes. The war for control of the city centre drug trade and of club and pub doors was on the verge of exploding. Factory's Dry bar was another target.

The situation was neatly packaged by the media as a battle between black gangs from Cheetham Hill and white gangs from Salford. But there were far more complex relationships at play, labyrinthine links between families and associates, and what appeared to be a tactical retreat by Manchester's most powerful crime firms. It was a situation exacerbated by a rise in the popularity of freebasing cocaine and the increased availability of crack and firearms. In any event, undercover operations by Greater Manchester Police revealed evidence of mass drug taking and dealing in The Hacienda and applied to withdraw its nightclub/drinks licence.

With Factory having just bought the building, it was imperative that The Hacienda remain open, and Wilson hired QC George Carman, at a reputed cost of £250,000, to represent the club. In an attempt to prove to licensing magistrates that they were clamping down on drug use in the club, searches on entry were introduced alongside a ban on trainers and shell suits. 'When it was clear we had to clear the drugs out, we had to almost destroy the culture,' said Wilson. Carman was able to pick holes in the police case and at the licence hearing on 23 July managed to secure an adjournment until January 1991.

While the Mondays were reaching the height of their popularity, chaos seemed still to follow them wherever they went. A rare front cover featuring the whole band together appeared in *NME* before their Glastonbury headline show. The interview inside, however, was as usual dominated by Shaun. 'There's the proper musicians in the band and then you get Bez and me,' he said. 'I don't even think of myself as being a singer in a band really.' He shot down Manchester. 'I hate the fucking place. There was nothing going on here before we started things anyway. There are one or two good bars and a bit of decent music, but that's about it. The place is bollocks.'

The journey down had seen the luxury double-decker coach crash. 'We were all tripping,' said Day. But that was only the start of it. Even though Happy Mondays had previous when it came to tours that brought with it certain levels of violence and crime, no one could have anticipated what was to come. Into a genteel field in south-west England that had been the home of hippies and palm readers for more than thirty years, the Mondays tornado descended in a weekend of riotous anarchy that left Michael Eavis, the bearded and softly spoken organiser of the festival, so shaken that when it was all over, he decided the following year's Glastonbury would be cancelled, something that had never happened before in the festival's history. The Mondays were told that they would never be invited back, blamed for turning the backstage area into an out of control free-for-all with over a thousand of their entourage using fake passes to come and go at will. Men in balaclavas offered Ecstasy and crack, tent crime was rife and stallholders were reportedly robbed. 'We heard stories about what was going on but we were oblivious,' said Whelan. 'It wasn't us doing it. I never thought we'd get tarred with that.' He admits he was 'naïve' to think that way.

The band had joined in the madness with Shaun smoking, he said, 'gram after gram' of heroin. Bez had been high on acid for three days solid. Paul was consuming vast amounts of cocaine and drinking heavily. 'I stopped myself thinking about the enormity of these gigs – G-Mex, then Wembley and now Glastonbury – by drinking and drugs,' he said. 'I don't know how I would have handled it otherwise.' The band were in some state, then, before they hit the stage to face a crowd of 50,000. 'It was chaos,' said Whelan. 'It always was.'

Incredibly they played a giant-sounding, well-received set. 'As soon as we got on stage it was us and we gave a hundred per cent,' said Paul. 'Rave On' was the perfect opener and the crowd started to dance. Shaun, in a new white jacket, drank booze and mistimed and forgot the lyrics to the James Anderton-inspired 'God's Cop', one of the two unreleased songs intended for the new album. 'Do It Better', 'Step On' and 'Clap Your Hands' all got huge applause, with Paul Davis sounding wilfully off-kilter. Shaun acted nonchalant, saying little between songs but occasionally firing daggers at Davis. 'Lazyitis', an enduring fan favourite, was followed by 'Hallelujah', which was met with huge cheers from its opening sample. Shaun and the band stumbled through the second new song, 'Kinky Afro', as Shaun again forgot the lyrics. The crowd did not care and the extended version of 'Wrote For Luck' had all 50,000 people joining in the Mondays party, which had been going on for three days and seemed to have simply continued on stage. It was not the slickest show ever to headline Glastonbury, but the Mondays had definitely pulled off the biggest gig of their lives. There was little celebration afterwards and the exhausted band found separate ways to travel back home.

Four days later they became the first rock band to play at Ibiza's famous 4000-capacity club, KU. DJ Paul Oakenfold was support. He and Osborne, following the success of 'Step On', had been asked to produce the band's third album. The band had shipped an entire PA system out to Ibiza for the show, fearing the club PA was not up to the task, costing them £10,000 of their £16,000 deal. Rowetta turned up unexpectedly, having won the trip in a radio competition, and sang with the band on stage. The band, higher than at Glastonbury, could recall little of the show. Whelan admitted they 'could be terrible' at some gigs and this was one of them. Nonetheless the crowd, many of them holidaying Brits – the popularity of Ibiza as a party resort had continued to increase – were swept up in the atmosphere, in just 'being there', said Whelan, 'caught up in the whole thing, a part of the Ecstasy revolution'. The Ibiza trip put the band on the cover of *Sounds* again – this time the picture was simply of Bez, dancing on stage.

The party now headed for America, where Wilson was predicting the country's imminent capitulation to the Madchester scene. He had told the British press, who swallowed it, that the Mondays were playing a rave at the 18,000-capacity Madison Square Garden in New York. Their successful and enjoyable small club tour with The Pixies a year previously had convinced Elektra of their potential, but Madchester had still to make any impact in America, where hip-hop was the dominant cultural force and the pop music of Janet Jackson and Vanilla Ice dominated the *Billboard* Hot 100 – the American equivalent of the UK charts. There were, however, pockets of interest in the Madchester scene, specifically among alternative rock radio stations in New York, Los Angeles and San

Francisco and college radio stations around the country. A wave of late 1980s American alternative acts that included not only The Pixies and REM but bands like Jane's Addiction had prompted *Billboard* to set up a 'Modern Rock' chart to run alongside the Hot 100, listing the forty most-played alternative songs of the week on modern rock radio – a kind of equivalent of the UK indie charts. 'Step On' was already receiving good airplay on modern rock stations and had been picked up by some dance stations – *Billboard* also ran dance charts based on twelve-inch sales, club plays and airplay. The aim was to use these avenues to try and break the Mondays into the Top 40 of the Hot 100 where the real sales were – a breakthrough into the mainstream similar to what they had achieved in the UK.

The Stone Roses had stalled on America, never even set foot in the country, and Happy Mondays were the first Madchester band to play significant dates in the US after the scene's explosion in the UK. The band's US agent Marc Geiger had skilfully used the publicity being generated by the Mondays and the strength of 'Step On' to book the band a short two-week tour in 1000-plus-sized venues in major cities from 9 to 24 July. These were cities the band had already played and where there was the best chance of building a fan base. Wilson had his own theory about breaking the Mondays in America: 'The culture will sell the band and the band will sell the culture.' Despite it being based on American club music, he hoped to popularise the UK's Acid House scene to the US – something he saw as akin to The Rolling Stones and Beatles reawakening America to their native blues music in the first British musical invasion of the early 1960s.

Wilson had organised for the Mondays' tour to coincide with a 'United States of the Hacienda' DJ club tour of major US cities featuring Mike Pickering, Graeme Park and Paul Oakenfold. He had also engineered a five-date Hacienda/Factory residency at the famed Sound Factory club in New York, under the banner 'From Manchester with Love', as part of New York's New Music Seminar – the music industry's major annual conference, featuring hundreds of seminars and band showcases. Northside, 808 State, A Guy Called Gerald and the Mondays were all scheduled to play the club during the residency. There was a buzz of excitement about Madchester building ahead of the seminar that would benefit the Mondays on their tour. The 'trance dance' Mondays featured, alongside New Order, 808 State and the Roses, in a feature on MTV's popular *120 Minutes* show about the 'wild new bands' from Manchester, 'a city that has become the centre of the biggest musical buzz in all of England'. The presenter explained that 'Manchester pop' was 'not just a sound' but 'also a distinct subculture with its own ways of dressing, getting high and dancing'. Another injection of hype came when the second largest news weekly in the US, *Newsweek*, put the scene on its front cover under a headline 'Stark Raving Madchester'.

Howard Thompson at Elektra was predicting great things for the Mondays. 'It looked like there was actually going to be no stopping them,' he said. He and McGough had convinced Brad Hunt, the label's general manager, to allocate a large budget for promotion to attempt to break the Mondays into the mainstream via Top 40 radio stations (a separate entity from modern rock stations or college radio). 'Elektra spent the money, and they really spent the money,' said McGough. 'It was a fortune.' Elektra prepared to spend in the region of $1 million on promotion of the Mondays, chiefly to woo the Top 40 stations. The band was travelling on a luxury tour bus that would accommodate them, a six-man touring crew and Rowetta, on her first tour. Central TV had paid £20,000 up front to film a 'fly on the wall' documentary about the tour, a deal brokered by Wilson.

The Mondays felt like rock stars, and away from the luxury tour bus and the TV cameras, spells in top-class hotels awaited them. They could also hear 'Step On' being played on radio stations in every city they visited, and Elektra organised publicity for the band that seemed to almost rival the attention of the UK. Their visit to Chicago, for instance, made the front page of the culture section of the *Chicago Tribune* and the tone of the piece was typical of America's reaction to Madchester: 'Dust off your bell-bottoms for the next music craze. If Manchester is the world capital of this dance movement, the ambassadors are the Happy Mondays.' 'Step On' was described as a 'visionary combination of disco and rock'. The band were headlining the city's Metro club only a week after

1200 ravers had packed it for the Hacienda DJ night – Wilson's well thought out plan benefiting the Mondays, who played to a capacity and appreciative audience. There were glitches – in Ann Arbor, the band found the sound system woefully inadequate and cancelled the show – but they adapted quickly from playing huge shows in the UK to these smaller club venues and to travelling hundreds of miles overnight between cities such as Detroit and Toronto, both filmed for the documentary. 'We knew America had to be worked at, same as Europe had to be worked at, we didn't mind, we knew we had to put the work in,' said Paul.

The inclusion of the bubbly, upbeat Rowetta – who amused the band with her wit and whip-hand treatment of male groupies – seemed to defuse any serious ego clashes between band members, and the journey through America was an adventure enjoyed by all, enhanced by the new levels of luxury they were being afforded and the sense that they were making giant inroads into success in the States. They worked hard, not just at the gigs (which they still routinely taped and listened back to) but by promoting them-selves at radio stations and with the local press. It was an ethic at odds with their reputation in the UK. In New York, the band checked in at five-star hotel The Mark, their base for the 'From Manchester with Love' Sound Factory show. Some things didn't change: they caused a disturbance by setting off the fire alarm, instigating the arrival of several fire engines, and Muzzer was in trouble again after another fight. The band partied at the hotel with actor Tony Curtis and would check out with a bill totalling a staggering £26,000.

Wilson had stirred up advance publicity for them in New York, chairing a New Music Seminar panel he'd titled 'Wake Up America – You're Dead', during which a confused *Billboard* writer had asked McGough: 'Your boys are drug dealers, they're not musicians?' 'Correct,' said McGough. The furore made more impact in the English music press than it did in America, where a hip-hop beef featuring rapper Ice Cube at another seminar event dominated headlines. Still, the Mondays' gig at Sound Factory was one of the hottest tickets of the New Music Seminar, not bad considering there were 350 bands playing over five days. A crazed-looking Bez shaking maracas was the picture used on the poster advertising the gig, and in the US he was often singled out as the band's chief attraction, compared to Flavor Flav, Public Enemy's infamous 'hype man'.

Two thousand people, with many more locked outside, witnessed the Mondays' triumphant Sound Factory appearance. The powerful, bass-heavy sound system at the legendary dance club suited the Mondays and there was a strong Mancunian presence and plenty of Ecstasy in the club. Despite Shaun's preference for clothes shopping, spending £1000 in Armani rather than attending the soundcheck, the band delivered a superbly polished set, a climactic 'Wrote For Luck' provoking the familiar stage invasion. In Los Angeles, a city where many more Mancunians were already involved in the underground Acid House dance scene, the band played their biggest show of the tour at the 4000-capacity Hollywood Palladium, headlining a 'From Manchester with Love' night that also featured A Guy Called Gerald and 808 State. The gig was reviewed positively by the influential *Los Angeles Times* and the Mondays were warmly received in the city, where the English music weeklies were popular imports and 'Step On' was a favourite of hip local radio station K-ROQ. The single was at number nine on the *Billboard* Modern Rock chart and three in the Dance chart. It had climbed into the *Billboard* Hot 100, where it was at number fifty-seven. The Mondays were so close, and there was a potentially big audience out there for them. But to reach it, to truly break America as a band would take more extensive touring, more meet-and-greets with radio stations, shaking hands, smiling gamely and playing the game. More time and hard work.

The publicity surrounding the band, as a sort of 'Ecstasy Sex Pistols', had limited impact in America, where hip-hop stars boasted of hardcore sexual exploits, gun battles and crack dealing, gangsta rap tracks such as NWA's 'Fuck Tha Police' revolved around violence, poverty and gunplay, and heavy rock acts such as Jane's Addiction and Guns N' Roses were supposedly addicted to crack, smack, crystal meth and hard liquor. The rumour that the Mondays were dealing a few pills did not exactly mark them out as bad boys as it did in the UK. 'Shaun didn't really have a personality here,' said the band's agent Marc Geiger. 'Neither did Bez.'

It was one of the reasons Shaun liked Los Angeles. The band were popular among a curious but cool hip crowd but he felt nothing of the pressure of the UK, where he was recognised on the street, everyone seemed to want a piece of him and to some extent he had to live up to the bad boy reputation he'd created for himself. Then there was the sunshine, the sense of space, and the new culture to absorb. He realised the band had made a great decision: that recording their new album here would work and he was glad they had turned down his alternative suggestions to record in Amsterdam or Barbados. *All* the band liked Los Angeles, relaxing finally into a comfortable lifestyle after so many years of struggling and then the bewildering blitz of success, a chance to take stock and recharge. Although they were all staying at the same lush Hollywood apartment complex – with communal pool, Jacuzzis and tennis courts – they had their own apartments and hire cars and could live their own grown-up lives. Girlfriends flew over to join them.

Before they were due to start the new album with Oakenfold and Osborne, there was a tour date to play in San Francisco. The show had sold out but the Mondays decided instead to take ketamine and see a Soul II Soul gig in Los Angeles. 'We were getting our heads into studio mode,' said Paul. It was unlike the band to cancel on a whim, especially after Wilson, McGough and Geiger had pleaded with them to get on the plane and do the show. Elektra, who had set up meet-and-greets and publicity, were not pleased and it was a foolish thing for the band to do. But this was the life: a million miles from Swinton, in the sun, shades on, cruising down Hollywood Boulevard in a red soft-top Chrysler LeBaron listening to The Doors' *LA Woman* on Gold Radio...fuck the gig in San Francisco and keep this vibe rolling. They were the Mondays and this was their time, the hippest band in the UK making an album in Los Angeles. *Los Angeles!* All they had to do was transfer the feeling onto record.

BOOK THREE
Stardust

19
Pills 'n' Thrills and Bellyaches

'Coming into the album we were on top of the world – not scared of anything,' said Whelan. 'It was a beautiful day outside every day: sunshine,' said Paul. 'That influenced the music, we were getting a different feel for things.'

After their recent gig at the Hollywood Palladium, Happy Mondays were the hottest, hippest new band in LA. They were the English lads everyone wanted to befriend. Factory and Elektra had rewarded the band by booking time in the studios at Capitol Records, a Hollywood landmark; to enter the building, the Mondays would walk past all four Beatles' Walk of Fame stars every day. Capitol was on Hollywood and Vine, the centre of the city's showbiz district, near Sunset Strip – a place where dreams came true. And the Mondays were living the dream, cruising down Sunset Boulevard and onto Hollywood Boulevard, the sheen on their hire cars sparkling in the sun, high on the best marijuana the city had to offer. Even New Order did not get this treatment.

Paul Oakenfold and Steve Osborne called Capitol the best studios in the world. In the basement complex some of the world's greatest music had been created; it had been a home for Frank Sinatra, Nat King Cole and The Beach Boys, who cut the famous *Pet Sounds* here. Oakenfold and Osborne had created a minor buzz in the UK with their mixes of the Mondays' tracks, particularly 'Wrote For

Luck' and 'Hallelujah', but this was their first major production job
after their work on 'Step On', their first time producing an album.
Oakenfold, fresh from the Hacienda tour of the US, had contacts in
LA and would DJ small and hip nights while he was there, but this
was his and Osborne's moment too. This was their gateway to multi-
platinum careers and ultimately, for Oakenfold, to superstar status.

The Mondays had seven songs and they were only booked into
the expensive Capitol studio for a week. In fact the dream was something of a mirage, as Factory and Elektra expected them to then
find a cheaper, less conspicuous home to record in. But the band
and their producers started out on such a high, the work in the
studio so remarkable, that the dream never ended: they were able
to force their labels to submit to paying for another three weeks
in Capitol's opulent surrounds. 'Kinky Afro' was the first track the
band recorded. It already sounded like a smash hit single, another
supreme moment, one to top even 'Step On'.

Osborne was hands-on, instrumental in getting the ultimate
'baggy' drum and bass on the track to groove. For a novice producer his talent for song arrangement was astounding. He too
was feeling good, the band's mood infectious. This was not the
intense live recording of *Squirrel* or *Bummed* but a more relaxed way
of working, the studio becoming another instrument. But Osborne
and Oakenfold had no great masterplan. 'Records tend to make
themselves,' said Osborne. 'It's about the vibe in the studio and
what people decide to do on certain days, which is affected by
what's going on around you.'

The band felt increasingly at home. They became pals with some
of the Mancunian, but chiefly Liverpudlian lads, organising Acid
House club nights in the city – Ecstasy was just arriving underground and weed and coke were plentiful. Their apartments were
lush and the sun shone. The backbiting and bitterness that had crept
into the band was held at bay. 'It felt good even though we were
carrying a lot of baggage by now,' said Mark Day, admitting that
it needed something successful to keep the band together. Shaun
had got himself a huge lump of opium and was happily stoned.
Mark Day's girlfriend Jane and Paul's partner Alison and their two
kids gave proceedings an air of maturity. Each band member, apart

from bassist and drummer, recorded separately so there was no sense of cabin fever or frayed nerves, just an easy rhythm. When the band members were together in the studio, listening to the playbacks, the mood was always encouraging and positive. 'There was never any tension in the studio,' said Osborne. There was none of the uptightness of Cale or the madness of Hannett, no *Apocalypse Now* scenarios deep into the night. Osborne ran a tight ship: the session started at midday and ended at midnight. Paul had never been happier, the sound the band were making was a progression from their first two albums and still distinctly their own. The whole groove of the record was down to his lovely, lazy style of bass playing – it sounded big. 'Absolutely the key part of the sound of the band,' said Osborne. Paul was so laid back he even let Osborne play bass on one song, telling the producer he thought it sounded better when he played it.

Whelan called the experience the band's 'first proper adult recording session'. He enjoyed the experience of recording his drums, creating loops from four bars of what he'd played and then playing over the loop. Whelan laid down the groove on another golden moment for the band, 'God's Cop', playing along with Oakenfold as he spun records. Oakenfold's record collection was his instrument, and he had his decks set up in the studio. He used his vinyl to suggest a mood or feel, sometimes to create loops to build a song around.

'Loose Fit', a third jewel, came from Paul and Oakenfold jamming in the studio. 'It was a different way of working,' said Paul. 'The other two albums hurt my ears a bit, the tone wasn't right on the bass. This one was a real clear production, easier on the ears. Oakenfold was great at getting those loops I wanted but as for everything else it was always Steve. He really helped with arrangements, something that we weren't very good at, still not knowing when to start and when to stop. The sounds on that album, the bass and the synths and drums, that's all Steve getting those sounds.'

Mark Day continued his understated journey to becoming the era's most innovative guitar player. 'He came up with amazing riffs,' said Osborne. But it was more than just the melodic guitar lines that buoyed the songs – and in some instances defined them

– but the textures and moods he seemed able to create. He enjoyed the stability and structure Osborne offered the band, the regular hours and polished sound. 'It was how it should be,' he said. 'Go in there, turn the guitar up loud, give it a load of distortion.'

The band were so relaxed they planned to record a cover of 'Everybody's Talkin'', made famous by Harry Nilsson in the film *Midnight Cowboy*. A plaintive song said to be about the rejection of fame and the return to the simple life, it was also possibly about heroin. Accompanied by Oakenfold, the band tried it out, one of the few times they played live in the studio. Steered by Oakenfold, they moved away from the idea of covering 'Everybody's Talkin'' but kept something of its feel. With a fuller drum groove, and the addition of acoustic guitar and a lazy bass line with a double bass sound, they were able to create the album's fourth inspired moment, 'Bob's Yer Uncle'.

Everything they touched was turning to gold. This was music that would define the era, a unique sound, rare alchemy at work. Paul was so happy with the music, the band, his life, he asked Alison to marry him. And there being no time like the present, he arranged for the ceremony to take place in Los Angeles while they were there. Day recalled that Whelan and Davis were 'spaced out' and missed the wedding.

The members of the band were falling into a routine: recording for extremely long hours, but then regularly blowing it out of their systems. Each had their own car, Bez as usual crashing on a regular basis, including one incident in which he started an argument with a couple of Mexicans before punching someone as the police were called. He ended up hiding in the studio for two days. On a night out, he'd turned down advances from film superstar Julia Roberts, although he hadn't realised who she was – *Pretty Woman* had only been out a few months. 'She quite obviously fancied Bez, she was talking to him all night,' said Whelan. 'The next day Bez came into the studio and we were asking, How did you get on?'

Bez said, 'Oh Julie, nice girl, Julie, really cool, but we left and she went off somewhere else, nothing happened.'

Shaun said, 'You fucking dick, it's Julia Roberts.' To which Bez replied, 'Who's Julia Roberts?'

The band had also failed to recognise The Cult's singer Ian Astbury — who lived in Los Angeles — on his repeated visits to Capitol to see the band record. 'Looking back, we were pretty sedated,' said Whelan. Bez calmed down a bit when his girlfriend Debs flew over, the two in a new hire car cruising Los Angeles feeling 'like millionaires'.

The others seemed to have taken the chance to turn down the volume on the usual anarchic routine. Paul Davis managed to put on almost two stone on a daily breakfast diet of steak and eggs. But the Mondays were not choirboys. It was here at Capitol that Davis picked up the nickname PD. It came from the studio's chief engineer, an old-timer called Ray Blair. Bez would have a lot to say about how the band should sound in the studio, but playing percussion on record was beyond him, and Blair had booked LA's lead session percussionist, Tony Castro, to play on the album. Blair didn't like the band smoking joints in the studio and reacted badly to the smell of cocaine being smoked in a spliff. 'Ray shouts, Hey PD, get the hell out of here,' said Paul. 'He didn't like it and I don't blame him, the smell was fucking awful. PD stuck, he was PD from then on.'

In the aftermath of the Glastonbury fall-out, which had since become legendary amongst the music press in the UK — the more so since the Mondays, for once, were unable to provide their account, allowing others to fill in the blanks — crews from two English TV shows, BBC's *Rapido* and the new Channel 4 show *The Word*, flew across to interview the band — largely, one suspects, to see whether they had brought their bad boy behaviour with them. There was certainly no real talk about music, the band now mining offbeat influences such as The Residents, Captain Beefheart (a favourite of Bez's) or the Stevie Wonder album, *(Journey Through) The Secret Life of Plants*.

Instead, there was an interview with a grumpy Shaun, at his monosyllabic worst, displeased after finally escaping the pressure of England to find it chasing him out here, and most memorably a mistake from Bez which made the band sound stupid and high-lighted just how unpolished and unprotected they were. Asked about future dates in Japan and what they knew about the country,

Bez said: 'I've heard it's wild, full of Chinese.' The rest of the band burst out laughing.

Manager McGough could not control what came out of their mouths, but he mismanaged these interviews, and neither really benefited the band, while another filmed interview with MTV became a farce when he mixed up the times. Alongside Tony Wilson, McGough was one of the chief reasons the band was here now, but there was a feeling he was enjoying himself a little too much in Los Angeles. While the band knuckled down, he partied 'a lot', said Paul. 'Nathan was as rock 'n' roll as the band, let's just say that,' said Osborne. Back in Manchester, Alan Erasmus had suggested the band needed a more experienced and heavyweight manager, particularly in terms of the American industry, who would supervise McGough, but Tony Wilson had stopped listening to his long-time partner.

Much of the band's cohesion was down to Shaun, who had pulled himself together in Los Angeles. Osborne had insisted he come to the studio every day to work, even if it was just to sing a few lines, and in his apartment he worked hard on his lyrics. Much of his newfound contentment and commitment was due to the seventeen grams of opium he scored – a drug with a history of inspiring romantic poets such as Percy Shelley and pop culture heavyweights such as Lenny Bruce, who described the experience of smoking opium in the following terms: 'I'll die young but it's like kissing God.' The drug calmed and inspired him. He reached deep into himself to produce the words for the sublime tunes he heard in the studio, for the first time working on paper, staring hard at ten poems and giving them serious thought.

He was not all blissed-out good spirit. He found it hilarious that, having long tried to get the drummer to try opiates, he'd tricked Whelan into smoking opium, tearing off a piece of the squidgy black lump and passing it off as hashish. And when it came to Mark Day, who'd wanted his girlfriend Jane to come to the studio to see what was going on, 'Shaun had a go,' said Day. 'All his drug dealer pals and scally mates could come but not my girlfriend. That sums it up.'

But, at the microphone, he was at his very best. And despite what he'd written, flights of fancy would still come tripping off his tongue, made up on the spot. Every day he and Osborne went about the same dance: Shaun pleaded with the producer that he didn't feel like doing his vocals, wasn't in the mood, and Osborne would talk him round. 'I knew from doing "Step On", Shaun's not somebody who is a super-confident vocalist,' said Osborne. 'Doing vocals for Shaun was not an easy thing.' Shaun even tried to get Whelan to sing 'Harmony', imagining it would be like The Beatles, where drummer Ringo often took on an album track. 'He wanted me to do it in a Ringo voice,' said Whelan. No chance. But Osborne's plan was working. Shaun was no perfectionist, but he worked harder than he ever had on his vocals and delivered not just some of his best lyrics but his most nuanced singing.

Shaun didn't like people in the control room, aside from the producer, when he was doing his vocals, but he had got used to Whelan hanging around 'a bit'. 'He liked the fact I used to buzz off his lyrics,' said Whelan. 'With "Kinky Afro" I didn't know what he was going to sing and I heard him start with "Son I'm thirty, I only went with your mother 'cos she's dirty", and I thought, Fucking hell, that is the best two opening lines I've ever heard, that is going to be huge – it sent shivers down my spine.'

Shaun, while writing the best lyrics of his life – 'Loose Fit' was inspired by the first televised war, the Gulf War that followed Iraq's invasion of Kuwait – continued to take liberally from a variety of sources. 'Kinky Afro' had in part been musically influenced by Paul listening to British soul band Hot Chocolate – the bass line to 'Brother Louie' had been an inspiration – and Shaun took the line 'no spook in my family' from the same song. He claimed to have taken the 'Yippee-ippee-ey-ey-ay-yey-yey' vocal hook from the movie *Die Hard*, although it was also reminiscent of Labelle's 'Lady Marmalade'.

Elsewhere he borrowed from Stretch's 'Why Did You Do It' (on 'Bob's Yer Uncle'), Donovan's 'Sunshine Superman' (on 'Donovan') and the New Seekers' 'I'd Like to Teach the World to Sing' (on 'Harmony'). For 'Holiday', a track on which the band sampled the seminal twelve-inch by Change, 'A Lover's Holiday', he drew inspiration from past hassles with customs officers. On 'Dennis and Lois', musically inspired by Stevie Wonder's 'Superstition', he referenced a book about the Kray Twins he was reading – *The Profession of Violence* by John Pearson – writing about the schoolboy 'Midget's Club' at Repton Boys Club where the Krays had learned to box. It continued the tradition of boxing references on the band's albums. On 'Bob's Yer Uncle', he sang a lyric full of sexual yearning in a deep husky voice.

It was the band at their most seductive and sublime, a moment of sudden maturity and the first track Wilson heard of the new material. He'd flown into Los Angeles with some trepidation, worrying that the band might have spent the past four weeks simply partying. He was blown away by 'Bob's Yer Uncle' – he would request that it be played alongside Joy Division's 'Atmosphere' at his funeral. In it he heard five years of promise come to fruition, and it was the moment he realised he was right, that his committed backing of the band, which had so alienated some of his best friends, was worthwhile, that they had created everlasting music. 'It was a real golden moment,' he said. 'I think I knew from then on that this would be one of the great Factory albums, actually one of the great British albums of the age.'

The Mondays flew back from LA on 25 August 1990. They'd been out in America for seven weeks, almost four of them in the studio. The band members, separately, put the finishing touches to the new album with Oakenfold and Osborne at Eden Studios in London, where Rowetta also added her backing vocals. McGough, back in the UK, started putting key arrangements in place, determined to achieve success with the album 'in as many markets as possible'. Aside from their US deal with Elektra, Factory's ad hoc licensing arrangements were far from ideal; the guy who handled their releases in Portugal, for instance, was just a fan of Factory who'd started his own label. The only sizeable European label Factory dealt with was Rough Trade Germany. McGough found even basic information such as sales figures hard to obtain, and was frustrated in his attempts to co-ordinate a European strategy for the band. With Wilson's blessing, and for a sizeable advance (split between Factory and the band), he negotiated a licensing and distribution agreement with major label London Records for the new album. For McGough it meant he had a clear idea what the release dates were, what would be spent on marketing campaigns and where he needed to take the Mondays for promotion. 'It was all centralised,' he said. Despite the sense that McGough was behaving too much as if he was in the band, this was another shrewd and well-executed move.

On 12 September, Mark Day returned to Manchester from a day in Eden with the final mix of the album. He listened to it coming home on the train. 'Fucking hell, this is it,' he thought. This album was going to be a massive seller, the one that propelled the band to new levels. 'I was buzzing.' He laughed to think of Paul Davis, who'd been suggesting replacing Shaun with Rowetta: Shaun had sung brilliantly on the album. It all sounded really clear and up, his guitar had never sounded better. This was it. He got home and proposed to Jane. 'I thought we could start a family now, get out of this two up two down, things are going to be happening this year,' he said.

Shaun was also expecting big things from the album. In the media he'd started talking more and more about doing this 'for the money' or how much he 'loved' money. He had kept the band going for seven years without any, so there had to be other motivations. His young girlfriend Trisha was pregnant too – although this was not made public, so perhaps he was hoping to provide security for them. But all the talk of selling hundreds of thousands of albums, and of 'Kinky Afro', lined up to be the album's first single, being a work of genius lyrically, had started to turn his head. And, back in Manchester, the drugs, not opium or Mexican weed but heroin and freebased cocaine, had quickly got a grip on him. He knew, McGough had told him, that legally a lyric writer was entitled to fifty per cent of a song's publishing copyright (a hit can be worth £100,000, often more over a lifetime, plus copyright of seventy years, earning money every time it is played on the radio or used in films or adverts). Separate from the income from record sales and live shows that all six members shared equally, this was considered to be the most lucrative portion of any band's earnings. Prior to this moment, the band – minus Bez – had decided to share the song publishing equally, taking twenty per cent each.

Shaun even felt he was being magnanimous in only demanding forty per cent of the song publishing when he could, legally, take fifty. He was giving the band ten per cent more to share, doing them a favour. Paul Davis's response pretty much summed up how the rest of them felt: 'You're giving me fuck all.' It was an issue that had split many bands, a source of tension within most, and Tony Wilson was keenly aware of the virtue of a band sharing their publishing equally. He had even warned the Mondays that should they not follow that model they would not be 'right' for Factory. Now it was too late. 'We'd been a Commie band, everyone's equal, everyone gets the same, but then Shaun decided he didn't want to be a Commie,' said Paul.

It was hard not to see greed and to feel upset – although perhaps not for Bez, to whom Shaun had promised five of his forty per cent. Mark Day wondered why he was working his balls off when Shaun, who didn't appear to be, was getting more than twice as much as he was. And then he thought, if Shaun was getting more than him, then he wanted a greater share than Paul Davis. The same thought crossed Paul Ryder's mind. Not only had Shaun shattered the band's fragile peace, he'd caused fresh animosities. The end of the band had already begun.

'That's when the band started to split up,' said Whelan. 'Shaun says it too but the irony is Shaun started it. If he hadn't done what he did then the other two wouldn't have done what they did.' Whelan and Paul Davis were called into a meeting with business manager Eric Longley and told that both Mark Day and Paul Ryder wanted to increase their percentages, which meant decreasing theirs. They asked why, said Whelan, and were informed that, as guitar players, Ryder and Day felt they were instrumental in writing the songs, 'whereas drums and keyboards aren't'. The Mondays had never been a band where one member brought a song in complete; the material had always grown out of endless jamming in the rehearsal room, often starting out with just drums and bass. 'It was a bone of contention,' said Whelan. Whelan recognised it for what it was: stupid, all about ego, not really money. He felt a tremendous sense of disappointment, but he was prepared to move on, although the issue was 'always at the back of my mind'. Davis couldn't.

'The moment we walked out of that meeting PD had left the band emotionally,' he said.

'Kinky Afro' was put on the A-list by Radio 1 and would receive heavy rotation. The video – shot by The Bailey Brothers in Granada Studios – showed the band miming to the song, surrounded by a handful of beautiful grooving female models, one of whom happened to be Gary Whelan's new girlfriend, Vanessa. The video captured none of the euphoria of 'Wrote For Luck' or 'Step On', and to some extent the band looked awkward, but it was also safe, easy on the eye. TV stations around the world could show it without fear of causing offence – and did. The song was single of the week in the *NME* – with Jack Barron writing: 'Prime time Rolling Stones are the Mondays' true godfathers...like them the Mondays bolt the lust and violence of great rock 'n' roll onto the blues and soul of black music' – and in *Melody Maker*, 'a stunning return to form' for the 'genuinely unique' band.

Tony Wilson rhapsodised about the song's lyric, suggesting it was 'the greatest poem about parenthood' since Yeats's 'Prayer for my Daughter'. The rest of the band knew better than to think too much about what the words meant, or whether they meant anything at all.

Although the Roses had gone to ground, The Charlatans, The Farm, Primal Scream and Inspiral Carpets were all scoring their biggest hits to date. Flowered Up and Northside promised to follow them into the mainstream charts after both gaining indie number ones. Undoubtedly popular as it still was, there was a sense of homogeneity and caricature now about the combination of House music, indie rock, Ecstasy and baggy fashion. This, combined with the now well-publicised gang problems in Manchester clubs and the establishment clampdown on Acid House parties, encouraged the UK media to talk up a new scene, 'shoegaze', a droning, guitar-heavy music popularised by southern bands such as Ride, Slowdive and Lush. The remarkable moment in time had passed; a Madchester backlash was in the air, enough with the northern oiks.

Factory, though, had a great deal riding on the Happy Mondays now. Not only had they invested heavily in the new album, new signings Northside and The Wendys were essentially tethered to them. There was no new album from New Order imminent, even a suggestion that they might never record another. Peter Hook's solo project, Revenge, continued to sell poorly and Bernard Sumner's more promising project with Johnny Marr, Electronic, had so far only amounted to one single – although an album was promised, Factory only had the UK rights. The new, hugely impressive Factory offices on Charles Street had just opened – a giant leap from Alan Erasmus's Palatine Road flat – and the bill was said to be close to £1 million. The decision over whether to extend The Hacienda's licence was still in the balance and the further £1 million Factory had recently invested in the building that housed the club would seem ill-advised if it was forced to close. Even now, as the management were forced to crack down on drug-taking in an attempt to extend the club's licence, numbers had dropped dramatically and the atmosphere had all but evaporated. Factory needed the Mondays album to be a worldwide hit.

In the UK, Happy Mondays' return breathed new life into the Madchester scene. Here was a band who seemed to offer something genuinely new. 'Kinky Afro' entered the Top 40 at number twenty and the band recorded their third appearance on *Top of the Pops*. Shaun wore his coat jacket buttoned and swayed slightly with his hands in his pockets. His new, if ill-advised, bowl cut hairstyle fringed his eyes and he smirked periodically. The band grooved convincingly, Whelan's long hair swishing with the beat and Bez, in white, dancing enthusiastically. The single climbed the charts to peak at number five – the band's second top five single. The Mondays, or more often than not just Shaun, were featured on a glut of front covers: *NME, Melody Maker, Vox, Record Mirror, Number One, Rave, Avanti* and *Rage*. He looked roguishly handsome (he'd started receiving love letters from admiring teenage girls) and regurgitated once more exaggerated stories of his and the band's past. It seemed to be working: the Mondays were routinely characterised as mad, bad, criminal and dangerous – 'the coolest band in the world', 'one of the last mad, bad rebel groups'.

Shaun was holed up in the plush Halcyon Hotel in upmarket Kensington with Trisha to handle the press interviews. He seemed to have the world at his feet, room service on tap, and it was difficult not to fall into rock 'n' roll caricature in this new fantasy world. Whichever way you looked at it, there was no doubt now that Happy Mondays were genuine rock stars, Shaun the biggest of all. His ego was massaged, the supply of drugs constant and the trappings of fame seductive.

But he was twenty-eight now and still part of him felt insecure about all this: that it would never last. He only had to look at the ill spirit in the band every time they met up to remind him of that. And he wasn't stupid. How much longer before Madchester blew out completely? And then what?

Part of him enjoyed all this – the doubt as his fame grew greater, the blanket of heroin, the sense that he wasn't sure exactly who he was any more as his press profile ate him up. It was classic, what all troubled rock stars had to go through. But his street instinct was still sharp and it kept coming back to this: make money while the going was good.

Bez had already seen which way the wind was blowing. His measly five per cent of the song publishing had come too late. Beneath the fug of drugs, the group's 26-year-old figurehead was a shy and deep-thinking young man. This wasn't the same gang of pals he'd joined in 1985. He sold his story to the *News of the World* – 'Jailhouse past of the Happy Mondays rocker' – for a reputed £8000, and was quoted as saying: 'Being in a band has saved me but now crime has gone it has left a big gap in my life. I get bored. I miss the buzz. I used to enjoy it.' He also spoke of his past dalliances with 'weed, acid, smack, speed and cocaine'.

The deal seemed to have Shaun's paws all over it. He'd admitted to selling stories to the tabloids in the past, even handing out his home number to select journalists at the *Sun*. And indeed, Shaun now gave the *Sun* an exclusive about his drug past for an undisclosed sum. Under a headline that read 'My Heroin Hell', he recounted a visit to rehab, at the '£160-a-day' Priory hospital, recalling how he discharged himself after he was found drinking beer in his room. As well as heroin addiction there was mention of his crack habit.

It seems unlikely that either gave any thought to how these 'exclusives' would impact on the band; they were rather more con-cerned with the impact on their pockets. But such was the image of the Mondays, such stories did little to dent the band's commercial prospects. 'You'd have thought it would have completely ruined it but it didn't,' said Paul. 'It was the rock star thing to do,' said Whelan. 'You get success, then after that there's some sort of addiction and then rehab, isn't that what you do?'

Jeff Barrett had quit as Factory PR to focus on his own expanding indie record label, Heavenly, home to Flowered Up, Manic Street Preachers and St Etienne. The Mondays' and Factory's new PR, Jayne Houghton, formerly Barrett's number two, told the press that Shaun had now 'kicked the habit'. In a statement she said: 'Shaun has a lot of teenage fans and he does not want them to think it is cool to use heroin. The matter is over and done with and Shaun is fine now.' There was nothing privately to suggest Shaun was in any way serious about kicking his habit. But it was not, for now, getting in the way of the band's activities 'at all', said Whelan. They had long come to accept that Shaun and Bez were what the press wanted, and while tensions simmered, they did nothing to prevent it from happening and just rolled with the media circus that they had become accustomed to. The one exception was when Shaun and Bez did an interview for *Penthouse* magazine photographed in a bubble bath with three topless models, boasting about having just bought a BMW 325i. For the rest of the band it was a complete sell-out; it turned them into just another washout group who would do anything for a pay cheque. Even McGough, whose proximity to Shaun was being increasingly questioned by the band, felt that there was a risk of it backfiring, especially when *NME* used the photos with the caption 'lather louts in these groovy out-takes from … top undressed chicks mag'.

Shaun had chosen to call the new album *Pills 'n' Thrills and Bellyaches*, a title that came 'off the top of his head'. 'We were trying to come up with something mature, a rock classic title,' he said, 'but we thought fuck it, just give it something that everyone's expecting.' The album was said to have 150,000 pre-orders and was expected to debut at number one, which would have been a first for the band. It was given a nine out of ten rating in *NME* by Stuart Maconie, who called it 'the trendiest music in the world'. 'Guitars are back on the Mondays agenda with a vengeance,' he wrote, praising 'a huge fractured delta blues riff that runs through God's Cop'. In *Record Mirror* the album was given four and a half stars out of five – 'sheer class'. In *Sounds* it was four out of five – 'the guitar consistently elevates potentially mundane tracks to greatness...Happy Mondays are so far ahead in their disorganised progress that they have left behind the culture they represent.'

Factory pushed the boat out at a launch party for the album, on 5 November, at London Zoo in Regent's Park. The group travelled there separately, Bez and Mark Day bumping into each other on the train. 'Second class,' said Day. 'Everything was budget for us.' Whelan travelled down from Manchester on a coach organised by Factory, one of many the label filled full of Mancunian party-goers. Paul was already in London, holed up at a hotel. 'I had my little one with me in a pram at the party,' he said. 'I just went down for a mooch and then went back early and sat snugly in the bar at the hotel.'

The 'star-studded' party made the Showbiz page in the *Sun*: 'Happy Monday party guests go ape in zoo'. The story suggested that Bananarama, Morrissey, The Farm and Radio 1 DJ Gary Davies were at the £10,000 album launch, during which 'hundreds of boozed up ravers caused mayhem'. It was reported that someone had 'hurled a park bench into a tank full of expensive giant koi carp', someone else had 'provoked the zoo's gorilla into a violent rage by rattling his cage and shouting obscenities', while others 'urinated on flower-beds and openly took drugs'. The zoo's miniature train was also derailed.

Pills 'n' Thrills and Bellyaches came dressed in another Central Station cover collage – this time of popular American sweet wrappers, with the name and the band and title in distinct and stylised cartoon lettering. Mick Jagger and David Bowie were said to be fans of the designers, having seen their recent exhibition at Manchester City Art Gallery. The album entered the UK charts at number four – the Mondays were unable to shift 'best of' albums by Elton John and Madonna – on its way to sales of around 400,000 during a remarkable twenty-six weeks on the charts. This was the Mondays' artistic and commercial peak in the UK, the album that in future would regularly be voted into lists of the greatest ever made.

The band had a highly lucrative short tour of the UK planned during which they would play a series of stadiums. The Stone Roses meanwhile had run out of momentum. Though they were supposed to be writing a follow-up album to their eponymous 1989 hit, their creativity had dried up and the group spirit was lost. Instead they had spent much of the year fighting charges of criminal damage after attacking the offices of a former record label with paint. Although they had avoided jail, a very real threat, and escaped with a fine, they were now at war with their current label. They were preparing to go to the High Court in a bid to escape their contract, leaving them free to sign to American label Geffen for a reported $4 million advance.

The slow disintegration of the Roses, who would win the High Court case in May 1991, during the Madchester boom period, did much to weaken the movement. After Spike Island they would not tour again until 1995, and 'One Love' would not be followed up until 1994. The Mondays were the winners of Wilson's phoney war, but perhaps they would have benefited from the Roses sticking around a little longer – for instance, the Roses never played America during this era and Madchester was denied its most potent twin-headed attack in that country.

For now, though, it was *Pills 'n' Thrills* and the Mondays that abated – or at least postponed – the Madchester backlash. It was full steam ahead to take this very special group and their third astonishing album in a row around the world, to Europe, America and Japan, where the bonds that held them together, already stretched almost to the limit, would get stretched a little further.

20
World

On the day Margaret Thatcher resigned as Prime Minister, 23 November 1990, the Mondays appeared at Whitley Bay Ice Rink, the first in a sold-out seven-date UK tour of huge 10,000-plus-capacity venues. The UK was slipping back into recession. Manufacturing was down, bankruptcies up, inflation at its highest since 1981 and unemployment rising again; it was soon to hit 2.4 million, with Labour accusing the Tories of fraudulently fixing the figures to hide a further one million who were without work. John Major took over as Prime Minister with Labour well ahead in the polls.

Thatcher had resigned a deeply unpopular and divisive figure, the Poll Tax riots a highly explosive reminder of her poisonous effect. She was widely vilified in the indie music scene – The Smiths had called for her head in a song, The Stone Roses had said it was a shame the Brighton Bomb had not done for her, and Paul Weller was a long-time and outspoken critic. Happy Mondays had never talked about politics in print but many journalists had written about them in relation to Thatcher's long rule, during their rise, as emblematic of the forgotten north's downtrodden and unemployed council estate underclass, a consequence of her policies. More recently Shaun, the contrarian, had to the band's horror said he'd vote Tory, if it meant paying less tax, and professed a warped admiration for Thatcher. 'We listened to her every word and said,

Right bitch, we'll take you at your word. I've got to fucking cheer the bitch 'cos she got me off my arse.'

Later he expanded on this view: 'Thatcher turned straight people into criminals. We dealt, we did the lot. We sold Evian water that came straight out the tap. They called us criminals but the way we saw it, we were enterprising business people. She laid the cards out and us people had no choice but to play her fucking game. All that applies to us . . . and millions of others.'

In a way, Shaun was right. The chemical generation had taken the Thatcher ideology of unrestrained entrepreneurialism and the mid-80s collapse in employment and applied it to their own desperate situation, organising parties, selling pills, making clothes and records, DJing, bootlegging, selling tickets. The Mondays were not Thatcherites, yet Shaun's comments would in time come back to bite him.

Prior to the gig in Whitley Bay there was a bomb scare. 'It was some bloke trying to put on an Irish accent,' said Whelan. 'The police traced the call back to the house right next to the ice rink and they arrested him within ten minutes.' The man had been upset over the noise levels. 'It was the first time we'd had a quad PA system,' said Paul. 'Speakers at the back, in the corner and at the front, and you could do tricks with this joystick, spinning the sound around the room.' Bez walked out on stage having 'forgotten how big we'd actually become' and 'nearly died'. He said he was 'physically hit by a wall of sound from the crowd'. Bodies were pulled over the barriers before the band had even started. 'The music sounded massive,' he said. The Mondays had invested much of their own money in sound and lighting equipment. On stage they had their own 10k rig rather than simple foldback, so they got a taste of what the audience was getting. 'They wanted a gig as well,' said Derek.

The band's crew remained tight, the same reliable eight faces, and the gigs ran smoothly, although on stage the band remained unpredictable. At the second date, at Wembley Arena, the *Daily Mirror* claimed the 'brat rockers' had halted the sell-out show, in front of 12,000 fans, while Shaun and Paul Davis 'threw instruments and yelled foul-mouthed abuse at one another'. The *Guardian*, at the same show, called the band 'rock 'n' roll counter-revolutionaries' making a 'rough and magical noise'.

Not everyone was convinced. To some, although the band had never sounded better, or bigger, it appeared Shaun was going through the motions. He never soundchecked, and he sat down on the drum riser for extended periods, leaving Bez and Rowetta – in black leather corset, thigh-high boots and brandishing a cat o' nine tails – to entertain the crowd. He seemed strangely absent and disconnected on stage, and there were grumbles over the price of tickets, £15, especially considering the band was still turning in short sixty-minute sets. While the Mondays had revelled in earlier comparisons to the Sex Pistols, this seemed more akin to the great rock 'n' roll swindle. But it wasn't as if the band were making fortunes; they had spent much of the projected profit on hiring in and transporting extra sound and lighting systems.

An unguarded Bez said he felt they'd let fans down as the mammoth dates continued in Glasgow, Birmingham, Manchester and Dublin. At Manchester G-Mex on 29 November, there was little of the triumphalism that had surrounded the band's appearance earlier in the year. The place was packed, but it felt more like a show than an event now. The mood in the band had been badly affected by a full-scale brawl between Shaun and Paul earlier in the day. They'd argued inside McGough's office about the song publishing, and the fight had spilled out into the middle of the street. On stage, inter-band grievances bubbled beneath the surface, but they managed to hold it together.

The band were in a better mood, the fight quickly forgotten, on 19 December as they partied with Paul McCartney and Bill Wyman at the Q magazine awards. The Mondays were nominated for album of the year and Osborne and Oakenfold won the best producer award. From the evening emerged the McCartney quote: 'The Mondays reminded me of The Beatles in our Magic Mystery Tour phase.'

'It was like, Yes, fucking hell, that's amazing,' said Paul. 'I had it on my wall,' said Whelan, the band's Beatle obsessive. 'But I couldn't see it, maybe he was trying to be hip at the time.' The NME and Melody Maker voted Pills 'n' Thrills the best album of the year.

Shaun was on the 1990 Christmas issue covers of both *Melody Maker* – with Bernard Sumner, dressed as wise men – and *NME*, where he clutched a bottle of Jack Daniel's beside Bez, dressed as Father Christmas and holding a large, comic spliff. Despite the band's rich and diverse musical output over three albums, drugs and drug dealing were the dominant theme of the interviews – much to the exasperation of Shaun, who complained that 'Nobody wants to talk about music anymore, they just want to hear crazy stories.' Whether he was being ironic about this, since he had been the prime peddler of such a line of narrative for years, is anyone's guess.

Shaun was also on the covers of *Q* magazine, new music monthly *Select* and *Vox*, where he was asked to pose with an object that had been 'particularly significant' to him during 1990. Shaun chose a Kit Kat, stating 'they've kept me going through our long arduous tour this year'. What he didn't mention was that he would throw away the chocolate and use the foil to smoke heroin from. In appreciation, Rowntree's, who didn't know the full story, sent him four boxes of Kit Kats to take on the next tour.

'The only other person who had more front covers than Shaun in the UK in 1990 was Princess Diana,' said McGough. 'This, for a lad who was where he was from, who has not been well served by the education system, where they probably told him he was never going to amount to anything, was difficult to deal with. All of a sudden he was hugely famous and notorious and everywhere – it really became like a huge phenomenon. Heroin is a narcotic, a pain-killer, a good place to hide, like rolling yourself up in bubble wrap. For Shaun it was a safe place. The thing is, unless you're a very organised, functioning heroin addict it impacts on every other aspect of your work, life and family, and Shaun's not someone who is organised about heroin supply. So it started to get problematic.'

In early January 1991 The Hacienda won a six-month reprieve in its expensive licensing battle. But after reports that his doorman had been threatened with automatic weapons, Tony Wilson announced the closure of the club, stating that it would reopen when it could be run in 'a safe manner'. The closure, intended to send out a message to police and gangsters alike, would last three months and was later estimated to have cost the label £200,000. It came at a time when Factory were buoyed by sales of the best-selling Mondays album and felt they could take the hit, but unlike earlier years when a New Order album could fund a year of fun, the label was now dangerously stretched. With the country back in recession after a period of rapid economic growth, interest rates were rising and property prices falling. Not only were Factory paying higher interest on the £2 million borrowed to buy and renovate the new headquarters and the Hacienda building, but the value of both properties had plummeted to less than half of what they'd paid for them.

Yet despite the problems the city's gangsters had caused at The Hacienda, for Wilson these powerful, rich, often young men, living beyond all society's norms, had something of a glamorous bad boy appeal. Shaun felt the same way. 'Shaun loved it all,' said Mark Day. 'He loved all the gangster movie films. The gangsters all wanted privileges. It was a spider's web, how do I get out of this. I kept saying, Someone's going to end up dying.'

On 12 January 1991, the Mondays were in London shooting a new video for 'Step On'. It was to be directed by famed French fashion photographer and video maker Jean Baptiste Mondino, who had made videos for acts such as Madonna, David Bowie and Prince. In America, Elektra Records were convinced that with the *Pills 'n' Thrills* album the Mondays had a shot at breaking into the mainstream. The band's US tour the previous summer had created ripples of excitement and, even without any band promotion, 'Kinky Afro' had risen to number one on the *Billboard* Modern Rock chart. It was quite an achievement, but Elektra hoped the album would do better still, and hit the Top 40 of the *Billboard* Hot 100.

There was a huge six-week American tour scheduled for March, with the band scheduled to visit uncharted territory away from the main cities: they were still willing to work hard in the effort to succeed in a market where many English indie bands had failed. As part of the push Elektra planned to re-release 'Step On' to help promote the *Pills 'n' Thrills* album, which would be released to coincide with the tour. British rock/dance records by EMF and Jesus Jones had recently reached number one in the *Billboard* Hot 100 singles chart. Although when Shaun, accompanied by McGough, flew out to New York to undertake a couple of days' promotional work in preparation for the tour, he said the two bands were 'full of bullshit', there was hope 'Step On' might now follow them to the top of the US charts.

In the UK, the Mondays' transition from underground cult band to chart-topping superstars was cemented by nominations for Best Group and Best Newcomer at the Brits, the British Phonographic Industry's annual glitzy, corporate pop music awards – the UK's answer to America's Grammys. Oakenfold and Osborne were also nominated for Best British Producer. On 18 January, the Mondays capped their triumphant year by playing Wembley Arena, for a third time in under a year, as part of the Brits-affiliated Great British Music Weekend, which was being heavily trailered before its live broadcast on Radio 1. The Mondays headlined a Madchester-styled Friday night bill that also included The Farm, James, 808 State and Northside. They kicked off with 'Step On', but Shaun brought proceedings to a halt thirty seconds in, despite the show being broadcast live. 'Start the fucking thing again,' he demanded. It was a short, lacklustre set from the Mondays, though it ended with a surging 'Wrote For Luck'.

When it became clear that there was to be no encore the audience began booing, but by then Shaun was backstage flicking through *Penthouse*. 'I didn't know it was taken so seriously,' he said. 'I thought it was just something to fit into the BPI Awards. I wasn't treating it as a proper gig or anything.' What about fans, he was asked. 'Yes,' he said, 'but who the fuck would turn up for something like this anyway?'

The Mondays had failed to grasp the prestige of the event – either that or they didn't care. The Cure headlined on Saturday night, a gig that featured indie stars The Wedding Present and Ride, while Ozzy Osbourne closed the event on Sunday on top of a line-up dominated by heavy metal. The Mondays then failed to show at the Brit Awards ceremony and The Cure beat them to the Best British Group award, while Betty Boo picked up Best British Newcomer. These snubs, and the band's negligent attitude towards the music business establishment, were predictable given their reputation, but these were important moments being tossed aside. Amid the major awards presented at the Brits that year to George Michael, Elton John and INXS were bands with strong indie roots making an effort: The Beautiful South and Depeche Mode as well as The Cure. The Mondays seemed too ready to accept that they would never be a part of it, or were happy to sabotage their own chances rather than try. It was rock 'n' roll, it was Factory, but it was time to grow up.

Instead the band – now a huge stadium concern in the UK – continued to operate like there was no tomorrow. A trip to Brazil, to play the gigantic and prestigious Rock in Rio Festival alongside Guns N' Roses, George Michael and Prince, was seen as the chance to have a holiday and a drug orgy rather than an opportunity to establish some sort of foothold in South America. The band's pay cheque was huge – a reputed $60,000 – and they took along as many of their entourage as possible. Shaun had handled some promotional interviews over the phone, and the band arrived to find themselves on a national newspaper's front page under a headline about them smuggling thousands of Ecstasy pills into the country. It was a joke that had backfired. It didn't dampen the mood.

The band, and entourage, soon found that cocaine was not just plentiful but ridiculously cheap in Brazil compared to the UK. No sooner had they settled into the Intercontinental Hotel, overlooking Copacabana Beach, than the party started, and it continued to rage through the night. At five o'clock in the morning the pool was full of the Mondays and pals, all out of their heads, accompanied by a plentiful supply of hookers and, said Whelan, 'all sorts of strange characters...It was madness – Sodom and Gomorrah in the six foot end.' No one seemed to care that Paul Davis and Mark Day were rarely seen, holed up alone in their hotel rooms, nor that there was a substantial British press pack at the festival. The road crew were having a ball and Shaun continued to push the band, in the name of publicity and another easy pay cheque, organising with Piers Morgan of the *Sun* for them to visit fugitive Ronnie Biggs, the Great Train Robber, who was still holed up in Brazil at the time.

It was a cheap stunt and the resulting double-page spread, with the headline quote from Shaun, 'I was a villain, just like you

Ronnie – Biggsie is my hero', did the band's credibility few favours. The fag end of the Sex Pistols had pulled a similar stunt after John Lydon and Sid Vicious had left the band, recording a single with Biggs in Rio in 1978. It had been seen as a bit of a jape and pretty naff back then, and now it seemed to encapsulate even less of the outlaw spirit. Mark Day refused to attend a barbecue at the convicted criminal's house: 'I didn't want to glorify him.' He thought the whole thing pointless, as by now the press were only interested in Shaun and Bez anyway. His upset at the chaos around the band and the bad relations within ate away at him: 'It was pathetic, us being the band, the people who write the songs – we never ended up on the front cover.'

The Mondays' scheduled slot in Brazil, supporting George Michael, was postponed. 'But there were also journalists saying, Don't go on the beach, people are getting their kidneys stolen,' said Paul. It gave them another few days to party, and to try and consume their remaining small mountains of cocaine. 'I ended up using it as talcum powder, two hours before we were on the way to the airport I just had too much of it, whacked a load under my arms and up my arse,' said Paul.

On the eighth night of the nine-day event, 26 January, the Mondays finally took to the stage at the Maracana Stadium. They had barely given the gig a second thought. It was a Saturday night, and in front of them were 198,000 people, a record that still stands. The event was also being televised live to over sixty million people. The Mondays started their set with a rambling version of 'Rave On', as they struggled to get their sound together. Vegetables, Coke cans and plastic bags full of rubbish were pelted at the stage.

This was shaping up to be the band's biggest fuck-up of all time. 'It wasn't going too well,' said Whelan. Then came a torrential downpour. Many such rainfalls had plagued the festival, the bands evacuating the stage for fear of being electrocuted by the equipment all around them. The gig couldn't have gone much worse if they were dead. Shaun looked at his brother, just fifteen feet away. Paul looked back and flicked the hood up on his coat before starting the bass line to the next song. 'It's rain, isn't it? No big deal to us, we're from Manchester,' he said.

Shaun smiled as the band followed Paul into the song. This was why there would never be another band to touch them. The crowd, who had started to retreat looking for shelter, let out a huge cheer, surged back to the front of the huge stage and began to dance, to join in the party. 'We just carried on, off our heads, in the pouring rain,' said Whelan. 'Everything was soaking wet, the microphones, my drums, Shaun. There were people at the side of the stage trying to get us off and Shaun was pushing them away.' The Mondays played for another half-hour in the rain. With the lyrics his dad had written out for him and placed on stage for him to refer to now smudged and unreadable, Shaun simply ad-libbed.

It is often claimed to be the band's greatest set. 'It was brilliant,' said Whelan. 'We came off and said, Wow they loved us.' But he recalled what Muzzer had said to him in response: 'Yeah, only because you stayed on in the storm, you could have got electrocuted – you all could have been dead.'

Again, briefly, there was a sense the band could come back together; moments like this would unite them. They'd all come from the same place, all been in this from the start.

Back in Manchester, Tony Wilson, who had missed the Brazil trip, and the rest of Factory were busy preparing the next single from the *Pills 'n' Thrills* album. Wilson chose 'Loose Fit' although the band would have preferred 'God's Cop', with its soaring chorus and guitar hook. But many inside and outside Factory were tipping 'Loose Fit' to be the band's first number one. Shaun was interviewed by *Smash Hits* magazine and The Bailey Brothers persuaded the Mondays to half-heartedly drag up for the video. Immediately, however, the single ran into problems with the BBC over the lines 'Gonna build an airforce base/gonna wipe out your race' and 'kill who you're killing'. The Gulf War was now in full throttle as coalition forces attacked Iraq and the BBC, ever cautious as to their responsibilities, cut out any lyrics that might offend. As a result the release date of the single was delayed while the track was edited to conform.

On 16 February 1991 Shaun and Trish became parents to a baby girl – an event deserving of a full page in the *NME*. The couple were now living together in a townhouse in affluent and fashionable Didsbury. A week later the Mondays started a three-week

European tour. The band had spent little time playing Europe and when they had it had been chaotic, more like lads on holiday than serious business, but their records, particularly the singles 'Step On' and 'Kinky Afro', had been attracting a good deal of media interest. This was also their first trip to major territories such as Germany, France, Scandinavia and the Netherlands since they had signed a licensing deal with London Records to release the band's music across Europe, and the plan was to promote *Pills 'n' Thrills* and establish strong fan bases in those territories. The band were booked into good-sized 1000- to 1500-capacity venues that quickly sold out, and Mark Day was pleased to note that both Shaun and Whelan came to him pledging to adopt a more professional attitude in the future.

In Hamburg, on the second date of the tour, Debs went into labour and Bez, like Shaun, became a new father. There was a sense of renewed vigour and determination about the German dates that continued into Paris, where the Mondays played two triumphant sold-out shows at La Cigale, reviewed by both *Sounds* and *NME*, the latter suggesting the Mondays were 'on the edge of greatness'. The delighted French promoter set about planning a return show in Paris at a 6000-capacity venue in the summer.

The calm could never last. And by the time the band were in Scandinavia, where they were less well known, life on the road had returned to the familiar pattern of lurching from one chaotic scene to another; even father Derek partied after every gig for a change. While Rowetta had briefly brought a sense of sanity to the male-dominated, ego-driven atmosphere, Shaun, on the road with sidekick Muzzer and away from Trisha and the baby, was out of control. He clashed with Paul Davis, who was left visibly upset. In Holland, he refused to get out of bed and the band missed their scheduled flights. There were even rumours that he needed to be airlifted off the tour and returned to rehab.

The band returned to the UK to play 'Loose Fit' on *Top of the Pops*, and were nearly thrown off the show because of their behaviour. When they finally made it on stage, Shaun resembled Brian Jones on his last legs – caked in make-up to hide the bags under his eyes. Bez looked like a spare part on this downbeat groove of a song.

The camera panned in on Whelan, who rolled his eyes, bored with the charade of miming. It seemed a lifetime ago, but it was just fourteen months since they had stood on the same stage with The Stone Roses as the vanguard of a new movement in British music. The intervening time had not been kind to them, least of all Shaun. But the real malaise was the old cliché that success wasn't what they wanted, or expected it to be. They had dreamt of doing something unique, something creative – going darker and dirtier than ever before. Instead they had to settle for this, and the overall feeling was that they were exhausted and fed up with it all – the TV miming, the interviews, the videos – and wanted it to be over with.

As if to reflect that malaise, 'Loose Fit' peaked at a disappointing number seventeen. Shaun had been begging for time off. He was exhausted. It was obvious the Mondays were doing too much and needed a break. Instead they headed off for a seven-week tour of America, to play over thirty dates from the end of March, through April and into May. *Pills 'n' Thrills and Bellyaches* was picking up prom-ising reviews in the States. The *Los Angeles Times* said the 'mature mix of dance-soul-psychedelia' was among the favourites at US college and alternative radio stations and was now climbing, slowly but surely, up the pop charts. 'It could be the foothold for the forecast US success,' the review concluded.

The band redoubled their efforts to try and break into the American mainstream. They were so serious about the gigs that they hired and travelled with their own sound system, hoping to blow people away with the fantastic sound. 'Kinky Afro' was a popular alternative radio hit, and this extensive tour of North America would see them play to new audiences in small venues in places such as Atlanta and Milwaukee alongside bigger gigs in cities like Los Angeles and New York. Some of the theatres they were booked into held between 2000 and 4000 but the tour was peppered with smaller gigs in virgin territory. Looking at the itin-erary, Derek wondered how the band would cope: 'It was weird playing the massive gigs in the UK and then back to the little clubs in America. It was a step back to the nerves again, people right up to you.' Back to a few hundred people curious but needing to be won over, not the tens of thousands there because they loved the band. But, despite Shaun's grumbles, they were looking forward to the tour. 'Still loving it,' said Derek. 'We were touring the world, having the time of our lives, going to all those places you've read about and thought about … a tidal wave rolling round the world.'

America was where the wave hit the shore hard and began to recede. It needed little excuse for the unrest within the band to flare up. On arrival, the Mondays checked into their hotel in Los Angeles to find Shaun's suitcase was missing. He blamed Mark Day and they went head to head. At the tour's opening date, in Ventura, California, forty miles from the centre of LA, only 270 people showed up in a venue that held 850. The show was reviewed in the *Los Angeles Times*, which praised their 'marvelous music' but immediately raised an issue that would dog the tour: the band did not stick to their advertised start time and did not do long enough sets.

Worse was to come, with Wilson receiving complaints back in Manchester, and the problem was succinctly put by the *Chicago Tribune*, reviewing a show at the large 2500-capacity Riviera Theatre: 'Few bands have captured a pop moment so perfectly as the Happy Mondays did recently on their latest album and even fewer bands have blown it so quickly, as the British sextet did in a scandalously brief 50-minute concert Friday night at the Riviera … drummer Gary Whelan and bassist Paul Ryder may be the best rhythm section in rock, defying the listener to stand still but it's difficult to appreciate a band that wobbles onstage nearly two hours after the opening act has cleared off and then plays only 10 songs. With tickets more than $17, the 2,000 or so fans who packed the Riv deserved better.' The band, reckoned the *Tribune*, 'just didn't appear to care'. Chicago until that point had been a key city for the band.

'We never played on stage long enough for the Americans,' said Derek. 'They wanted three hours – not a chance.' After an easy couple of days in LA, where Paul Davis was seen moving a table and chair into the shallow end of the hotel pool and ordering a full tray of food, having decided to have dinner there, the band played a big show at the 4000-capacity Hollywood Palladium. There were noticeable pockets of empty seats, a fact the Mondays felt keenly. Then the tour moved across the vast swathes of America, zigzagging from the north-west through the mid-west and up to the north-east. The band was expected to travel hundreds of miles overnight and they were finally seeing the real America, marvelling as they travelled across the Rocky Mountains.

Every day was a new day, but the coach travel was tiring, everyone living on top of one another. And the gigs and crowds could be dispiriting, the band playing in tiny venues, sometimes to straight-looking audiences seated politely in rows. But these were the people who had heard of the band and bought the album; the Mondays needed to deliver and just move on. Instead, they argued. Mark Day wanted his guitar turned up, a sensible call given the make-up of many audiences on the tour, but the band's sound remained bass heavy. Shaun continued to miss his cues on stage, leaving the band to adjust as best they could. The partying offstage got wilder.

It was a relief to finally make it to New York, about halfway through the tour. Here the audiences were hipper and bigger – the band playing at the 1500-capacity Academy. Crucially they would be staying at a hotel for a few days, as Marc Geiger had also organised for them to support Jane's Addiction at the 14,000-capacity Madison Square Garden. It gave the band a chance to escape the cabin fever on the coach. 'It just all got more chaotic,' said Mark Day. 'I would go out early in the mornings sightseeing, while the others festered in bed, abusing room service.'

New York was home to Elektra Records and the Academy show went well. The band had shrugged at Elektra's re-release of 'Step On' but it was a bad idea, convincing few Top 40 stations to back the band. McGough pressed the label to release either 'Loose Fit' or 'God's Cop' as a single, new material for the modern rock stations who were backing the band. Instead, 'Bob's Yer Uncle' was given a hasty American release and the slow, growling, overtly sexual tune failed to follow the success of 'Kinky Afro', peaking at twenty-three in the *Billboard* Modern Rock chart. The album Elektra hoped would signal mainstream success for the Mondays in America, *Pills 'n' Thrills and Bellyaches*, had only reached number eighty-nine on the *Billboard* Hot 100. Many at the label were beginning to wonder if their investment in the Mondays had been a waste. Head of A&R Howard Thompson hoped the Madison Square Garden gig would convince his bosses otherwise.

The band had organised for extra PA to be set up on stage at Madison Square Garden. This was their biggest gig in America yet, and Derek and the rest of the road crew had put a great deal of effort into making it sound huge. They were aware too that the venue was unionised and that if they did not stick exactly to schedule, they would be charged thousands in overtime fees. Still, Whelan and Shaun conspired to arrive well after they were due on stage. Their cab had got stuck in traffic, they'd forgotten their passes and had trouble getting into the venue. Eventually, having made it inside, they ran backstage, ready to apologise to the band and beg for forgiveness. But nobody was there. 'None of them had fucking turned up,' said Whelan. 'Eventually they all strolled in one by one.'

Twenty minutes after they were due to appear, the band went on stage. There were boos simply for that. Yet the sound was mammoth, and the band felt comfortable performing in front of a crowd this size. Although they only had time to play a handful of songs, by the time they got to 'Wrote For Luck' they had the crowd on side. Unfortunately they were now running late, clocking up thousands of dollars in overtime charges. Attempts were made to get them off stage – which they resisted – and the show ended in an unsightly squabble between the band, venue staff and their own road crew.

Backstage the band shrugged off suggestions that they should meet and greet the Elektra bigwigs in favour of losing themselves in drugs. It was a clusterfuck, said the band's American agent, Marc Geiger, of their repeated disasters. 'They really didn't care, from what I could tell, at all.'

Already the band had cancelled gigs in Salt Lake City and Madison, Wisconsin, due to technical difficulties or nonsensical travel arrangements. But an opinion was forming that not only were the cancellations commonplace – in fact they were a rarity – but gigs were being cancelled because the band couldn't be bothered to play. As they headed south for the final two weeks of the tour, things started to unravel. Rowetta left after an argument with Shaun but was persuaded to return. What was supposed to be a relaxing break between dates turned into an emergency rescue mission when Paul Davis found himself stranded while skiing in Austin, Texas. A helicopter finally picked him up and carried him to safety.

Mark Day withdrew into himself and Shaun grew increasingly grumpy, especially when faced with more small venues and unenthusiastic crowds. McGough recalled him demanding to cancel one gig because there was no barrier in front of the stage: 'He wasn't concerned for people's safety, he just didn't want people looking up his nose while he was singing. They wanted to cancel a college gig because they said, Why are we playing on a college campus?' There were laughs, such as golf cart races at an outdoor gig in Houston Amphitheatre, but the band were frazzled and, for all the excitement of seeing the south of America, had exhausted themselves. McGough was unsympathetic and blamed drugs: 'They partied so hard, everyone would get tired, that was the deal.'

Dates were cancelled in Tampa, Dallas and Austin. Now the reasons for the cancellations were unclear. McGough was exasperated. He knew that fans would have spent their money on a ticket and travelled many miles to the shows, only to be let down: 'It's hard to carry on being a fan of a band who does that, and they've done it not because anyone is ill or there's been a bereavement but because someone can't be fucked for it to happen.' The Mondays weren't making fans, they were losing them.

Not only that, they were fast losing the support of Elektra's senior management. They had read the reviews about the band's short sets, experienced the chaos of Madison Square Garden, and now reports filtered back that important promotional meet-and-greets with local radio stations had been cancelled or, often, simply left hanging. Elektra realised making a priority of the band had been a mistake, the million-dollar promotional campaign misplaced. They would only ever amount to a cult phenomenon, chiefly in Los Angeles and New York and a few other cities. They would never, like previous Modern Rock chart acts such as U2 or Red Hot Chilli Peppers, make the transition to the mainstream. 'Elektra gave up on the campaign because they spent so much money to break them on radio, it hadn't worked, and the band were cancelling shows,' said McGough.

Marc Geiger saw it as a culmination of events. 'The label was struggling to break them and we were pushing for more funds, more commitment, more resources, more priority,' he said. 'It's a fragile thing and if the band starts fucking up, the band lets the label off the hook and it becomes an excuse.' He believed Elektra's withdrawal was due to a number of factors: 'delivery dates for recording, dates that get missed, artwork that's not turned in. It's an aggregate of issues.' Geiger acknowledged that McGough was doing his best, but Elektra had had enough.

The Mondays meanwhile were sunning themselves in Texas. 'All plotted up around the hotel pool, boiling hot, beautiful,' said Paul. The relentless pressure of trying to maintain the momentum they had sustained since Madchester took off, had finally cracked them. If they cancelled the last few dates of the American tour they could have a week off around this pool and, said Paul, 'everybody needed a week off'. The band had given everything they had: 'When we were on the stage it wasn't just playing the songs, not for me anyway, I'd give it 120 per cent every night. And by the time you're getting close to thirty dates, I was exhausted. It was brilliant, we loved it, all of us loved it, even me with stage fright, but people do get tired. It does catch up with you.'

Pills 'n' Thrills and Bellyaches went no higher in the *Billboard* Hot 100. The band's American career had promised so much: they had been the hottest ticket in New York last summer, the hottest band in Los Angeles – playing huge dates there – and with the backing of modern rock radio had scored a number one on America's alternative chart. They had even promised to burn up the dance charts. Now here they were, burned-out husks, laid out in the sun, unable to finish the tour. Not only had this extensive tour been a disaster, it had cost the band an estimated $150,000.

The band was not, of course, entirely responsible. Blaming the drugs was an easy get-out for McGough. His management style, he said, had been based on that of Rob Gretton. But he had not followed Gretton's lead, despite the repeated suggestion of Alan Erasmus that an American manager should be appointed to handle the band's US career. New Order's rise to playing 20,000-capacity venues in America had been orchestrated not by Gretton but by

American manager Tom Atencio, and the band's Stateside success had been helped by clever videos that were hits on MTV and the positioning of their songs on the soundtracks to hit films such as *Pretty in Pink*.

Happy Mondays had made mistakes but so had McGough – and so had Tony Wilson, who had also closed his ears to suggestions the Mondays needed influential and powerful full-time American management. In Wilson's eyes his own ideas for the Mondays and Madchester had been enough. It was hard, for instance, not to see his hand behind misguided decisions such as the release of 'Bob's Yer Uncle' as a US single. Wilson may have dreamed of the Mondays breaking America and starring in their own *Mad Fuckers!* film but in reality, he and McGough had guided Elektra towards a strategy that had been a failure. This, their final US tour, had almost finished the band, and certainly their chances of mainstream American success.

21
Baby Big Head

Back in Manchester the Mondays needed to quickly put their American travails behind them as they prepared for their biggest ever UK date, with 33,000 tickets on sale for an event titled 'Match of the Day' at Leeds United's football stadium, Elland Road, on 1 June 1991. It was the Mondays' first UK show in over six months and had been part organised by the band's notorious merchandisers, John Kenyon and Jimmy Sherlock. Although there was always inevitably some suspicion around Kenyon and Sherlock, the men who also controlled the illicit bootlegging of Mondays merchandise, they remained part of the Mondays' close circle of associates.

Little of the band's disappointing tour of America had been reported in the UK. It was noteworthy if left-field indie bands cracked the Top 40 in America, not if they failed – the 1990 release of 'Step On' had been the only Madchester single to break into the *Billboard* Hot 100 – and the Elland Road gig was seen as a return to brilliance for the band following the disappointing chart placing of 'Loose Fit' in the UK.

Madchester-related acts continued to profit – The Farm had gone to number one with their debut album, James had reached number two in the singles chart with 'Sit Down' and new albums by Inspiral Carpets and 808 State went top five. Blur were seen to be catching the coat-tails of the scene as their debut album entered the top ten. Although Factory could gain no traction with

The Wendys, Northside's debut album had reached a respectable number nineteen in the charts and the debut album by Electronic, Bernard Sumner and Johnny Marr's supergroup, reached number two, while their second single, 'Get the Message', made the top ten. Though Simply Red, Eurythmics, Queen and Michael Jackson were the year's big sellers and guitar rock-orientated indie bands such as My Bloody Valentine, Teenage Fanclub and Curve also found success, Madchester remained UK indie music's key scene. The Madchester backlash postponed by *Pills 'n' Thrills and Bellyaches* still refused to materialise. But there was a sense that the scene was, after over a year and a half of dominance in the UK, on the wane. The dance scene was also splintering, and indie/dance was no longer the cutting-edge sound it once had been; instead, straight-ahead electronic rave sounds from groups such as The KLF, Oceanic, Altern-8 and The Prodigy were finding favour.

Elland Road was the Mondays flexing their muscles. It was predicted that the gig would be the 'loudest ever' in England and the band hired a huge sound system for the purpose; the biggest PA ever assembled, it had eighty-foot speaker towers, with spikes planted in the ground so that the bass would rumble through the pitch. 'We had enough sub-bass for three-quarters of a million people,' said Derek. An environmental health officer had measured the sound at the mixing desk at a remarkable 134 decibels, a volume equated with hearing loss and permanent damage to hearing (The Stone Roses at Spike Island had been limited to 97 decibels). He told Derek the event should be shut down – that 134 decibels was ridiculous – but 'it sounds perfect, it's not ripping your head off'. 'There were no high frequencies,' said Derek. 'He chose to turn off the sound level meter and go away.' There was also a £30,000 light display and a remarkable nineteen different Mondays T-shirts for sale, as the band looked to cash in on a summer of festival dates – although, of course, Glastonbury would not be among them this year.

The day began at 2.30 p.m. and the Mondays were on stage at 8.45. The Farm and DJs Mike Pickering and Paul Oakenfold were among the entertainment. No alcohol was allowed on site, a ban blamed by Shaun for the event's failure to sell out, but 23,000 neverthe-less witnessed the Mondays deliver one of their tightest and longest ever shows, playing for almost ninety minutes. It was a stadium gig unlike any other. Shaun had a new smart, short haircut and his lack of rock bombast was perfectly captured in his between-song banter: 'I've got fuck all to say, if the band don't hurry up I'll just have to stand here and say nothing.'

Remarkably, given that the band had been touring some of these songs for over two and a half years, it was the first gig that they had played that stuck to a proper programme, with the backing tracks and many of the electronics pre-programmed as they played live versions of Oakenfold and Osborne's remixes. It might even have been the first time that the band played sober, so paranoid were they about making a mess of it. They were certainly all focused. And they pulled it off. The show received glowing reviews from *NME*, *Melody Maker* and *Select* with the Mondays now called 'The Rolling Stones of the 90s'. Those watching in the wings confirmed what the band felt – it was the best show that the Mondays had ever played – and within minutes of coming off stage plans were afoot to put together and release a bootleg album of the show.

The bootleg, titled *Baby Big Head*, was on sale by the end of the month, a fourteen-track double album priced at £15 – available by mail order from a Manchester address, suspected to be Kenyon and Sherlock's office, with a personal guarantee from Shaun that '100% of people will receive this record'. McGough too backed the bootleg, and was quoted in *NME* as saying he'd be personally responsible for making sure everyone got a copy or their money back. The cover featured the name of the band and the title, with the description 'bootleg album' stamped repeatedly on the cover. Although this was in effect an illegal release, James Brown in the *NME* gave it a full page, nine out of ten lead review, comparing it to The Who's famous *Live at Leeds* album. The 'sound quality is excellent', he noted. 'The songs are looser than the LP versions but never lose their pace...Shaun's charm, if you can call it that, permeates every lyric.' He chose 'God's Cop' as the pivotal moment, praising Day's 'mighty wah-wah'. The review concluded: 'Baby's got a big head for a reason, hunt it down.'

Tony Wilson told the press that he thought it was 'absolutely great this bootleg is available'. He enjoyed the frisson of illegality surrounding the release and the idea that this outlaw band was bootlegging themselves without the permission of their record label – an act of full frontal rebellion not even the Sex Pistols had managed – even though he was the label's prime mover. Not everyone at Factory felt the same, but the label had more pressing concerns. The Mondays had felt empowered to release the bootleg after learning that Factory owed them, and was currently unable to pay, an estimated £100,000 in royalties.

It later emerged that the label was steadily sinking under a debt burden estimated to be around £2.5 million. Interest rates had hit ten per cent and the bridging loan that was keeping them from going under stood at twenty-three per cent. By the end of the year The Hacienda and Charles Street between them were estimated to be worth less than £1 million. The Hacienda had reopened with metal detectors on the door, but the gang violence had persisted; in one highly publicised incident, six doormen were stabbed and beaten. There had been a remarkable thirty-five shootings in Manchester over a six-month period. The club had little option but to take on new door security with ferocious reputations in the city, reportedly paying them a massive £375,000 annually. 'The door was connected – had to be – a matter of survival,' said Wilson. 'And where did security stop and protection start? We lost on that one.' He said The Hacienda was losing money again.

Electronic's recent hit album, meanwhile, had not generated the same sort of money for the label as New Order. Factory had committed a large marketing budget to the project, but the band's manager, Marcus Russell (who would go on to manage Oasis), had made deals – with Virgin for Europe and Warners for America – that meant Factory could not benefit worldwide from the group. Wilson's investments in Cath Carroll, Peter Hook's Revenge, The Wendys and new signings The Adventure Babies proved fruitless – none of them could crack the Top 40.

Nor was it just the banks and Happy Mondays to whom Factory owed money; crucially, New Order were also owed vast sums. And the label needed to find more money to fund the recording of new albums by New Order and the Mondays in the hope of generating cash. The Mondays had no new material, and New Order, if they could overcome their personal differences, would be effectively making an album to get back the money Factory owed them. 'It was demoralising,' said Bernard Sumner. After so many years of the good times, the party was, very suddenly, almost over.

Ever the opportunists, Shaun and Bez generated other income streams for themselves. For a generous fee they agreed to guest edit *Penthouse*. They would select models, supervise a photo session and reply to letters. They arrived – Shaun in his new Issey Miyake blazer – at the magazine's offices in a limo, to be greeted by a swarm of photographers and Sky TV. While journalists like Barbara Ellen at *NME* felt that it did the band's credibility no good at all, they were unaware of the backstory of the amounts that were owed to the band and the financial imperatives that were driving such decisions. Everyone else in the band disapproved, but neither Shaun nor Bez cared, and the divisions between the members became even more distinct.

Over the summer the Mondays played a handful of huge European festival dates, appearing before 50,000 people in Holland and Belgium and 30,000 in Ireland. Although a lucrative date in Paris was cancelled, the promoter citing the band's links to 'drugs, unreliability and violence', the Mondays were well paid for these shows, and although Shaun appeared to be bored the crowds in Europe were enthusiastic. Unlike America, Europe appeared to be a market the Mondays could capitalise on. It seemed more than ever an oversight that a third single had not been pulled from *Pills 'n' Thrills* for the UK and Europe – 'God's Cop' remained the obvious choice – to further drive sales.

At a show in a bullring in Valencia the lighting equipment collapsed on the Mondays, almost killing them. Their equipment was destroyed, the gig was cancelled and the Mondays badly shaken, but when they got back to the hotel they were swamped by thousands of Spanish fans, all dressed as if they had just walked out of The Hacienda. If they hadn't realised it before, they certainly knew now how big it had all become.

The Mondays' business partnership, Wabash, continued to hold regular directors' meetings, routinely without Shaun, but the band's finances were a mess. Eric Longley had been poached by Factory to carry out a financial audit on the company and it was unclear who his long-term replacement might be. There was talk of cash flow problems, delays in all payments going through Factory, the possibility that the band's wages wouldn't be paid. 'It was chaos with the money,' said Whelan. 'Money was coming in from all over the world at different times and it was hard to keep track of what was happening. We were making a lot of money from gigs but God knows where it was going.' The band were now on approximately £600 a week each, and publishing royalty cheques had started to come through, but there was a sense that McGough had lost control of the situation. The office ran on unusual hours, and even when he could be reached – he was often out partying – what he said could not always be believed. Managing the band now was an impossible job.

However, at a meeting of Wabash's board of directors on 30 July 1991 – again without Shaun – there was good news of a new £50,000 merchandise deal with major company Bravado and the band were allocated £8000 to replace the equipment destroyed in Spain. There was also an exciting offer on the table from famed Sex Pistols manager Malcolm McLaren. He'd long admired the band and now wanted them to appear in a forthcoming Christmas TV show called *The Ghosts of Oxford Street*. The show, about the history of the street, would be a musical, with contributions from acts such as Tom Jones and Sinead O'Connor, as well as McLaren himself. He had in mind that the Mondays would play convicted highwaymen led up Oxford Street and hanged from a replica of the Tyburn gallows at Marble Arch, in an imitation of the public executions that had taken place there for over 500 years. The Mondays suggested that they record a cover of the Bee Gees' 'Stayin' Alive' for the film. McLaren, who would be paying for the recording session, loved the idea.

In early August the Mondays were paid a rumoured £50,000 to headline the final night of a Manchester music festival in Heaton Park called Cities in the Park. Playing after a triumphant set from Electronic, Shaun roused himself to deliver a committed performance, looking healthy and keen, as the band rolled out their stadium show one more time in front of a sweltering 30,000 people.

The band came together again for Mark Day's wedding, which took place in a plush marquee in the grounds of a five-star Worsley hotel with 1400 guests. With the money apparently about to start rolling in, maybe the band's members were willing to try and paper over the cracks between them. However, while Mark was busy celebrating, Paul Ryder's marriage had collapsed. Paul knew only one thing could alleviate the emotional pain; he drove straight to Shaun's house and told him to get some heroin. His life would never be the same again.

Whelan and Paul had always been the ones who kept the band going, their obsession being enough to counter pretty much anything that Shaun, in particular, threw at them. Once his marriage fell apart and he found comfort in heroin, Paul lost that motivation. 'It was the start of the descent into the end,' Whelan put it succinctly on seeing Paul doing heroin for the first time.

Factory officially released the Happy Mondays' Elland Road bootleg in September, retitling it *Live* and hoping to generate some much-needed income from this relatively cheap project. Unfortunately many fans had already bought the bootleg and the album peaked at twenty-one in the UK. The dodgy dealings that had surrounded its original release, the rumour it was now being released purely to alleviate Factory's financial difficulties, and the fact that the sound-desk recording omitted the roar of the crowd, clouded the album's perception. It was panned by *Melody Maker* as 'an unflattering picture of the most important group of the past ten years' and picked up lukewarm reviews elsewhere, *Select* suggesting that the format, a live double album, was outdated and conjured images of self-indulgent heavy metal bands. The overall impression was grubby, when in fact *Live* was a clean and lean release of a perfect live set, only the lack of crowd atmosphere preventing it from bearing comparison with the very best live albums of all time. This, the Mondays' fourth album, proved beyond doubt that they were the pre-eminent live band of the era. It sounded huge, the band immaculate. The Mondays had everything.

But it had no effect on the ill feeling within the band, who seemed to barely register its release. Shaun was trying to come off heroin but had been bingeing on crack and freebasing cocaine.

Morale had sunk to an all-time low, not helped by the fact Shaun had been in charge of the video camera at Mark Day's wedding and, it now transpired, had spent an inordinate amount of time filming a horse's cock. Even the recent European festival dates, and injections of merchandise cash that showed they were still considered a huge force in the UK, could not stop the downward spiral. Whelan, who was depressed, had begun drinking heavily at home alone. He was dismayed at what he saw as the media's current reading of the Mondays – after years in which Shaun had constantly derided the band's talent and made a succession of buffoonish statements, cemented by the high-profile *Penthouse* pantomime – as 'a load of fucking idiots'.

Two albums were circulating that would only compound his bleak perception. Although it peaked at UK number eight, Primal Scream's *Screamadelica* would pick up a slew of best-of-year album awards. This remarkable psychedelic dance/rock album was produced by DJ Andy Weatherall, who had risen to prominence after remixing, with Paul Oakenfold, 'Hallelujah' from 1989's *Madchester Rave On* EP. Weatherall had taken much of the Mondays' sound and method from that period and applied it to Primal Scream, who had thrown off their mid-80s winklepickers and leather-trousered indie rock jangle and embraced Ecstasy. Many critics heralded *Screamadelica* as the high point of the Acid House/indie rock crossover that the Mondays had pioneered – and with the Mondays stuck now in a deep hole and having recorded no new material in over a year, it was hard to disagree. In retrospect *Screamadelica* came nowhere close to the originality or musical depth of either *Bummed* or *Pills 'n' Thrills and Bellyaches*, yet it was seen at the time as a crown-stealing effort. But the killer blow would be the release of Nirvana's *Nevermind*, an album of violently alive rock 'n' roll that would glide on the back of hit single 'Smells Like Teen Spirit' to sell thirty million copies worldwide and precipitate a 'grunge rock' movement that would bring down the curtain on the Madchester scene.

Although, ultimately, electronic dance music, and DJ culture, popularised by Acid House, would come to dominate modern music, especially in America, Grunge was a return to a familiar 'rock' sound of the 1970s – heavy, distorted electric guitars and growling vocals. Madchester, without the Roses and without any new musical moves from the Mondays, had been exploited to exhaustion. The Grunge scene, an extension of the alternative rock sound of American bands such as The Pixies, Sonic Youth and Dinosaur Jr., was fresh meat. In America, where Madchester never caught on, Nirvana led alternative rock to become a mainstream phenomenon, and bands such as Pearl Jam and Soundgarden enjoyed huge commercial success – changing the musical landscape forever, as Madchester had done in the UK.

Grunge in the UK was a respite from the dominance of Madchester and another subculture to be championed – and the two had many striking similarities. The Grunge scene was linked to one city, Seattle, a fiercely independent-minded place with one dominant independent record label, Sub Pop. It was also antishowbiz and stood in opposition to the rock 'n' roll theatrics of bands such as Guns N' Roses and Motley Crue. Like Madchester, the scene was heavily marketed, with Grunge fashion, really an antifashion, becoming popular – unkempt appearances and flannel shirts. The escapism and optimism of Acid House and Madchester was however completely absent from Grunge – and this resonated among a huge demographic that felt social alienation, apathy and pessimism towards the future. It made Madchester and the Mondays' hedonism seem less vital, out of touch, and its strippedback rock made Madchester sound flabby by comparison.

The Mondays' rehearsals in New Order's Cheetham Hill space, which took place over the late summer of 1991 with the intention of producing some new material, were devoid of any sense of unity or direction. They spent most of their time complaining or arguing. Mark Day was reluctant even to attend, so pissed off was he with the heroin in the band and the deceit and greed and bad moods it brought with it, and he would routinely leave early. At least he was there. Shaun was a consistent no-show. 'We actually knew the end was coming and I don't think any one of us had the bottle to end it,' said Whelan. 'For me it was, Let's just milk it while we can. Trying to resolve anything, to turn it into something creative and enjoyable, was gone – let's just ride this wave as long as we can, because it's going to end any day. It had become a monster and there was just no way of controlling it.' Heroin had come between Whelan and Paul Ryder, Mark Day had not spoken to Shaun properly in well over a year. 'We were in a bad, bad way,' said Whelan.

The Mondays were due at Real World Studios in Bath on 17 September 1991 for a five-day session to record 'Stayin' Alive' for McLaren's TV project. Paul Oakenfold and Steve Osborne, who were again producing, had hoped to use the time to also make a start on new material. There was none. 'We had no ideas,' said Paul Ryder. 'No bits of ideas, no half a bass line, nothing.'

Following the slew of awards they had won for their production of *Pills 'n' Thrills*, the two producers were in great demand. They had worked with trip-hop group Massive Attack, and U2 were sounding them out. They found the decline in the group that had been so focused in Los Angeles a year previously shocking. No one seemed to be in control or really to have a clue. On the first evening, the band drank all the booze – two barrels of Guinness and two of lager – the studio had laid on for the week. McGough had in mind that, simply by repeating the formula of 'Step On', 'Stayin' Alive' would be a smash hit; the Mondays thought they were just recording it for the TV show and treated it almost as a throwaway. Factory, like Osborne and Oakenfold, were expecting new material, imagining the band would conjure it up in the studio as they had done on a couple of *Pills 'n' Thrills* tracks. But the session was disastrous. 'Everything we'd done before was a great vibe and really positive,' said Osborne. 'And there wasn't that positivity on this session.'

Mark Day, who refused to stay at the residential studio and would travel down each day from Manchester, struggled with the guitar on 'Stayin' Alive', finding it impossible to rethink for the Mondays. Despite their problems, Whelan and Paul Ryder managed to put together a couple of new tracks that showed promise. One of these, 'Baby Big Head', was to lie unfinished – but the other, with a driving keyboard riff and some smart slide guitar, would become the band's next single, 'Judge Fudge'. Shaun had no lyrics prepared but an evening in a local pub, and a chance encounter with the cheating wife of a local aristocrat, inspired him and they came tumbling out the next day: 'She's healthy, wealthy, dripping wet and wise, sending out those plate me eyes, stinking rich tell stinking lies has no friend just alibis'.

The band were impressed, and Osborne and Oakenfold thought the track had potential, enough to work on it further back in London at Eden Studios. But in London any optimism was destroyed when Shaun turned up at the studio in a ski mask, looking like an armed robber, and refused to remove it, saying his head would fall to bits if he did. Oakenfold called McGough to come and rescue them and Shaun. 'Paul and Steve were scared,' said McGough. 'It freaked them out.' Despite talk of the sessions being the start of an album to follow up *Pills 'n' Thrills*, it was clear the band were not in a good place. Osborne and Oakenfold told them that if they started work now it would be chaos; they should wait until they had rediscovered some of the vibe they had going into *Pills 'n' Thrills.* 'You can't do a record now because it will go wrong,' said Osborne.

McLaren was disappointed with the Mondays' version of 'Stayin' Alive' and did not warm to the band as they filmed their part for the show one cold October night. They were dressed as convicted highwaymen, put in a metal cage on a cart and drawn by a horse up Oxford Street and through the gates of Marble Arch, before being hung from a 25-foot replica of Tyburn gallows. 'I liked the idea of working with McLaren but I found him a bit pompous,' said Paul. 'Stayin' Alive' was included on *The Ghosts of Oxford Street* soundtrack album (released by RCA) alongside contributions from Kirsty MacColl, The Pogues and Tom Jones, the *NME* calling it the highlight of a 'pretty useless soundtrack'. Although Shaun told *Melody Maker* it would be released as a future single, Factory shelved any such plans.

The video for 'Judge Fudge', shot with The Bailey Brothers in Stockport, was a slick, cinematic, black and white affair in which film of the band playing in the rain – Bez made a rare appearance on guitar – was intercut with a narrative built on the band committing a jewel heist. But they were ill-prepared to face the media, starting a run of ruinous promotional engagements by performing the track live on Channel 4's *The Word*. Bez again pretended to play guitar, which was odd, but it was Shaun you could not take your eyes off: he looked horrific, unrecognisable from the handsome man who had recently headlined a show at Heaton Park. He was fat, bloated and ill, his hair shorn back to a crew cut. Next Shaun recorded an interview on MTV during which he joked about a past as a rent boy, just as he'd joked about being sexually molested as a child. This time the story was picked up by the tabloids and on 12 October the *News of the World* ran a page lead with the headline: 'I was a rent boy says Happy Mondays star – Singer Shaun sold sex for £40-a-day.'

'I was pissing myself laughing,' said brother Paul. 'I thought it was him having a laugh.' But when he phoned Shaun and told him there was a hilarious funny piece in the paper about him being a rent boy, Shaun went ballistic. 'What? I'm a fucking rent boy? He didn't think it was funny one little bit.' Once he found out where the journalist had taken it from and how out of context it was, Paul had to admit it was bad. That evening Shaun and Bez were involved in an incident at Dry during which Shaun smashed a huge mirror. 'I had to show my head,' said Shaun. 'I wanted people to see I was annoyed.' This incident again made the press, enlivened by claims that Shaun was brandishing a .375 Magnum.

'Judge Fudge' was released on 18 November and Shaun was back on the cover of *Melody Maker*, airbrushed to a reasonable state. He memorably summed up his current condition with the line: 'The last two years have been one long blur. I remember something about becoming a dad and being on *Top of the Pops* but not much else.' He also appeared on the cover of *NME*, having been persuaded, as rumours about him going crazy circulated, to appear trussed up in a straitjacket. It was intended as a joke, but looked like anything but, especially once the interview inside was digested.

Well-established, politically provocative *NME* writer Steven Wells had come up to Manchester with the idea to attack the band over their casual sexism, homophobia, lack of morals, material-ism, and what he saw as a right-wing political drive. Wells, a former ranting poet, tended to champion socialist or anarcho-punk bands, and while he often also fell foul of flights of fancy over camp pop acts, the Mondays were clearly not his sort of band. Nor was Wells the band's sort of journalist; they viewed him as something of a joke as he took the band to task about having betrayed their roots.

'His questions were things like, Do you feel embarrassed you've come from working-class roots yet you're making good money and are buying new cars?' said Whelan.

It was clear, just looking at Shaun, that he was deeply ill. He was trying to kick heroin, but even on the substitute methadone he was still suffering withdrawal symptoms, sweating and anxious. He was drinking and smoking marijuana heavily and freebasing cocaine and hitting the crack. Wells asked him about the recent *News of the World* 'rent boy' story, framing the question like this: 'What's wrong with being a rent boy, you already said you were a drug dealer?' Shaun grunted: 'Lads who come from where I come from don't like being called a fucking faggot. I have nothing against them but I have my rights and I ain't a fucking faggot and that's it.'

Wells had already riled Shaun by saying that being a rent boy and being gay were not the same thing. Shaun had acknowledged this and then reiterated his point bluntly: 'I don't suck dick.' Now Wells said he found the word 'faggot' offensive.

The interview was set to explode and effectively end the Mondays' career. So it is worth pointing out that the Mondays had used the word 'faggot' in interviews in the *NME* before, without censure, while on the streets of Manchester and Salford at the time, 'faggot' was used in a similar way to how the word 'gay' has been used more recently as a general term of disparagement – wrong but common-place and not intended to be aggressively homophobic: a cultural epidemic and certainly not the Mondays' fault. In answer to Wells's concern over the word, Shaun simply said: 'I don't give a fuck. I'm not bothered. I haven't got any problems [with gays] and I ain't a fucking rent boy and it was a dirty story on me.'

Shaun sighed. Bez had been buzzing around the interview, getting increasingly wound up. His emotions were raw and he engaged his mouth before his brain, giving Wells all the ammuni-tion he need to bury the Mondays. 'I hate faggots,' Bez shouted. 'Anyone who is straight finds them disgusting. Faggots might find shagging pussy disgusting but we find shagging a bloke not right. The majority of people in Britain aren't gay, are they?'

The band all looked at him in horror. 'Don't listen to Bez,' they admonished, 'he says things when he's wound up, or off his head, but he doesn't mean them.' The band then pointed out to Bez – and this was quoted in the article – that he had been out partying with well-known homosexual pop star Paul Rutherford, of Frankie Goes to Hollywood. Bez responded: 'If he'd started getting his cock out in front of me, I'd have fucking filled the bastard.'

McGough was aghast. 'You're sat there thinking, fucking hell,' he said. 'It all came out and it looked bad.' Hundreds of outraged letters poured into the *NME*, attacking the band not only for Bez's homophobic remarks but also for their promotion of drug abuse, their misogyny and their 'nasty little right wing politics', typified by Shaun's tongue-in-cheek quote about voting Tory. Stripped of all context such things were a lethal weapon in the hands of the press when they turned on the band. Largely in reference to Shaun's words and compounded by his materialistic outlook and individualistic viewpoint, the Mondays would be called 'Thatcher's children' and 'the worst of Thatcher', or 'Thatcher's philosophy made sexy'.

All the chickens were coming home to roost. Shaun, who seemed most under attack, was asked not to attend a World Aids Day event he'd been due to guest at; it became another story in the tabloids, the Mondays labelled as the 'gay slur' band.

Bez was capable of deep and profound thought – in past interviews he'd talked about his admiration for Emmett Grogan, founder of the Diggers, a radical 1960s community-action group from San Francisco. In his head what he'd said to Wells wasn't intended to be homophobic, it was just the way it came out. However you dressed it up, though, it was impossible to defend, and the band was furious. 'It was bullshit,' said Whelan. 'A complete stitch-up – none of us were homophobic.'

McGough tried. He had to – the band's career was in the balance. Bez had witnessed lads being raped by older lads when he was in a Young Offenders Institute and that was where the outburst had come from. Bez would later say that on three different occasions men had tried it on with him, 'and that's what my opinions are based on'.

To the rest of the band, Shaun was guilty only of using the word 'faggot', and they had never seen Bez act in a homophobic way before. Shaun said that as a Roman Catholic he'd been raised to believe a certain thing about homosexuals, but now he'd travelled the world he realised that was wrong. But everything they said just made it worse. The message became: Shaun Ryder and the Happy Mondays hate gays. And there was no clear way back.

'Judge Fudge' peaked at twenty-four in the UK at the end of November. The band was not invited to appear on *Top of the Pops*, nor was the video for the single widely shown. The music industry had its fair share of homosexuals in powerful positions. Last year, at the same time, Shaun was being readied to appear on the Christmas edition covers of *NME*, *Melody Maker*, *Vox*, *Q* and *Select*, while *Pills 'n' Thrills* was widely acclaimed as the album of the year. This year he was a pariah. Nirvana, Primal Scream, The Wonder Stuff, REM and Carter The Unstoppable Sex Machine had replaced him. In the *NME*'s end-of-year 'in' and 'out' list, Manchester, Ecstasy and Bez were top of the 'out' column. At one point, the band had joked that they could go on stage and 'curl a turd out' and still get a good review in the music press. Now they were virtually untouchables.

22
Barbados

Happy Mondays had already recorded three studio albums in exceptional circumstances, but the events surrounding the making of their fourth would ensure it went down in rock 'n' roll legend. Tales of the chaos inflicted on the exotic location, the drug rampages, near-death episodes, unflinching mental instability and dead-eyed depravity would be told through the ages. It was an album that would come to signify rock 'n' roll excess and meltdown, one that eclipsed every troubled and drug-afflicted album ever made. In comparison the Stones' *Exile on Main Street*, The Beach Boys' *Smile* or The Stone Roses' *Second Coming* seem like a Sunday walk in the park. It was this infamous, chaotic recording that the name of the Happy Mondays would be forever remembered for.

After the *NME* interview, the band did not, as many expected, sack Bez. It was tempting, especially since even before his outburst some of the band felt he was a hindrance to them being taken seriously as a musical force. But 'when push came to shove', said Whelan, they just told him to take a break, 'a long holiday'. The band all needed a long holiday. What had once been an ultra-tight gang of friends who spoke a language only they understood, was now a ball of confusion, animosity and feuds. They were badly damaged, worn out and fed up. Bez thought that Shaun needed to get clean before embarking 'on anything more challenging than a photo shoot'.

Instead the Mondays had to make a new album. Factory's financial concerns were now acute. The recession continued, employment rose to 9.4 per cent, the highest level since 1987. Takings at The Hacienda were down and gangs were still a heavy presence among the young party crowd. Factory were stuck in a spiral of negative equity, while interest rates on their property loans were crippling the label. Tony Wilson, under increasing pressure, continued to charm and plan and plot, outwardly unruffled. He had struck up a relationship with the long-time and experienced general manager of London Records, Roger Ames, a man who knew the value of both New Order and Happy Mondays. Ames could easily see the Mondays' financial worth – their publisher FFRR was owned by London and the label had also licensed *Pills 'n' Thrills* for Europe. Even though they had not recorded an album since 1989's *Technique* that had sold close to one million copies worldwide, New Order were worth a lot of money, both their future and their past; so too, now, were Joy Division, whose catalogue and history Factory had curated with rare and immaculate taste. If Factory's property investments were flawed, as a record label they were still a more than attractive proposition.

Wilson argued persuasively on three fronts: everyone who had spent a lot on buildings before the financial collapse was 'fucked'. If the people who built Canary Wharf were fucked, what chance Factory? The gay furore surrounding the Mondays was, said Wilson, 'like a Socialist Worker meeting a worker and not knowing what the fuck had hit him'. 'I treat it the same way as I used to treat the accusations that New Order were a bunch of Nazis,' he told the *NME*. 'It's crap. If one of our groups was being homophobic or Nazi, that's it, we'd just say bye-bye.' Third, Happy Mondays and New Order were both now making new albums for Factory, certain to be two huge money-spinners. Everything was fine.

So Ames and London Records, for what Wilson called 'a substantial advance', struck a worldwide licensing and distribution deal for Factory product, though it excluded various deals that were already in place, such as Elektra's US deal with the Mondays. Ames was said to be interested in taking London's stake in Factory further and Wilson was considering selling shares, as much as forty-nine per cent, in the label. 'We had a very tough summer during the recession but we're pulling through,' he told the *NME*. Creation Records, home to Primal Scream, My Bloody Valentine, Teenage Fanclub and The Boo Radleys, were negotiating at the time to sell forty-nine per cent of their shares to Sony for £3.5 million. Factory, it was felt, had to be worth double that.

Wilson and McGough agreed a £250,000 recording budget for Happy Mondays' new album. It was a high figure, more than the label had ever spent before on an album and over twice the cost of *Pills 'n' Thrills*. But Factory had recently spent £100,000 on The Adventure Babies' debut album, which had failed to enter even the indie charts. A lavish budget for an indie album, rivalling the quarter of a million Creation spent on My Bloody Valentine's *Loveless* (which would peak in the UK at twenty-four), it was – the current state of the band notwithstanding – a reasonable figure for a band coming off the back of a huge hit like *Pills 'n' Thrills*. Factory desperately wanted everything that happened with that album to happen again, and quickly.

The Mondays, however, did not have the material and complained there was not enough time to get new songs together. Christmas 1991 was rancid and bitter for the band. Shaun never came to rehearsals. Worse, he would send along various hopefuls he'd met as he went about feeding his habit. 'That happened three or four times,' said Whelan. 'Some random bloke would turn up and say, Shaun said come down, I play a bit of guitar and I sing, I'm here to help you write some songs.' Paul, so long the band's driving force, was drifting away into deep heroin addiction. There were just seven or eight loose ideas and no vocals. 'I was worn out,' said Mark Day. 'The fire wasn't there any more, there was too much damage.' Factory announced that the band's new album would be released in six months' time, in June 1992. 'We said, we're not ready,' said Whelan. 'They said, Well you need to do it.'

The same applied to New Order, who along with manager Gretton and Factory boss Alan Erasmus had serious doubts about Wilson's dealings with London Records. They knew Wilson had not made clear that Factory had no contract with, and did not own, its major assets. Both New Order's and Joy Division's back catalogue belonged to them, not the label, and they had long operated on a 50/50 profit-sharing deal. Wilson tried unsuccessfully to rectify this but Gretton would not entertain making a deal. In effect New Order were being told to record an album to keep the label alive – all profit, even likely their fifty per cent, would be eaten up by a mountain of bad debt. They feared Wilson might try and use their assets – i.e. their back catalogue – to guarantee loans. Their own internal issues were exacerbated by the dilemma and confused by the vast amount of money they had already invested in Factory and The Hacienda.

The Mondays too had strong emotional ties to Factory. 'Nobody else would have signed them,' said Derek, thinking back to 1985. 'Good job Factory was there. It was exactly the correct label for them, pure stroke of luck ... Thank God for Factory.'

McGough could not convince Oakenfold and Osborne to change their position. 'We were gutted to not make the next record, absolutely gutted,' said Osborne, but he reiterated that if they tried to record it now, it would simply not work; the band had no material and a cloud still hung over them because of the bad press. So the search for new producers commenced. 'Quite a few names were being thrown around,' said Paul. 'I'd heard a Ziggy Marley album with a song on called "Tomorrow People" and thought it was a great record.' He found out it had been produced by Chris Frantz and Tina Weymouth, formerly the rhythm section of Talking Heads – one of his favourite bands.

For a band built on groove and rhythm, Frantz and Weymouth seemed an interesting choice. Not only had Talking Heads' eight albums brought them huge success and formidable reputations in America, they were one of the most critically acclaimed bands of the 1980s. In the UK, moreover, Talking Heads were seen as super-cool art rockers – so the association would help the band's rehabilitation. Paul saw a new direction for the Mondays with the pair producing; perhaps they would be the key to unlocking Top 40 radio in America.

Paul and McGough flew to meet the married couple at their home in Connecticut. Frantz, the drummer, and bassist Weymouth had forged a strong reputation outside of Talking Heads with their acclaimed, self-produced, dance-orientated Tom Tom Club records. The Ziggy Marley album, *Conscious People*, had been the pair's first production job for another act and they were keen to do more. Singer David Byrne had recently announced that after fifteen years he was going solo – effectively splitting Talking Heads. The offer of producing the Mondays' next album was perfectly timed for them. They had not followed closely the band's recent troubles, nor were they made aware of the internal problems, but they were impressed with *Pills 'n' Thrills* and felt they could bring something to the Mondays' sound.

'We thought they were great people,' said Paul. 'From Connecticut we went on a journey to find a studio. We flew to Miami to go to the Bee Gees' studio. It was a huge place but weird, on an industrial estate.' They went from there to Jamaica and saw a studio in Ocho Rios, but it was really small and not well equipped – they would have to rent lots of gear and transport it to Jamaica. Paul wanted to go to Compass Point in Nassau, where Frantz and Weymouth had a home and had often recorded in the past, as had Bob Marley, Bowie and James Brown. 'Some amazing stuff had come out of there but I asked Chris about it and he said it was under two foot of water, place was destroyed.' Then somebody mentioned Eddy Grant's studio, Blue Wave in Barbados, where Sting and Mick Jagger had both recorded.

'We had this meeting with Nathan and Tony,' said Whelan. They told the band there were three options, the first of which was a studio in Amsterdam. 'Everyone looked at each other and went, Well, obviously that one's out.' Another option was a new studio located in a former church in Manchester and run by Pete Waterman, the man behind Kylie, Jason Donovan and a host of other pop megastars. 'Waterman had even put in a pitch to produce the album and me and Paul were really against it, we wouldn't even discuss it. Nathan had spoken to a few of the others and they were up for it; Shaun was up for it. I said if you do that, I won't be getting involved, I'll be leaving.'

The third option was Barbados. Everyone opted for Barbados apart from Mark Day who said, 'Can't we do it in Manchester?' They all looked at him: 'Why the fuck would you want to do it in Manchester?' 'Well,' said Day, 'we've all got homes and stuff now.'

A Wabash Communications meeting took place at the Dominion Hotel on 10 February 1992 to finalise details. Eric Longley had been laid off by Factory in a recent round of cost-cutting and was back as the band's business manager. Shaun wasn't at the meeting and, unusually, nor was Mark Day. McGough revealed to the rest of the band that Shaun had sacked him. Don't worry, he said, he and Shaun had been to see former Smiths and current Electronic guitarist Johnny Marr about replacing Day. The band were shocked. What the fuck was going on?

'He was fired,' said McGough. 'Mark was unhappy and Shaun felt culturally he wasn't on board. Mark's a great guitarist, it wasn't an issue for me, but Shaun made it an issue and for half an hour one afternoon Johnny Marr was in the band and was about to get on the plane to Barbados.'

After nine years in the band, Shaun had sacked Day with an abrupt phone call and no explanation. Day was hurt and confused: 'I'd done nothing wrong.' He felt the whole band had turned on him; it was as if they were saying it was all his fault — as if, he said, 'I was the one going to make the next album shit.' That was not the case. Communication within the band was now being conducted via Chinese whispers. 'We thought he didn't want to play anything else with us,' said Paul. 'Then the Johnny Marr wheels started turning.'

Eric Longley asked Gary Whelan to try and get Day back in the band. Although still resentful of Day's grab at an increased portion of the band's song publishing, Whelan acquiesced. He and Paul met with Day. 'Mark said, Don't you want me in the band?' said Paul. 'We said, Yeah, but you don't want to be here. Mark said, No, I don't want to leave. He just needed a bit of time off like everyone else. We said, We thought you wanted to leave, thought you were unhappy? We made sure he wanted to be in the band and that was it.' It was a disturbing episode, one that left an already drained Day traumatised.

The band met at Manchester airport to fly to Barbados the day after Day had been reinstated. Despite the poor state of relations between the band members, there was still understandable excitement about flying out to Barbados to record. The Mondays would be joined by their partners and children and the sunshine would

bring out the best in the band, just as Los Angeles had for *Pills 'n'*
Thrills. They would whip up some grooves with the Talking Heads
pair at the helm and Shaun would write. It was going to be alright.

Then McGough dropped the bag containing Shaun's
methadone – four 500ml bottles of the heroin substitute that
would see him through the recording. Shaun had not bothered
packing the bottles properly and they shattered. There was glass
and green gloop inside the bag, seeping out, mixed with Shaun's
clothes. 'We ran downstairs to where they sold little bottles of
water, emptied the water out and tried putting the methadone
in this little water bottle,' said Paul, who had his own small stash.
'There were pieces of glass in it and all sorts of stuff.' Shaun didn't
want to fly. Derek reassured him they'd get something sorted
when they reached Barbados.

They arrived on the island in the middle of the night and in the
midst of a torrential downpour. Shaun was already experiencing
withdrawal symptoms after the thirteen-hour flight. They were
tired, and no one could look anyone else in the eye – there was a
sense of great trepidation, fear almost. Mark Day began to cry. He
had been sacked and reinstated, they had hardly made a start on
the demos, it was going to take a lot of hard work to finish; they
were carrying two junkies – Shaun and Paul – and he could not
see a way of galvanising Bez, Davis and Whelan. The emotions he'd
bottled up for close to two years, the abuse he'd felt, chiefly at the
hands of Shaun, came spilling out. 'I had a breakdown,' he said.
'What am I doing here with these fucking nutters?'

Whelan and Davis had been drinking on the plane and carried
on consuming the local rum at the luxury complex, Sam Lord's
Castle, where most of the band were booked to stay in their own
five-star apartments. They drank through the night and then
through the next day; two days later they were still drinking.
There was a cabaret-style calypso band called Spice playing at the
complex and Davis took a dislike to them. Whelan finally collapsed
and awoke the next morning to hear that Davis had gone on stage
and attacked Spice. 'He throated one of Spice,' said Whelan. 'It was
a thing PD used to do, grab people round the throat.' The band
were asked to vacate Sam Lord's Castle.

Blue Wave studio was in a beautiful, serene location, surrounded by sugar-cane fields and jungle. It was in the grounds of Eddy Grant's large family estate, where he lived in his own giant colonial-style house. Reggae superstar Grant, best known for his 1980s hits 'Electric Avenue' and 'I Don't Want to Dance', was away but his wife was at home. The studio was at the end of a long driveway, behind high whitewashed walls. It was one of several buildings in the grounds, near an outdoor pool the band could use. There was also a recreational space for the band, where a live-in cook would feed them. Bez and Shaun had been given their own accommodation in the grounds to reduce the chances of them disappearing entirely during the recording. Weymouth and Frantz had already settled in, bringing with them percussionist Bruce Martin and engineer Mark Roule. They reassured the studio manager, who had heard many worrying stories about the band, that they had things under control.

Bubbling with ideas to make the songs groove in a dirty, Mondays sort of way, Weymouth and Frantz set the band up live in the studio. They ran through the half-finished songs they had put together and, encouraged by the Talking Heads pair, started chasing new ideas. It was like being in The Boardwalk, but elevated to new levels by Martin's percussion and the producers' input and enthusiasm. Whelan, Day, Davis and Paul found they were having fun. They would meet at the studio at midday and all throw in ideas, slowly becoming a band again. Day had been listening to Eastern music, becoming particularly keen on the sound of Arabic instrument the rebab, and he played a bewildering selection of off-kilter but killer guitar parts. Paul and Whelan locked into some ferocious grooves and allowed themselves to be swept along by Weymouth's ebullience in particular. A new Mondays sound began to emerge, less aggressive, more nuanced, and Paul Davis was cooking up huge keyboard sounds. Here was the basis of the album and an unlikely resurrection seemed now possible.

But it was too late to save the Mondays. Drug abuse within the band was endemic and there was one drug in particular that was about to take these promising beginnings and shred them: crack. The band had been unable to locate any methadone on the island.

Paul's supply had run out and he started to experience severe stomach cramps, the stress-related pains he'd been experiencing since his marriage breakdown exacerbated by heroin withdrawal. He fell seriously ill. Shaun was in some sort of hell – once he'd drunk the small amount of methadone he'd managed to rescue from the airport disaster, he was in all sorts of pain. McGough found a doctor who put Shaun on Largactil (aka Thorazine), a heavy anti-psychotic. 'They use it in prison to dumb people down,' said Paul. 'You can tell who's on it because they do the Largactil shuffle, they just shuffle along, it zaps you of energy.' It rendered Shaun incapable of working. 'He tried doing one vocal and then stopped and said I can't do it.' Without a bassist and singer, work in the studio continued, but without any real sense of direction or input from the band. Then the crack dealers showed up.

'I was just having a walk around and there he was, Bobby the Diver – do you want anything?' said Paul. The Mondays had scored a huge quantity of marijuana as soon as they arrived, something that had alerted the local dealers to the fact there was a big-spending band up at Eddy's place – the 'white niggers', as they would become known to the dealers. Barbados, the Mondays now discovered, had a plentiful supply of cheap crack. The island was one of the many transshipment points for narcotics bound for Europe and the US. And on the beach the Rastafarians were giving rocks away like sweets. 'In Manchester a rock of crack could cost £30,' said Shaun. 'In Barbados it was 20p.' Even Bez said they may as well have packed up and left right then.

Frantz and Weymouth worked with the recordings, adding parts where they could, but chaos now reigned. Bez was hospitalised and feared he would lose his arm after flipping his brand new hire jeep on rough terrain near the studio. 'He knocked on the studio door with his arm hanging off,' said Paul. 'He was white, pure pale white. Tina came out and tried to help him through it. His eyes were rolling into the back of his head.' Derek hurried the mile to where Bez's upturned jeep lay, unsure if the police would be arriving soon and wanting to check the vehicle for drugs. He was horrified at the state of the jeep and the tiny space in the driver's window through which Bez had managed to escape: 'How the fuck he got out of there I don't know.' Specialists on the island advised Bez to return to the UK but he refused and was given a powerful painkiller, Pethidine.

It was the first of a series of car crashes. Paul Davis, who celebrated his twenty-sixth birthday in Barbados, had only just learned to drive and wrote off three hire cars. It was common to see the band's cars upturned at roadworks on the way to the Six Cross Roads in St Philip where they went to score crack. 'We'd all come in separate cars and blank each other,' said Davis. One night Whelan, who stayed off the crack, was in a bar drinking rum and having a spliff when a car ploughed straight through the front of the bar. It was Shaun. 'So we had to pay off the guy who owned the bar,' said Whelan.

All the band's partners and children were on the island now: Davis's girlfriend Belinda, Whelan's girlfriend Vanessa, Jane Day, who was pregnant, Shaun's Trisha and their baby, Bez's Debs, who was also pregnant, and their baby and Paul's two children. Shaun and Paul's mum Linda had arrived too, concerned over Paul's stomach pains. There was much to enjoy about Barbados – the good weather, pure white beaches, fresh fish and fruit. Soca music played on the radio and trips to the capital unearthed great tunes by The Congos and Barrington Levy, whose 'Love the Life You Live' was a favourite of Shaun's. There were barbecues on the beach and everyone seemed to settle to their own rhythm. Whelan and Day, who had both finished recording their parts, found beautiful houses to rent by the beach with stunning views and outdoor pools. Frantz and Weymouth continued to work on the music, and felt they had the basis of ten great tunes down on tape. The next step was getting Shaun's input. Weymouth spent days and nights playing Shaun the music. Nothing came, no lyrics, no inspiration. His head was scrambled. While the others settled into some sort of calm, his rambling descent picked up pace.

All he cared about was the crack pipe. He was, said Bez, 'way beyond reasoning'. Even Bez could not stand being in his company for 'any minute longer' than he had to. When he was not sleeping, he was scouring the island for drugs. There was now real concern among Frantz and Weymouth that Shaun wouldn't be able to get himself together and the album wouldn't be finished. The band were less concerned, having had years of Shaun leaving his lyrics to the last minute. Finally Whelan was persuaded to have Shaun stay at his and Vanessa's rented house in the hope he would find some peace to write in. The first night he returned from an aborted trip to score crack covered in blood, having written his car off. He begged to borrow Whelan's car. He wouldn't relent. Whelan handed him the keys. 'About two hours later he was back. Sorry Gaz, I've written yours off as well,' said Whelan. He was covered in even more blood, but refused to go to the hospital.

Frantz and Weymouth, doyens of the wild, late-1970s New York punk scene, were reportedly 'staggered' by the band's capacity for hedonism. 'A lot of times in Barbados Chris and I were really scared,' said Weymouth. 'These guys didn't know where the edge was. They were about to fall over the cliff.' In the fourth week, Whelan visited the studio to see how the album was progressing. 'I walked up to the pool and they had all these sun-loungers piled up into a crack den,' he said. 'It was hilarious.' As Whelan drove back across the island in a Mini Moke, a jeep/golf cart with no gears and a maximum speed of about 20 mph — the only vehicle the rental company would loan the band since the number of cars written off by the Mondays had reached double figures — he started to notice 'a lot of the local blokes dressed like Mancunians'. Obviously they'd been giving their clothes away, swapping them for rocks when they'd run out of money. There were also reports of furniture being stolen from the studio to exchange for crack — although the band claimed they just wanted something to sit on in an otherwise bare crack den.

Stories of the car crashes, chaos and crack binges were filtering back to the UK tabloids. There was even a story in the press about the band holding the album tapes to ransom, implying that the money being demanded from Factory, a reported £30,000, was needed to supply their drug habits. Although Whelan denies it, stuck in the middle of the carnage it was hard to tell the difference between the truth and the rumours that were flying around in Manchester.

After five weeks, and having burnt through most of the £250,000 budget, 'Cut 'Em Loose Bruce' was the only song completed in Barbados. 'The last thing we did, right at the end,' said Whelan. 'That was the only one where Shaun had lyrics.' Shaun had heard a story in a crack den about a judge called Bruce who was letting crackheads loose and proudly announced he had an idea for a song. 'So we decided to have some fun and try and make some Caribbean music, but dark.'

By this point Bez had left, an indication of just how out of control things had become, and McGough too had flown home. The band, some of them angry and frustrated, returned to Manchester in mid-March with Shaun heading straight to rehab at the famous Charter Clinic in Chelsea, his third attempt at drying out. He would be treated there for six weeks, at a reputed cost of £10,000, detoxifying and undergoing aversion therapy. The *NME* reported that the band were 'in disarray'. There were even rumours that Shaun was dead. McGough spent weeks trying to nurse him back to health.

Meanwhile, after almost three years of arguing over their future, and amid persistent rumours that they had broken up for good, New Order had finally entered the studio to record the follow-up to *Technique*. They were being kept in the dark about Factory's finances but were in no doubt that the label was in serious trouble as increasing pressure was exerted on them to get the album done. It would prove, however, to be a long drawn out process. According to Phil Saxe, still head of A&R at Factory, the label was precariously juggling various income streams to pay the studio bills on the album. The end result, Happy Mondays having spent like 'lunatics', was two albums that cost half a million pounds to produce, something that Factory would have struggled to cope with even at their most financially stable. Wilson continued to talk positively about the tie-up with London Records as lawyers on both sides looked at a deal that was said now to give the major label a controlling percentage. Gretton and Erasmus were unable to find alternative solutions and were resigned now to losing control and fourteen years of independence. Electronic bailed out, terminating their Factory contract, and signed with EMI subsidiary Parlophone. It was the first in a series of events that would weaken the Factory portfolio still further.

In May, a sober Shaun spent two weeks with Frantz and Weymouth in Comforts Place studio in Surrey completing the album. Weymouth encouraged Shaun to use the cut-up technique, popularised by William S. Burroughs, for his lyrics. Factory were desperate for the income streams a completed album would bring; in addition to the income from UK sales, they would trigger various licensing advances from Elektra and London Records. Wilson, who was busy organising In the City, an idea of his to host a UK equivalent of the New Music Seminar in Manchester with forums, delegates and showcase performances, talked about the album out-selling *Pills 'n' Thrills*. He imagined the Mondays and Guns N' Roses headlining In the City.

The fragile Shaun seemed to find a little of his old verve in Comforts Place, but the lyrics touched on deeply personal issues and were almost uniformly dark. On many songs, including 'Angel', he came across as repentant, but on others he appeared scornful of the band and seemed to try and deny responsibility for his brother's heroin addiction. He tried singing softly and he tried screaming. He was pliable and part of his brain seemed to have shut down, and the flights of fancy he had so often been able to turn into avalanches of winning non-sequiturs had virtually deserted him. The lyrics seemed forced, with only flashes of the agile wordplay displayed on *Squirrel*, *Bummed* and *Pills 'n' Thrills*. Unusually for Shaun, they also tended to conform to obvious patterns of verse/chorus/verse. They were still good, just a little more straightforward. And he was short of them. One track stayed instrumental.

Now that he had emerged from the crack psychosis, Shaun began to wish he'd taken more interest in the music. He was listening to a lot of hard-edged American rap, Bushwick Bill and Redman, and was frustrated at where he'd found himself – struggling to get into what the band had recorded even though it was some of the best playing of their career. He organised for Kermit, from well-liked Manchester rap band Ruthless Rap Assassins, to add a rap on 'Cut 'Em Loose Bruce'. Rowetta was once again asked to supply backing vocals, but on this album she played a more significant role, inject-ing her own melodies and much-needed character to many of the tracks. The overall impression was of an odd contrast between the smooth, almost too clean, uptempo soul/funk art rock, Rowetta's sweetly powerful melodies and Shaun's venting of breakdown and disintegration. It was not as immediate or as positive as *Pills 'n' Thrills*, but it had a direct lyrical meaning and musical sophistication that suggested mass appeal.

'Sunshine and Love' seemed to have all the elements of an obvious first single. It had the sleazy, lazy feel of a great Mondays track, combined with a Talking Heads percussive lilt and Rowetta's gospel-tinged chorus. 'Angel', too, was a Mondays classic, Shaun finding a groove and Rowetta and the band building waves of surging power behind him.

With the album complete, McGough was able to start generating much-needed cash for the band. Factory were struggling to pay the bills, which would total almost £400,000, on the album (the final mix took place in New York) and were unable to pass on the nearly £100,000 in licensing advances triggered from Elektra and London Records by its delivery. Wilson remained optimistic of selling shares in Factory to London Records for £4 million but the complex deal was still not completed. So McGough looked elsewhere. The band had recouped their £69,000 publishing advance from FFRR and he negotiated a further advance on publishing royalties of a quarter of a million pounds from them in staggered payments. The band was able to immediately share a much-needed £45,000. But this payment only highlighted the inequality in the band as Shaun demanded his fifty per cent legal entitlement of the songs' publishing copyright and got a £20,000 pay cheque. Paul, Whelan, Day and Davis agreed to a deal that saw them share the remaining fifty per cent equally and took home just over £5000 each. Bez got nothing. There were two similar payments due late in the year – same split. Dissension within the band reached new highs. 'We were all pissed off about the money,' said Mark Day. In fact, they really weren't a band any more.

Shaun and Paul chose 'Stinkin' Thinkin'' to be the first single released from the new album. Factory organised for the track to be remixed by American producer Stephen Hague, famed for his work with the Pet Shop Boys and New Order, and Boy's Own, the hip London crew centred on DJs Terry Farley and Andy Weatherall.

The band were shipped to London to shoot the video, but it was clear the director was only interested in Shaun and Bez and didn't really want the rest of the band there.

Promotion of the single was excruciating. Nirvana and grunge rock bands such as Pearl Jam were the new dominant force on the indie guitar scene, while upcoming UK glam guitar band Suede were the new rock press darlings. The Shamen, The Orb and The Prodigy were leading UK dance music away from the indie/dance sound. Interviews focused on the band's problems with Factory, among themselves and with drugs. In the *NME* the band were described as 'sullen' and 'awkward', Shaun's apologies for the homophobia controversy 'anxious and panicked . . . his voice squeaking'. 'When you start defending yourself,' he said, 'it's like, is he lying now to put the record straight, to get the sales back up or to get people coming back, and I am not.'

Shaun's brief period of sobriety ended, and he started to drink heavily and once again reached for the comfort blanket of heroin. Back in Manchester, he was arrested and charged with drink driving, failing to stop at the scene of an accident and driving without due care and attention.

'Stinkin' Thinkin'' entered the UK charts at thirty-nine in August 1992, four places below the latest release from Inspiral Carpets. Nonetheless Nicki Kefalas managed to get the band on *Top of the Pops*. She soon wished she hadn't. The band members travelled to London separately, while Bez didn't show at all. Rowetta was dressed as a schoolgirl, clutching a teddy bear. Shaun had opted to sing live on the show in an attempt to prove he was capable, at least, of that much. He looked smart too in his new Issey Miyake jacket and clipped short hair, slim and handsome, something of the smirk returning. Midway through the performance, however, he forgot the words and was forced to take a crumpled piece of paper with the lyrics on it from his back pocket and grimace at it. 'Stinkin' Thinkin'' peaked at number thirty-one. It was not the comeback Factory had been expecting and hardly the encouraging sign Wilson was looking for as he continued to try and push through the London Records deal. The Mondays were looking a less attractive proposition by the minute.

Roger Ames travelled to Manchester for Wilson's In the City music convention in September 1992. The London Records boss was being lined up to take over as chairman of the label's parent company, Polygram. The event was a success but the Mondays showcase did not happen; instead, new British bands Suede and Radiohead, who were being tipped as the UK's Nirvana, proved popular attractions. A new Manchester band, Oasis, who channelled Madchester via Sex Pistols-style guitar rock, were ignored, and despite their repeated visits to Factory to see Phil Saxe could not get a deal with their favourite label. Their huge breakthrough was two years off. The Bowie/glam rock-influenced Suede would hit number one with their debut album in 1993, and remain popular throughout Grunge and the coming Britpop era. Radiohead were a more difficult sell, and their success would not come until 1995 when their artful guitar rock sound became popular in America.

In Manchester, Ames heard worrying stories about Shaun's relapse and the Mondays' inner turmoil that the upcoming positive reviews of the new album could not entirely put out of his mind. Then there were the stories about New Order – it was rumoured that Factory did not hold the rights to any of the band's recordings. If that was true, and if the Mondays were truly spent, what did the label have? It was becoming an increasingly desperate situation for Factory. There was also an armed robbery at Dry during which £10,000 was stolen. Advance orders on the Mondays album were poor – nowhere near the 300,000 Wilson had hoped for – and New Order had not yet completed even the basic recording on their new album. If the London deal didn't go ahead soon, they would run out of money.

The title of the album – not one of Shaun's, he was keen to point out – was *Happy Mondays . . . Yes Please!* It was how the Blue Wave studio manager used to answer the phone in Barbados. Considering the state the band had been in before they started recording and what had happened during recording, it was amazing that it was here at all, even more so that it was a more than worthy addition to the band's catalogue. It suffered from the vocals being recorded in a different place and time to the music but it was grown-up music, adult in its instrumentation and complex rhythms. The influence of Frantz and Weymouth was clear but not heavy-handed and the album still sounded like the Mondays – as ever, unique. Many reviews focused on the chaos surrounding the band and the amount the recording had cost, with the band being presented as wasteful, ungrateful and, if you had to put it in words, a bit thick. A full-page review of the album in *Melody Maker* ran under the headline '*Happy Mondays... Yes Please!* No Thanks', though the review suggested the album was actually 'pretty good'. The band was not being judged on their music. *Select* panned the album mainly because of the band's 'loathsome behaviour'.

In the past, after the excitement of the avalanche of praise for *Squirrel*, the Mondays would scarcely have paid attention to their album reviews, the page after page of glowing praise and strange interpretations of their music. Now the bad reviews hurt and they drew strength wherever they could find it. Not everyone hated them. *Q* magazine awarded the album four out of five stars: 'Somehow despite everything, Happy Mondays are back on the case...against all odds, they've pulled it off again.' In the *NME*, Stuart Bailie wrote, 'the last 20 lines of Angel read like T.S. Eliot with cheap crack in his blood...one of Shaun's richest and darkest creations', concluding: 'Some people will never forgive Happy Mondays for what they've done and said in the last couple of years and that's a perfectly cool reaction. All I'm saying is that they're back again, unflinching and honest...and there's life in the band still.'

The album entered the UK charts at number eight, selling 30,000 copies. It proved beyond doubt that there was still commercial life left in the band, but sales needed to be substantially higher to have any impact on Factory's finances.

The band, if not Shaun, were proud of the album. Paul had told *NME* they should be 'accepted as musicians' and were not the crazed characters suggested by the media stories. He found something of his old self, able to point out the positive reviews, the promising sales, to bolster the band's fragile state. All 17,000 tickets for the first seven dates of a UK tour sold out quickly and six more dates were added. McGough had booked the band into medium-size 2000-capacity venues such as the Free Trade Hall in Manchester and Brixton Academy in London. These were not the stadiums they had been playing but they were more than respectable. Finally there was some respite from the interminable downward spiral.

McGough organised for the band a huge, expensive and impressive rehearsal room in Ancoats and they had two weeks to rehearse for the tour. In Shaun's continued absence, and supported by their faithful road crew, they worked up thunderous versions of the album tracks. The songs sounded powerful and newly bass heavy – and all the better for that. All four musicians were suffering – Paul with heroin, Whelan, Day and Davis with negative thoughts about the future of the band – but they had something rare together and a bounty of great songs to call on. They even started writing new songs, determined to have something new to play to Shaun to reinvigorate him.

It was not the same, and the longstanding problems over drugs, booze, egos and money were never far from the surface, but it was workable. They were – a word rarely used to describe the Mondays – professional. And they needed the money this tour would generate. Shaun didn't: Mr Fifty Per Cent pocketed another easy £20,000 from the publishing advance. Except he did – his drug habit was now out of control. There didn't seem to be any ups and downs with Shaun any more, just one long down.

British hip-hop stars Stereo MCs, whose recently released album *Connected* was at number two and whose single of the same name had cracked the top twenty both in the UK and on the *Billboard* Hot 100, were the support act. They had played with the Mondays on the band's ill-fated 1991 US tour and taken much of the band's back beat for their new album, adding rap and sassy samples. They were on a giant high. Nothing could have depressed Shaun more. He looked at the modern hip-hop vibe and the vitality, the upbeat live show, the band's unity, and then at his band, his gang – he disliked much of the new album, they were burned-out. It was a fucking nightmare. There was no unity, no band, no one was communicating. They were nasty and filthy.

The band were aghast with Shaun, seen smoking heroin at the side of the stage in Glasgow and smoking crack while being interviewed for *Q* magazine. He was also drinking a bottle of vodka or whisky a night. During an interview with BBC2 show *The O-Zone* he looked broken, as if he would rather be anywhere else. 'He was just so deep into heroin,' said McGough. The tragedy was that even now, ruined and hopeless, the Mondays were such a huge and powerful band. Their heads were gone, full of negativity and drug addiction, but they were still everything Saxe, Wilson and McGough had always believed – the band of their generation, astonishing, distinct and important.

The show at Brixton Academy was filmed for Japanese TV, where the new material sounded fresh and mature. 'Monkey in the Family' in particular throbbed, the bass booming and the band grooving. The following night's show, also in London at the Kilburn National, was reviewed by David Sinclair in *The Times*. He found that despite Bez, the arm he'd broken in Barbados still in a sling and shaking one maraca, cutting a 'rather pathetic sight' and Shaun's 'portrait of loutish indifference', the band 'still displayed unmistakable clout'. He wrote how the 'guitarist glued songs together with sequences both imaginative and melodic'. The *NME* review of the same show praised the rhythm section that 'drives them forward like never before . . . someone cares deeply for the band for them to sound like this'. Anyone who thinks this is all wishful thinking, selective revisionism, can listen to the now infamous bootleg from Kilburn National, *Kill Nat*. They were pure funk. They were attracting new fans, while those who had stayed loyal appreciated there had always been a real band beneath the Madchester hype.

Once they got on stage, 'nothing else mattered', said Paul. 'Everything else was forgotten: what was on stage was real, we weren't just going through the motions.' Offstage, they couldn't get away from one another quick enough. Privately they seethed. Davis and Day talked of forming a band with one of the band's road crew as vocalist. They tried to rope in Whelan. Paul went back to the warmth of heroin. Shaun and Bez slid endlessly towards rock bottom. 'I was putting fires out everywhere,' said McGough. On 5 November 1992, Bonfire Night, after finishing the UK tour and with European dates scheduled for December, the Mondays played to 20,000 screaming fans at the Budokan in Tokyo. It was a reminder that there was a world out there, where the band could still prosper. They had postponed, rearranged and then cancelled several Japanese dates previously and the gig was attended by the city's fashionable crowd. The Mondays impressed. But in the aftermath of the gig the fractured band died. In a dark room backstage, shooting up heroin, and later amid blank stares and conspiratorial whispers in a modern bar in a luxury Japanese hotel. A long way from Swinton. Spirits broken. Confused. Exhausted. Enough.

23
EMI

By the time the Mondays returned from Japan, Factory Records was also dead, killed by the band that breathed life into it in the first place. 'I still believe Tony Wilson can run a successful company,' Roger Ames told *Music Week*, the industry's trade weekly. 'But we just couldn't make a deal. The numbers just didn't add up.' New Order didn't want to kill Factory, quite the opposite. But 'the twat', 'the arsehole', 'the cunt' – Tony Wilson, in the words of New Order and their manager Rob Gretton – had behaved so recklessly with the label's finances that they had little choice.

Even now, deep down, New Order knew in their hearts that Wilson's intentions were good. There was just too much debt. Everything was such a mess. They had to save themselves. In the end, Ames and London Records had been told that, due to the radical nature of Factory in its infancy, New Order owned the copyright on the recordings they made for the label; the same applied to Joy Division. Factory had nothing to sell, certainly not New Order or Joy Division – nothing worth the £4 million London had reputedly offered for controlling shares in the company.

Negotiations had begun between New Order and London, without the burden of Factory. The numbers were never revealed, only that London were prepared to make good the money Factory owed New Order and pay to complete their new album. Factory might have owed New Order half a million pounds or more. 'Our hands were tied,' said Bernard Sumner. To make matters worse for Factory, who had nurtured them for over ten years and five studio albums, the album New Order were close to completing, over four years since their last, would be a number one hit worldwide in May 1993.

Manchester's Utopian vision had expired. Factory was £3.5 million in debt and the banks (NatWest was owed close to £1 million) could no longer be charmed by Wilson. The label went into administration, a decision made public on 23 November 1992. Factory's official statement read: 'Factory tried to do too many things, from adventurous buildings to ambitious recording projects, at a time when some foresight of the economic climate might have suggested restraint.' The receivers, Leonard Curtis, added: 'It's a real muddle...a fairly complex situation.' They expressed disbelief that Factory and Joy Division/New Order had worked together for so long on the strength of a gentlemen's agreement. The list of creditors was frighteningly long. The Factory headquarters were put up for sale with a guide price of £350,000, a fraction of what they had cost to buy, renovate and refurbish. The falling price of property in the recession, the loans taken out to buy and make good the property, and the rise in interest rates – up recently to a panic-inducing fifteen per cent in the UK, without any significant income after a succession of backfiring projects and problems at The Hacienda – had done for them. Wilson had gambled everything on the deal with London Records. His plan B seemed to be based on hoping for a miracle.

Having struck a deal with New Order, London also hoped to make one for Factory's other major artist, Happy Mondays. As an indication of recent poor A&R decisions and the rapid decline of Madchester, the label's other pop acts, The Wendys, Adventure Babies, Cath Carroll and Northside, were left to wither. London made an offer for the Mondays but it was abject. The band currently had an un-recouped balance with London of approximately £400,000 relating to the recently struck deals for advances on publishing and European licensing rights. *Yes Please!* had underperformed, having sold 50,000 to date, and London were anxious to try and recoup some of that amount. The deal they were offering would lock the Mondays in for three albums with a low-figure advance, a mountain of debt and a number of caveats including the ownership of the band's entire back catalogue – the one thing they owned that had significant worth. Their situation was so bleak McGough was forced to consider the offer.

Elektra, surprisingly, was keen to extend their deal with the group for America. The Boy's Own remix of 'Stinkin' Thinkin'' had been a hit in American clubs and remarkably had reached number one on the *Billboard* US Dance charts. The final Factory release, on 9 November 1992, was 'Sunshine and Love', the second single to be taken from *Yes Please!* It was never properly promoted or distributed in the UK, peaking at sixty-two. Wilson claimed he'd raised money to make a video but Shaun 'wouldn't get out of bed to do it'. In America the Boy's Own mix of 'Sunshine and Love' was proving to be another dance hit, reaching number five on the *Billboard* Dance chart. Elektra were offering $125,000 to the band to license their next album. But that was money that would be eaten up by London Records should the band accept its three-album offer.

McGough delivered a statement to the media stating that the collapse of Factory had rid Happy Mondays of all contractual obligations (*Yes Please!* was the final album of a contracted four-album deal with the label). He said: 'We are looking forward to a new start. We will negotiate a worldwide deal. It is not the end of an era, it's just business and in this climate, everyone has to be ready for things like this.' McGough hoped he might attract another label. One that did not know the extent of the band's heroin and cocaine problems. 'That's called spin,' he said of the statement. 'I wanted to make it clear we weren't going down in flames with the label.'

The fall of Factory compounded what the group had felt in Japan – that it was over. Heroin had ruined the Ryder brothers, cocaine made the band brittle, it was the end of an era – time to start afresh, get a new group going. Whelan was already experimenting with former Smiths bass player Andy Rourke. Davis and Day might join them, and Day was being sounded out by other Manchester acts, such as the well-respected Ed Barton.

The offer from London came amid a period where the band were unsure of where they stood, legally or financially. There was a suggestion if these three left that Paul, Shaun and Bez might try and keep the name Happy Mondays, and concern over what might happen to the demo tapes for their next album, put together during tour rehearsals and dubbed 'the unfinished symphony'. 'The boat was sinking and everybody was bailing out, getting what they could,' said Day. 'It was drugs and paranoia. Ten years of that – for what? Where did all the money go? The band didn't get it.'

There was no money left. The Mondays were broke. They were in pieces. The band was dead and the idea of carrying on was 'a joke', said Whelan. The London deal would just keep it alive by artificial means. Time to pull the plug.

The collapse of Factory clouded their thoughts further. Maybe the Mondays could only ever have existed on Factory? The label had allowed the band to operate with a unique looseness, so that they had an almost accidental feel. London would demand they work harder, do more promotion – but maybe that wasn't such a bad thing? They were dead and now they were cracking up. It didn't make sense. It was hard to make the break clean after all those years of closeness and adventure together.

The Mondays cancelled the European tour that was scheduled for December, claiming that it was due to the birth of Mark Day's first child. Many of their close associates were owed money by Factory – Nicki Kefalas at Out Promotions was owed £10,000, Jayne Houghton at Excess Press £15,000, Oakenfold and Osborne £40,000 in unpaid producer royalties. Via a statement the band offered their sympathies. For many, however, the collapse of Factory was their fault – and it was widely presumed that it was the chaotic and costly Barbados recording session that had tipped the label into bankruptcy.

Over the years this argument has often been aired. It was simply not true. Factory had agreed a £250,000 budget for the Mondays' album before the band had even begun the recording. Undoubtedly the label had overstretched itself trying to pay for the recording of both a Mondays and a New Order album at the same time, but at least the Mondays had delivered. Although they had gone over budget, Factory had been able to recoup close to £200,000 on the worldwide licensing of the record and the substantial revenues from 50,000 sales. *Pills 'n' Thrills* had generated over £1 million for the label, and some of the money from that was still owed to the band.

When Factory went under, they *owed* the Mondays money in unpaid royalties and their share of licensing advances. 'A sizeable amount of cash,' said McGough. 'It was at least £30,000 and it might have been double that.' That did not fit the convenient narrative – far easier to pin the blame on the crazy, crackhead Mondays.

McGough wrote a letter addressed to 'all the band' on 18 December 1992 to outline a future. In it he discussed the London Records offer and the situation with Elektra, but said no decision would be made on the London offer 'until we have heard from EMI'. Clive Black, the 28-year-old director of A&R at EMI Records, had taken an interest in the band and planned to visit Manchester in January to hear more of the group's 'new material'. In the letter, McGough said it was important they continue to work on the new songs they had started. In the Ancoats rehearsal room Shaun had freestyled lyrics to the tunes the band had written while rehearsing for the UK tour and his vocals had been recorded in the room by the band's soundman Si Machan. This was the material that Clive Black had heard: new titles like 'Did You Ever', 'Opportunity Knows', 'Dirty Bitch' and 'Walking the Dog', all, according to Paul, eighty per cent finished.

Black drove up to Manchester from London in January 1993 and was taken to the rehearsal room to meet the band and hear more of these new songs. The Mondays hadn't rehearsed and didn't much see the point of reconvening. Black was under the impression Shaun was off drugs and was unaware that the bizarre concoction the singer was drinking was a mix of methadone and brandy. The band started limbering up, as Shaun continued to free associate – using vocal melodies that sounded like 'She'll Be Coming 'Round the Mountain' and 'Old MacDonald Had a Farm'. He had the microphone tight up to his face and Black could have sworn Shaun was actually singing these children's nursery rhymes. But he could not take his eyes off Shaun, who despite looking unhealthy radiated, he said, an 'incredible charisma'.

The EMI man had gone to Manchester, if he was honest, largely out of curiosity and had expected the band to be a mess. But as he sat there absorbing it all, and the band worked out, he found he didn't want to leave the room, he was mesmerised. At one point Shaun wandered up to him and said, 'Don't die on me, man, don't die on me, I own fifty per cent of you.' Quick as a flash, Black shot back, '*Stardust*, David Essex,' having recognised that Shaun was quoting the film's final lines – spoken by the manager, played by Adam Faith, of Essex's pop star character, Jim McLean, who had overdosed on live TV. Shaun was impressed. They had a connection. 'That's my fucking favourite film, man,' Shaun said. 'That is my whole fucking life, everything is in that film.'

They were the only words Black exchanged with the band on this visit, but the day made him feel fantastic and he was simply spellbound by Shaun. Yes, he'd read the bad press about the band, but he felt now he wanted this. He called them 'one of the most important groups ever to come out of this country' and was experienced enough, he said, to know that all groups go through a low – they could come through it: 'They were too good to ignore, that was my view.' He spoke to McGough and found it would be, in his words, 'ridiculously cheap' to get the band.

The next morning, Black talked to his superiors and convinced them the Mondays were worthy of the investment. He said they were both excited and fearful at the prospect of working with the band. He was able to go back and make an offer to McGough by lunchtime: £175,000 – all in, including recording costs for the band's next album – for world rights excluding America. McGough leaked to the press that the deal was worth £1.7 million, and it would be if EMI decided to pick up the options on the four-album deal. Black, however, was focused on this first album: £175,000 was a good figure. If the band could record the album for £75,000 – which was possible – they would be able to share a £100,000 payday.

The Mondays were forced to look again at the situation they were in. Black had spent time around huge talents such as Kate Bush, David Bowie and Michael Jackson, signing bands the Mondays could only admire, such as Afrika Bambaataa and Lee 'Scratch' Perry. He was highly thought of in the industry and was on his way to becoming managing director of EMI. He had come at them in a clear frame of mind and made his decision. For months, all the band had felt was negativity. Now, they began to see things from Black's point of view. Maybe they were the group he thought they were. Here, now, was a last chance to rescue the Mondays. They told McGough to accept the offer.

The contracts were drawn up, negotiated and ready to sign. Before this, however, Black travelled by train to Manchester on 10 February 1993, ostensibly to discuss details about recording the album, such as what studio to use and what producer the band might choose. There was, however, something else on his mind: he'd heard Shaun was using again. McGough met Black at the station and took him for lunch in Chinatown. Here, Black asked McGough if what he'd heard was true.

McGough thought there was no point trying to deny it, because if he did the truth was bound to come out. 'I said, Well he is, and is that an issue?' Black answered calmly. He told McGough he knew of plenty of people in the music business with heroin habits, but you'd never know because they had it locked down, they were perfectly able to function. Black wondered if Shaun controlled the drugs or they controlled him. What was more important to Shaun, he asked: the drugs or the band? Was he going to get out of bed in the morning and go to the studio and make the record, or simply take the cash because he needed to feed his habit? McGough didn't have the answer. He said Black would have to ask Shaun himself.

They finished eating and McGough drove them over to the band's rehearsal room. McGough had warned the band and Shaun that this meeting with Black had to go well – no fuck-ups, everyone to turn up on time. They arrived in Ancoats and pulled up outside the rehearsal room, right next to another car. 'In the car was Shaun,' said Black. He looked startled and started frantically wiping at his nose. Black got out of the car and Shaun wound down his window. 'Go in mate, our kid's in there, I'm just going to Kentucky,' he said. Black answered, 'OK, see you in a minute.' Shaun repeated, 'Yeah, won't be long, just going to Kentucky.'

Black thought little of it and went inside the rehearsal room with McGough. The band were kicking a football around. Black smiled and watched as Whelan and Day juggled the ball between them. They came across one by one to say hello and started to jam a few of the new tunes.

An hour went by and they took a break. Where the fuck was Shaun? They passed some time talking to Black and McGough and went back to jamming. Three hours went by. Black asked, 'Where is this Kentucky?' The band was exasperated. Someone told him Kentucky was 'skag' – heroin. 'I gave it another hour and then we left,' said Black.

Here was the very essence of the dilemma at the heart of the Mondays. It was the band's attitude to drugs that had seen them become the defining band of the 'chemical generation'; it was what had marked them out from all the other bands. Ecstasy Shaun saw as the key. It was when things had started to turn for the band, when all the connections were made: when everyone was higher than high. Drugs. All his best lyrics had come from them. 'To him it was like the drugs are what have made us famous, that's why everyone is into us,' said McGough. He'd been as close to Shaun as anyone for the past five years and had spent the past year desperately trying to get him levelled out. 'Shaun couldn't make a cultural differentiation between Ecstasy/pot and heroin/crack,' he said. 'He was saying, No you don't get it, it's always been about the drugs. I said, It's not about that, mate.'

It was just an excuse. Even if Shaun did believe it was drugs that had built the band, he had forgotten about the music, didn't care about the band, could he stop? The answer was no. He hadn't gone chasing heroin instead of meeting Black because he thought it was cool. It was because he was an addict. He couldn't do anything without it. If it was a choice between the music and the drugs, he had no choice. And he knew how pathetic it looked.

McGough had been here before. He drove Black back to the station trying to look angry and pissed off, as if this was all manageable. He called someone on his state-of-the-art mobile phone, and Black heard a woman answer. McGough asked if Shaun was there. She said, 'No he's not, fuck off.' He phoned someone else. They didn't know where he was either, 'Fuck off Nathan.' It was a routine people were bored of.

Black had his answer. Shaun was not a junkie who had it under control. He was messed up. 'He took drugs to get obliterated, to try to destroy himself,' said Black. If Shaun couldn't turn up to collect a cheque for £175,000, 'which was basically what it was', said Black, then how could he ever work in a system like EMI, where there would be deadlines and demands and endless hoops to jump through? It seemed clear now. Shaun didn't really want to do this, he just wanted the money to pay his heroin dealer.

McGough asked if there was any way of rescuing the deal. Black said: 'Is Shaun capable, if he's got forty-eight hours' notice, of going to a meeting and conducting himself for twenty minutes? Can he at least do that?'

McGough finally got hold of Shaun on the phone to explain that Black wanted him to go to his EMI office in London to show he wanted the deal to go ahead. Shaun's reply was, 'If Clive Black thinks I'm going to come all the way to London to suck his cock, he can fuck off, Clive Black can suck my balls.' He then offered up his reasoning to McGough: Black was trying to split the band up. Black wasn't interested in signing the band, he just wanted to sign him – Shaun.

McGough knew it was over: 'This was absolute fantasy, none of this has been discussed or mentioned.' He called Black to tell him Shaun wasn't prepared to come to London cap in hand. Black laughed. It was why he loved Shaun, loved the Mondays. It was also what made his mind up. He asked McGough if he could get a number to call Shaun on. McGough set it up so that he would call Shaun at his mum and dad's house in Worsley the next morning. Trisha had left him and taken their daughter with her, blaming Shaun's crack habit and telling the press drugs were destroying him. Shaun was either incapable of looking after himself or lying low. The EMI lawyers told Black he should record the call. He did.

'I phoned Shaun at ten and his mother answered,' said Black. Linda fetched Shaun to the phone. Black told him straight: he was going to have to pull the deal. 'I'd love to do this, I think you're amazing, but I just don't believe EMI could take the upheaval and the unpredictableness of it.' Before Black could finish his sentence, Shaun interrupted. 'If this is about PD, he couldn't fucking play keyboards at all.'

Black said, 'Look Shaun, it's not about PD at all, it's about you, I'll be honest with you, it's about you.'

Shaun said, 'PD, right, he couldn't fucking play, PD couldn't do fucking nothing.' Black could not steer Shaun away from the thought that Paul Davis was to blame.

He next called McGough to tell him the deal was off, and McGough in turn phoned each band member to tell them he was quitting. 'We'd had the front cover of *Music Week* saying this EMI deal was going to happen,' said McGough. 'You don't come back from that. You're done at that point – you're cooked.'

'And that was that,' said Black. 'The end of it.'

The way Shaun had messed up the deal convinced Whelan it would never have worked out anyway. And Paul shouldered his share of the blame. Until he'd got involved in heroin the band had been able to function around Shaun; now he was an addict too. Two junkies in a band was one too many. When the drugs had become more important than the band to Paul, it had been over. Paul now needed money to feed his habit – they all needed money, they all had mortgages that needed paying. But there was nothing left.

In fact it was worse than that. The band had a tax bill to pay and their assets, their valuable back catalogue, was tied up until that was sorted. There was one final attempt to save the band. A meeting was called near McGough's office, and everyone turned up, even Shaun. Everyone was frazzled, on edge, and there was discussion about taking a break for twelve months, of people going off and doing other projects. Shaun apologised for the EMI debacle. By the end of it he was pleading with the others to give the band another chance. But they wouldn't have it – they just wanted to leave, make a clean break from him.

From there, Whelan and Day had to race to the rehearsal room and grab their equipment, pile it in the back of a car and disappear. They feared that otherwise Shaun would nick it all and sell it to pay for drugs. 'Everyone was just running into that rehearsal room and grabbing what they could,' said Paul. 'There was tax owed. There were no wages or payments or publishing until that was paid off. We owed a load of money for equipment, hire of the rehearsal place...I was back at my mum's, back in my old bedroom, thinking how did this happen?'

The band's business partnership, Wabash Communications, went into receivership on 17 February 1993. Shaun, Paul, Bez, Whelan, Day and Davis were issued with redundancy notices terminating their employment. 'There's no chance of reforming,' Paul Davis told the *Manchester Evening News*. 'I'd rather be on the dole than be in a band with Shaun.' Day said Davis was misquoted. 'I got linked in with it,' he said. 'What PD meant was, in his present state.' He and Whelan were forced into the humiliating position of having to sign on the dole. 'I didn't want to but I had a house and I couldn't afford the mortgage,' said Whelan. 'I heard someone three people behind me saying, Fucking hell, it's a bit of a comedown for him, one minute he's in Barbados the next he's signing on in Swinton. It's real life, it's what happened and I don't blame anyone. We stood by and let it happen.'

Shaun was said to be scouring the city carrying a hunting knife looking for McGough. On 25 February 1993 he appeared in court in Manchester on a charge relating to the drink-drive incident the previous summer. He admitted driving with excess alcohol, failing to stop and driving without due care and was fined £650 and banned from driving for eighteen months. It was revealed he'd crashed into a Lada driven by a church pastor.

In court Shaun stated he was penniless, that all his assets had been frozen, and requested two months to pay the fine. He was labelled 'a fallen pop star'. He sold a story to the *Sun* for some fast money, regurgitating stories about his troubled childhood. He said he couldn't recall anything of the Mondays' biggest gigs, talked about the pressure of stardom, drugs and the fool he'd made of himself on drink. But, and this was the message, he was clean now. He said he hoped the Mondays could get back together. 'Now I'm clean I've written a load of good stuff,' he said. It would be a long time before anyone would believe the half of it.

Afterword

It would be six long years, from 1993 to 1999, before Happy Mondays cleared their debts and the band members began to receive any revenue from their back catalogue. They were cited as one of the chief inspirations behind mid-90s Britpop, the UK-led scene that came to replace American-led grunge rock as the music press's next big thing. Leading Britpop bands Blur and Suede acknowledged the Mondays as a key influence, while the scene's towering presence, Oasis, not only came from Manchester but spoke of Factory Records and the Mondays in reverent tones.

Oasis' hit debut album, *Definitely Maybe*, went to UK number one in 1994, the same year Blur scored their first number one album with *Parklife*. These two bands began a rivalry that came to define Britpop and when the 'war' between them made *News at Ten*, indie guitar music finally became inextricably mainstream, paving the way for the huge success of acts such as Arctic Monkeys and The Libertines. Despite the success of Blur and Oasis in the UK, Britpop's impact on America, like Madchester, was limited. Happy Mondays meanwhile were seen – for better or worse – as a key building block in the rise of 'lad culture' during the 1990s, exemplified by Oasis and *Loaded* magazine, when beer, football, sex, anti-intellectualism and consumerism came to signify a new sort of maleness. During all this, the darkness, originality and artistic worth of much of the Mondays' music became largely forgotten, but they remained contemporary.

Throughout this period, the band members' fortunes diverged wildly. The musical careers of Paul Davis, Gary Whelan and Mark Day stuttered then collapsed. A band called Delicious, briefly featuring all three, disintegrated after a year without releasing any material. Davis then disappeared. Whelan admitted to having some sort of breakdown. Mark Day worked with Manchester poet/ songwriter Ed Barton before setting up a business selling educational books. He admitted that it was tough at first, but he made a career of it. He also started teaching guitar in schools, which would become his main employment over the years. He didn't seem to miss life in a rock 'n' roll band.

In the period straight after the Mondays split, brothers Paul and Shaun stayed together, working on a new band and new material. But soon even Paul could no longer put up with Shaun and walked out. He and his new girlfriend, Astrella, put together a band and recorded demos in Los Angeles, but Paul's heroin addiction grew worse and he went into rehab four times, finally being sectioned to a mental hospital. 'I completely lost it,' he said. Shaun stuck at the new band and in 1995, during the Britpop era, returned with Black Grape, featuring Bez and rapper Kermit, who'd appeared on the Mondays' final album, and embarked on a second magnificent run of success. The band's debut album, *It's Great When You're Straight . . . Yeah*, went to number one in the UK and spawned two top ten singles. Problems, however, with management, personnel and money meant the group was short-lived and they split after a weak second album in 1998.

The Hacienda closed in June 1997 and went into liquidation with debts of £500,000. Gang violence had continued to plague the club as it blighted the city. Labour, under Tony Blair, won a landslide victory that year, returning to power after eighteen years of Tory rule; Manchester began to emerge from its post-war malaise and the recent, horrific era of 'Gunchester' or 'Gangchester' (Oasis had quit the city as soon as they achieved any success) and regenerate itself to compete on a world stage. Bids to host the 1996 and 2000 Olympics paved the way for the revitalised city to host the 2002 Commonwealth Games. The Hacienda was demolished and luxury apartments built on the site. Tony Wilson continued to run the popular In the City, the UK's leading annual music industry convention. He, and Factory, rightly took much credit for Manchester's renaissance and Wilson was often credited as the man who put the city on the map for its music and nightlife – some dubbed him 'Mr Manchester'. His attempts to revive Factory, as Factory Too and F4, failed. Factory's Dry bar, however, is still open today amid the now thriving Northern Quarter of the city.

In 1999, Happy Mondays reformed but without Paul Davis and Mark Day, and with Rowetta taking a more central role. They sold out the 20,000-capacity Manchester Arena and toured extensively around the world, performing alongside Oasis on many stadium shows. A new single, a cover of Thin Lizzy's 'The Boys Are Back in Town', put them back in the charts, peaking at twenty-four. For a moment they were press darlings again, appearing on the front cover of *NME* with the music weekly also handing Shaun a 'Godlike Genius' award in 2000. Shaun did much to disparage the musical worth of the enterprise. In one of the many interviews undertaken to promote the comeback, he was asked if he thought the Mondays would go down in musical history. His response: 'I couldn't give a fuck.' He said the reunion was all about the money, admitting his motivation was the need to pay off a tax bill. It was too much for brother Paul, who quit saying he never wanted to work with Shaun again. Paul finally kicked heroin, relocated to Los Angeles and formed his own band, Big Arm. The whole Mondays enterprise ground to a halt in 2001 with Shaun reputedly hooked on Valium and Temazepam.

The following year the Mondays were fictionalised in *24 Hour Party People*, a feature film based on the history of Factory with Steve Coogan playing Tony Wilson. It did much to fortify the image of the Mondays as depraved, criminal and lucky, hooligan idiots, the music a by-product of their laddish antics. In 2003 Shaun released his first solo album, the astonishingly warped, musically minimal, and brilliant *Amateur Night in the Big Top*. It sold poorly and Shaun continued to be mired in financial problems, all of which were laid bare in the shocking 2004 BBC3 documentary *Shaun Ryder: The Ecstasy and the Agony*. In it Shaun appeared ill, bloated and lost, his current woes relating to a lawsuit with the management of Black Grape that prevented him from working.

The same year, Rowetta took part in *The X Factor*, reaching the final four. She admitted to battling alcoholism and her ex-husband sold a story about how he'd violently beaten her during their marriage. She would become a high-profile figure in raising awareness of domestic abuse. In 2005, Bez, declared bankrupt and facing a large tax bill, took part in *Celebrity Big Brother*. It was rumoured that he'd smuggled a stash of Ecstasy into the house. In any case, he won the show but was soon claiming that the £50,000 winnings and raised profile caused him nothing but problems. He was declared bankrupt for a second time in 2008. He had personal difficulties and was pictured taking part in a bare-knuckle boxing fight.

Shaun was rescued from purgatory when Damon Albarn, formerly of Blur, used him to provide vocals on a UK number one hit, 'Dare', by his cartoon band Gorillaz. From 2005 until 2010, Shaun, Whelan and Bez gigged intermittently as Happy Mondays, even releasing an album, *Uncle Dysfunktional*, which reached seventy-three in the UK. In April 2007, at America's huge Coachella festival, they were introduced on stage by an ailing Tony Wilson, who was suffering from cancer. It would be Wilson's final public appearance. He died on 10 August 2007, aged fifty-seven. Despite Wilson's clear undying love, this version of the band, with Whelan – now living in Canada and with his own band Hippy Mafia – often absent, seemed to drain much remaining goodwill towards the band and to further damage the Happy Mondays' reputation. In 2010 Shaun took part in *I'm a Celebrity...Get Me Out of Here!* and was a popular contestant, coming second to Stacey Solomon. In the immediate publicity blitz after the show's finale, watched by ten million viewers, he announced his intention to launch a solo career. Many expressed surprise that he was not dead already and he cut a likeable figure on a variety of light entertainment shows. His solo career, however, amounted to nothing more than a greatest hits album packed with Mondays songs.

In January 2012, inspired by the recent hullabaloo surrounding the reformation of The Stone Roses, who had imploded shortly after releasing their critically mauled second album in 1994, Shaun announced that the original line-up of Happy Mondays was reforming – all six of them, plus Rowetta. 'The whole was always greater than the sum of the parts,' he said. A few months later they played a sell-out tour of the UK including, again, Manchester Arena. The band also played South America for the first time, and festival dates across Europe. These greatest hits sets were warmly received. Despite the loss of Davis the band played more high-profile festival dates in 2013 before embarking on a brave UK tour, where they played the *Bummed* album in its entirety twenty-five years after it was released.

It was a turning point, both critically and within the band. New hip British bands were now, and still are, often being shoehorned into a lineage of bad boy rockers that leads from The Rolling Stones to the Pistols, through the Mondays to The Libertines. And there were hints of the Mondays, musically and image-wise, in many new upcoming guitar acts. But *Bummed* was an album like no other, the Mondays a band like no other, and the tour a reminder of that – to themselves as much as anything. The band played solidly and above all with honesty, something that had always marked them out. More festival dates followed in 2014 and the band sounded vital. There were more great reviews and thousands upon thousands of happy dancing fans, plus tantalising talk of a new album.

The band's former American agent, Marc Geiger, is now one of the most powerful men in the American music industry as head of William Morris Endeavor's music division. He flew from Los Angeles to see the reformed Mondays play in Manchester and remains a fan. 'The Mondays wasted their talent and potential,' he said. 'More than the Roses, more than the Primals [Primal Scream], who both only had one great record, the Mondays, pretty much, all their albums were great. I don't think historically they've earned their due.' Geiger hoped this book would go some way to readdressing that.

Mark Day still lives in Swinton. In early 2014 he was putting the finishing touches to a new extension to his house and a lovely modern kitchen. He was as down to earth as ever. He'd kept the original cassette tapes of the Mondays' first ever rehearsals and the master tapes of the band's final 1993 'unfinished symphony' recordings. Gary Whelan was moving from Canada to Los Angeles where he would be closer to Paul Ryder, the rhythm section still the heartbeat of the band — and both, despite themselves, impossibly pop star elegant. Shaun still lived round the corner from his mum and dad in Worsley, an enigma even possibly to himself. Bez had cast aside all bourgeois conceits, such as owning a home and bank accounts, and was promoting his interest in permaculture and making a stand against fracking. Rowetta continued to be one of Manchester's best-loved personalities. Paul Davis remained unknowable. But he'd more than played his part. And the remarkable journey of possibly the most remarkable band ever continues.

Gigography/Discography

1983
September: Wardley Community Centre
24 October: Blackpool, GPO Social Club

1984
15 March: Manchester, The Gallery
date unknown: Manchester, The Hacienda, The Hometown Gig
11 December: Manchester, The Hacienda, The Year's Best of the
Hometown Gig (cancelled)

1985
27 January: Leeds, Tiffany's, supporting New Order
17 April: Salford University, Maxwell Hall, supporting New Order
19 April: Macclesfield Leisure Centre, supporting New Order
27 July: Manchester, International, supporting Flag of Convenience
September: *Forty Five* 12″ single: 'Delightful', 'This Feeling', 'Oasis'
21 September: Manchester, Belle Vue Stadium, Cumberland Suite,
supporting A Certain Ratio
27 October: Manchester, Corbieres, with The Weeds
3 November: London, Clarendon Hotel Ballroom, with Section 25/
Stockholm Monsters (cancelled)
3 December: Manchester, The Hacienda, supporting New Order

1986

20 February: Hull University, supporting The Colourfield

21 February: Reading University, supporting The Colourfield

22 February: Leicester University, supporting The Colourfield

1 March: Newcastle University, supporting The Colourfield

18 March: Manchester, Ritz, supporting A Certain Ratio

28 March: Brighton Centre, supporting New Order

1 April: Peel session – 'Kuff Dam', 'Freaky Dancin'', 'Olive Oil', 'Cob 20'

6 April: Manchester, Boardwalk

7 June: 'Freaky Dancin''/'The Egg' 7" and 12" single

7 June: Barrow-in-Furness, venue unknown

12 July: Hull, Adelphi

15 July: Manchester, PSV club, supporting James

17 July: Manchester, Rafters, with The Weeds/Easterhouse

21 July: Liverpool, Bootle Fire Station

23 July: London Kennington Oval, The Cricketers

26 July: London Hammersmith, Clarendon Hotel Ballroom, supporting The Weather Prophets

10 August: Manchester, Boardwalk, supporting Julian Cope

27 August: London Covent Garden, Rock Garden

August: Leicester, Fan Club

12 September: Blackburn, Windsor Suite, with The Railway Children

30 September: Leicester, Fan Club, supporting The Weather Prophets

2 October: Birmingham, Tower Ballroom, supporting New Order

3 October: Malvern, Winter Gardens, supporting New Order

7 October: Leeds, supporting The Weather Prophets

8 October: Leeds, Adam & Eves

9 October: London Ladbroke Grove, Bay 63, with Blurt, The Young Gods

10 October: Edinburgh, Hoochie Club

11 October: Hull, venue unknown

16 October: Rochdale, Tiffs, supporting The Bodines

31 October: Blackburn, King George's Hall, supporting A Certain Ratio

December: Hull, venue unknown

1987

31 January: Manchester, Boardwalk

22 February: London Camden, Black Horse

March: 'Tart Tart'/'Little Matchstick Owen's Rap' 12″ single

April: *Squirrel and G-Man Twenty Four Hour Party People Plastic Face Carnt Smile (White Out)* album

18 April: Blackburn, Top Hat

20 April: Manchester, International II, supporting The Fall, The Bodines

23 April: London, Rock Garden

24 April: Liverpool & Merseyside Trade Union and Resource Centre

1 May: Liverpool, Upstairs at the Picket, supporting The Farm

3 May: London Camden, Black Horse

12 May: Stoke, Shelleys

15 May: Brighton, Zap Club

16 May: Cardiff Polytechnic, supporting The Weather Prophets

17 May: Cheltenham, Humphreys, supporting The Weather Prophets

18 May: Liverpool University

19 May: Bristol, Bierkeller, supporting The Weather Prophets

20 May: Leeds Warehouse, supporting The Weather Prophets, The Bodines

21 May: London, Astoria, supporting The Bodines

22 May: Wolverhampton Polytechnic

23 May: Hull University

28 May: Manchester, The Hacienda

29 May: Middleton, Civic Hall

6 June: London Finsbury Park, supporting New Order, A Certain Ratio and The Railway Children

9 June: Glasgow, Barrowlands, supporting New Order

3 July: Aldershot, The West End Centre

13 July: Glasgow, venue unknown

15 July: New York, Limelight

20 July: London Camden, Dingwalls

7 August: Manchester, Platt Fields, free concert

13 August: Manchester, Boardwalk

5 October: London, Portlands

7 October: Leicester, Princess Charlotte

8 October: Cambridge Technical College

9 October: Northampton, Roadmenders Club

10 October: Sheffield, Leadmill

15 October: Liverpool University

16 October: Manchester University, Solem bar

19 October: Nottingham, Trent Polytechnic

20 October: Newcastle Riverside

21 October: Hull, Adelphi

26 October: London Camden, Dingwalls

October: '24 Hour Party People'/'Yahoo'/'Wah Wah (Think Tank)'
12" single

10 December: Warrington, Legends

11 December: Manchester, International II

1988

12 February: University of London Union, supporting Stump

12 May: Manchester, The Hacienda, Temperance Club

May: Milton Keynes, Russian Centre

May: St Helens, venue unknown

5 October: Warrington, Legends, supporting James

11 October: Manchester, Ritz, supporting James

12 October: Newcastle, Riverside, supporting James

14 October: Aberdeen, Venue, supporting James

15 October: Glasgow University, QM Union, supporting James

16 October: Stirling University, supporting James

20 October: Liverpool Polytechnic, Haigh Hall, supporting James

21 October: Sheffield University, supporting James

22 October: Nottingham, Trent Polytechnic, supporting James

25 October: Birmingham, Irish Centre, supporting James

26 October: Bristol, Bierkeller, supporting James

27 October: London, Astoria, supporting James

31 October: 'Wrote For Luck' single

5 November: Birmingham, Irish Centre

November: *Bummed* album

28 November: London Camden, Dingwalls

3 December: London, Astoria, supporting Loop

4 December: Brighton, Zap Club

17 December: Manchester, G-Mex, supporting New Order

1989

9 January: London Camden, Dingwalls

14 January: Manchester University

date unknown: Hamburg, venue unknown

date unknown: Berlin, venue unknown

date unknown: Düsseldorf, venue unknown

30 January: Cologne, Luxor

date unknown: Switzerland, venue unknown

date unknown: Austria, venue unknown

date unknown: Cologne, venue unknown

date unknown: Heidelberg, venue unknown

10 February: University of London Union

21 February: Peel session – 'Tart Tart', 'Mad Cyril', 'Do It Better'

27 February: Birmingham, Irish Centre

28 February: Leeds, Warehouse

1 March: Newcastle Polytechnic

2 March: Sheffield University

3 March: Liverpool University

9 March: Nottingham, Trent Polytechnic

10 March: Leicester Polytechnic

11 March: Manchester, International II

12 March: Brighton, Escape Club

13 March: Bristol Polytechnic

14 March: London, Astoria

16 March: Belfast, Limelight, with The Shamen

17 March: Dublin, McGonagles, with The Shamen

20 March: Paris, venue unknown (cancelled)

21 March: Lyon, Le Truck, supporting My Bloody Valentine

22 March: Paris, New Morning, supporting My Bloody Valentine

23 March: Rennes, L'Ubu, supporting My Bloody Valentine

24 March: Reims, venue unknown (cancelled)

26 March: Birmingham, NEC, supporting New Order

3 May: London Kilburn, National Ballroom

6 May: 'Lazyitis' single

8 May: Manchester, The Hacienda

9 May: Manchester, The Hacienda

15 June: Valencia, La Conjura De Las Danzas festival

22 July: Seattle, Moore Theatre, supporting The Pixies

24 July: San Francisco, The Fillmore, supporting The Pixies

26 July: San Diego, The Bacchanal, supporting The Pixies

27 July: Hollywood, The Palace

30 July: Boston, Paradise

31 July: Long Island, Malibu Club, supporting The Pixies

2 August: Philadelphia, Chestnut Cabaret, supporting The Pixies

3 August: Hoboken, New Jersey, Maxwells

4 August: New York, The Ritz, supporting The Pixies

6 August: Washington DC, 9.30 Club, supporting The Pixies

8 August: Cleveland, Peabody's, supporting The Pixies

10 August: Chicago, Cabaret Metro, supporting The Pixies

11 August: Minneapolis, First Avenue, supporting The Pixies

13 August: Milwaukee, Odd Rock Café

14 August: Ann Arbor, Rick's Café

15 August: Toronto, Diamond Club, supporting The Pixies

16 August: Montreal, Foufounes Electriques

17 August: Boston, Axis, supporting The Pixies

19 August: New York, CBGB

September: 'Wrote For Luck' single

13 November: *Madchester Rave On* EP: 'Hallelujah', 'Holy Ghost', 'Clap Your Hands', 'Rave On'

15 November: Bradford, Queens Hall

16 November: Newcastle Polytechnic

17 November: Widnes, Queens Hall

18 November: Manchester, Free Trade Hall

21 November: Leeds Polytechnic (cancelled)

22 November: Birmingham, Hummingbird

24 November: Bristol University
25 November: London Kentish Town, Town & Country Club
27 November: Brighton, Top Rank
30 November: Lancaster, Sugarhouse
1 December: Leicester Polytechnic
2 December: Sheffield University
3 December: Cambridge, Corn Exchange
6 December: Hanley, Victoria Hall
7 December: Liverpool University
8 December: Nottingham, Trent Polytechnic
9 December: Strathclyde University (cancelled)
9 December: Leeds University
10 December: Glasgow, Barrowlands
December: *Madchester Rave On* VHS

1990
3 March: Hamburg, Große Freiheit
4 March: Berlin, Loft (cancelled)
6 March: Cologne, Luxor
8 March: Valencia, The Garage (cancelled)
9 March: Barcelona, Ars Studio
12 March: Lyon, Le Truc
13 March: Paris, Bataclan
14 March: Amsterdam, Paradiso
17 March: Reykjavik University
24 March: Manchester, G-Mex
25 March: Manchester, G-Mex
7 April: London, Wembley Arena
9 April: 'Step On' single
24 June: Glastonbury festival, headliners
28 June: Ibiza, KU
July: *The Happy Mondays Party* VHS
July: *One Louder* VHS
9 July: Chicago, Cabaret Metro
10 July: Ann Arbor, venue unknown (cancelled)

11 July: Detroit, St Andrews Hall

12 July: Toronto, The Diamond Club

14 July: Boston, Axis

15 July: Washington, venue unknown

16 July: Philadelphia, venue unknown

18 July: New York, Sound Factory

20 July: Los Angeles, Palladium

21 July: San Francisco, I Beam (cancelled)

24 July: San Francisco, Fillmore (cancelled)

October: 'Kinky Afro' single

5 November: *Pills 'n' Thrills and Bellyaches* album

12 November: *Call the Cops* VHS

23 November: Whitley Bay Ice Rink

25 November: London, Wembley Arena

27 November: Glasgow, SECC

29 November: Manchester, G-Mex

30 November: Birmingham, NEC

2 December: Glasgow, SECC

4 December: Dublin, The Point

1991

18 January: London, Wembley Arena (Great British Music Weekend)

26 January: Brazil, Rock in Rio 2 festival

February: 'Loose Fit'/'Bob's Yer Uncle' single

24 February: Berlin, venue unknown

25 February: Hamburg, Docks

26 February: Düsseldorf, venue unknown

27 February: Frankfurt, venue unknown

1 March: Paris, La Cigale

2 March: Paris, La Cigale

4 March: Munich, Theatrefabrik

6 March: Ghent, Vooeruit

7 March: Amsterdam, Paradiso

8 March: Utrecht, venue unknown

10 March: Copenhagen, venue unknown

11 March: Stockholm, venue unknown

12 March: Oslo, venue unknown

26 March: Ventura, Terrace Theatre

27 March: San Diego, Montezuma Hall

28 March: Los Angeles, Palladium

30 March: San Francisco, Warfield

1 April: Seattle, Moore Theatre

2 April: Vancouver, Commodore Ballroom

4 April: Salt Lake City, venue unknown (cancelled)

5 April: Denver, Gothic Theatre

7 April: Madison, Barrymore Theatre (cancelled)

8 April: Minneapolis, First Avenue Club

11 April: Milwaukee, Varsity Theatre

12 April: Chicago, Riviera Theatre

13 April: Detroit, Latin Quarter

14 April: Toronto, Concert Hall

16 April: Boston, Citi

17 April: Boston, Orpheum, WFNX anniversary supported by Iggy Pop and Jesus Jones

19 April: New York, Academy

22 April: Trenton, New Jersey, City Gardens

24 April: New York, Madison Square Garden, supporting Jane's Addiction

25 April: Long Island, Malibu Club

27 April: Poughkeepsie, Vassar College Amphitheatre

28 April: Washington DC, Citadel Center

30 April: Atlanta, Masquerade

1 May: Winter Park, Florida, Enyart Alumni Fieldhouse

2 May: Tampa, Janus Landing (cancelled)

4 May: Houston, Southern Star Amphitheatre

5 May: Dallas, Deep Ellum Live (cancelled)

6 May: Austin, Liberty Lunch, venue unknown (cancelled)

date unknown: Phoenix, venue unknown (cancelled)

date unknown: Irvine, venue unknown (cancelled)

date unknown: Santa Barbara, venue unknown (cancelled)

20 May: Landgraaf, Holland, Pinkpop Festival

1 June: Leeds, Elland Road

22 June: Hamburg, Stadtpark, with Deee-lite

5 July: Paris, Zenith (cancelled)

6 July: Torhout, Belgium, festival

7 July: Werchter, Belgium, festival

10 July: Valencia, bullring (cancelled)

27 July: Lisbon, Estadio Jose Alvalade

2 August: Tipperary, Feile Festival

4 August: Manchester, Heaton Park, Cities in the Park

September: *Live* album

14 October: Osaka, Japan, venue unknown (postponed to February 1992)

15 October: Nagoya, Japan, venue unknown (postponed to February 1992)

18 October: Kawasaki, Japan, Club Citta (postponed to February 1992)

18 November: 'Judge Fudge' single

1992

February: Osaka (cancelled)

February: Nagoya (cancelled)

February: Kawasaki, Club Citta (cancelled)

31 August: 'Stinkin' Thinkin'' single

September: *Yes Please!* album

10 October: Leicester, De Montfort Hall

11 October: Manchester, Free Trade Hall

13 October: Newcastle, City Hall

14 October: Glasgow, Barrowlands

16 October: Newport Centre

17 October: London, Brixton Academy

18 October: London, Kilburn National

20 October: Sheffield City Hall

21 October: Hanley, Victoria Hall

22 October: Preston, Guildhall

24 October: Wolverhampton, Civic Hall

25 October: Cambridge, Corn Exchange

26 October: Portsmouth, Guildhall

5 November: Tokyo, Budokan, with BAD II

November: 'Sunshine and Love' single
2 December: Hamburg, Große Freiheit (cancelled)
3 December: Berlin, Neue Welt (cancelled)
6 December: Munich, Nachtwerk (cancelled)
7 December: Cologne, Live Music Hall (cancelled)

Bibliography

Bez, *Freaky Dancin': Me and the Mondays* (Pan, 1998)

Champion, Sarah, *And God Created Manchester* (Wordsmith, 1990)

Collin, Matthew, *Altered State: The Story of Ecstasy Culture and Acid House* (Serpent's Tail, 1997)

Harris, John, *The Last Party: Britpop, Blair and the Demise of English Rock* (Fourth Estate, 2003)

Haslam, Dave, *Manchester, England: The Story of the Pop Cult City* (Fourth Estate, 1999)

Hook, Peter, *The Hacienda: How Not to Run a Club* (Simon & Schuster, 2009)

King, Richard, *How Soon Is Now?* (Faber and Faber, 2012)

Larkin, Colin, *The Guinness Who's Who of Indie and New Wave* (Guinness, 1992)

McGill, Colin, *Kickers, Flickers and Dippers* (self-published)

Middles, Mick, *Factory, The Story of the Record Label* (Virgin, 1996)

Middles, Mick, *Shaun Ryder: Happy Mondays, Black Grape and Other Traumas* (Independent Music Press, 1997)

Middles, Mick, *Shaun Ryder: In His Own Words* (Omnibus, 1998)

Nice, James, *Shadowplayers: The Rise and Fall of Factory Records* (Aurum, 2010)

Nolan, David, *Tony Wilson: You're Entitled to an Opinion* (John Blake, 2010)

Norris, Richard, *Paul Oakenfold: The Authorised Biography* (Bantam, 2007)

Reade, Lindsey, *Mr Manchester and the Factory Girl* (Plexus, 2010)

Robb, John, *The North Will Rise Again: Manchester Music City (1977–1996)* (Aurum, 2009)

Robertson, Matthew, *Factory Records: The Complete Graphic Album* (Thames and Hudson, 2006)

Ryder, Shaun, *Twisting My Melon: The Autobiography* (Transworld, 2011)

Sharp, Colin, *Who Killed Martin Hannett? The Story of Factory Records' Musical Magician* (Aurum, 2007)

Spence, Simon, *The Stone Roses: War and Peace* (Penguin, 2012)

Spence, Simon, *Still Breathing: The True Adventures of the Donnelly Brothers* (Black and White, 2013)

Strauss, Neil, *Motley Crue: The Dirt* (HarperCollins, 2001)

Verico, Lisa, *High Life 'n' Low Down Dirty: The Thrills and Spills of Shaun Ryder* (Ebury, 1998)

Walsh, Peter, *Gang War: The Inside Story of the Manchester Gangs* (Milo, 2003)

Warburton, John (with Shaun Ryder), *Hallelujah!* (Virgin, 2003)

Wilson, Tony, *24 Hour Party People* (Pan Macmillan, 2002)

http://www.cerysmaticfactory.info/
http://www.mdmarchive.co.uk/
http://www.happymondaysonline.com/

Acknowledgements

This book is based on interviews conducted in 2013 and 2014 and would not have been possible without the incredibly generous amounts of time afforded me, separately, by Gary Whelan, Paul Ryder and Mark Day. Huge thanks also to Keith Jobling, who introduced and recommended me to the Mondays, and to Pat Carroll and brothers Anthony and Christopher Donnelly, for their early encouragement. Special thanks go to Phil Saxe, Nathan McGough and Derek Ryder, who were all equally generous with their time. Industry heavyweights Clive Black, Steve Osborne, Nicki Kefalas and Marc Geiger also gave up precious time thanks to their longstanding admiration for the Mondays. Tracey Donnelly, David Young, Andrew Berry and Andrew Hardy all made invaluable contributions. Thanks too to Alan Erasmus, Rowetta, Paul Davis, Phil Grunshaw and Matt Carroll. And huge thanks to Anthony Young (aka T), who allowed me complete access to his astonishing Mondays archive.

Further thanks to Mark Day, Paul Ryder, Tracey Donnelly, Andrew Hardy, Peter Walsh, and T for supplying photographs and imagery, and to Joe Henry at *Glastonbury to Paris* magazine for liaising with Alan McGee. Also to my agent Kevin Pocklington at Jenny Brown Associates, plus the book's copy editor, Steve Gove, and, at Aurum Press: Sam Harrison, Andrew Compton, Liz Somers, Charlotte Coulthard, Lucy Warburton and especially, Robin Harvie.

Index